OFFENDER REHABILITATION IN PRACTICE

WILEY SERIES IN
FORENSIC CLINICAL PSYCHOLOGY

Edited by

Clive R. Hollin
Centre for Applied Psychology, The University of Leicester, UK

and

Mary McMurran
School of Psychology, Cardiff University, UK

COGNITIVE BEHAVIOURAL TREATMENT OF
SEXUAL OFFENDERS
William L. Marshall, Dana Anderson and Yolanda Fernandez

VIOLENCE, CRIME AND MENTALLY DISORDERED
OFFENDERS: Concepts and methods for effective treatment
and prevention
Sheilagh Hodgins and Rüdiger Müller-Isberner (*Editors*)

OFFENDER REHABILITATION IN PRACTICE:
Implementing and Evaluating Effective Programs
Gary A. Bernfeld, David P. Farrington
and Alan W. Leschied (*Editors*)

OFFENDER REHABILITATION IN PRACTICE
Implementing and Evaluating Effective Programs

Edited by

Gary A. Bernfeld
Behavioural Science Technology Program, St Lawrence College, Ontario, Canada

David P. Farrington
Institute of Criminology, University of Cambridge, UK

Alan W. Leschied
Faculty of Education, University of Western Ontario, Canada

JOHN WILEY & SONS, LTD

Chichester · New York · Weinheim · Brisbane · Singapore · Toronto

Other Wiley Editorial Offices

John Wiley & Sons, Inc., 605 Third Avenue,
New York, NY 10158-0012, USA

WILEY-VCH GmbH, Pappelallee 3,
D-69469 Weinheim, Germany

John Wiley & Sons Australia, Ltd, 33 Park Road, Milton,
Queensland 4064, Australia

John Wiley & Sons (Asia) Pte Ltd, 2 Clementi Loop #02-01,
Jin Xing Distripark, Singapore 129809

John Wiley & Sons (Canada) Ltd, 22 Worcester Road,
Rexdale, Ontario M9W 1L1, Canada

Library of Congress Cataloging-in-Publication Data
Offender rehabilitation in practice : implementing and evaluating effective programs /
edited by Gary A. Bernfeld, David P. Farrington, Alan W. Leschied.
        p. cm. — (Wiley series in forensic clinical psychology)
    Includes bibliographical references and index.
    ISBN 0-471-72026-7 (paper)
    1. Criminals—Rehabilitation. 2. Prisoners—Services for. 3. Social work with criminals.
    4. Criminal psychology. I. Bernfeld, Gary A. II. Farrington, David P. III. Leschied, Alan
Winfield, 1952– IV. Series.
    HV9274   O33 2001
    365'.66—dc21

                                                                                    2001026497

British Library Cataloguing in Publication Data
A catalogue record for this book is available from the British Library

ISBN 0-471-72026-7

Project management by Originator, Gt Yarmouth, Norfolk, UK (typeset in 10/12pt Palatino)
Printed and bound in Great Britain by Antony Rowe, Chippenham, Wilts.
This book is printed on acid-free paper responsibly manufactured from sustainable forestry,
in which at least two trees are planted for each one used for paper production.

To my wife Carol, who has been an invaluable support throughout the 3 years needed to submit the completed manuscript, and to my daughters Lisa and Katie, who represent the hope for the future—a future where human services will be implemented with care, integrity and quality, in the best interests of the clients that we serve and the front-line staff who labour mightily towards that end. — G.B.

To my wife Patti and our boys Benjamin and Christopher who, as well as tolerating many work-related absences due to travel demands, also taught me that a sense of justice without compassion would not move us along as a culture committed to assisting young people and their families in need. — A.L.

CONTENTS

PART II: IMPLEMENTING SPECIFIC PROGRAMS

PART III: IMPLEMENTING GENERAL PROGRAMS

ABOUT THE EDITORS

Gary A. Bernfeld

Dr Gary A. Bernfeld is a clinical psychologist and professor in the Behavioral Science Technology program at St Lawrence College, Kingston, Ontario. This program is unique in Canada. There, he teaches future front-line staff in corrections, and many other fields, how to use "best practices" in applied behavior analysis and cognitive-behavioral therapy to treat youths and adults with serious behavior problems.

Gary has devoted over 20 years teaching and supervising those who serve youth with multiple and severe problems. He has managed a range of children's services (child welfare, mental health, young offenders and developmentally handicapped) in both residential and community settings. He spent over 8 years developing and refining one of the first cognitive-behavioral and ecological family preservation programs in Canada for high-risk young offenders. He also was a psychologist for 3 years at Bath Institution of Correctional Services Canada.

Gary is a community educator with over 100 presentations to his credit. He is an experienced consultant and a program evaluator with experience evaluating multi-site, province-wide programs, in the children's services field. He has a number of publications and manuals in the area. As an Adjunct Assistant Professor in the Psychology and Education Departments at Queen's University, he teaches courses on developmental psychopathology and on at-risk adolescents.

David P. Farrington

Dr David P. Farrington is Professor of Psychological Criminology at Cambridge University. He has been President of the American Society of Criminology, of the British Society of Criminology and of the European Association of Psychology and Law. His major research interest is in the development of delinquency and crime from childhood to adulthood, and he is Director of the Cambridge Study in Delinquent Development, which is a prospective longitudinal survey of over 400 London males from age 8 to age 46. He has published 27 books and monographs and over 290 articles on criminological and psychological topics.

Alan W. Leschied

Dr Alan W. Leschied is an associate professor in the Faculty of Education at the University of Western Ontario. His work has focused on developing assessment strategies and treatment interventions for youth at risk. In addition, he has provided considerable input to legislation and policies in Canada that can influence the delivery of effective human service to young people and their families.

LIST OF CONTRIBUTORS

Gary A. Bernfeld

Behavioural Sciences Technology Program, St Lawrence College, King & Portsmouth, Kingston, Ontario K7L 5A6, Canada

Karen A. Blase

Executive Director, Calgary Women's Emergency Shelter, Box 51052, Edmonton Trail N.E., Calgary, Alberta T2E 8K9, Canada

Bradford M. Bogue

Justice System Assessment & Training, 2111 30th Street, Suite A, Boulder, CO 80301, USA

James Bonta

Solicitor General Canada, 340 Laurier Avenue W., Ottawa, Ontario K1A 0P8, Canada

Michael F. Crowley

National Parole Board of Canada, 516 O'Connor Drive, Suite 100, Kingston Ontario K7P 1N3, Canada

Daniel L. Edwards

MST Services, 268 W. Coleman Blvd, Suite 2E, Mount Pleasant, SC 29464, USA

David P. Farrington

Institute of Criminology, University of Cambridge, 7 West Road, Cambridge CB3 9DT, UK

Dean L. Fixsen

FYI Consulting Ltd, 671 Regal Park N.E., Calgary, Alberta T2E 0S6, Canada

Paul Gendreau

Director, Centre for Criminal Justice Studies, Department of Psychology, University of New Brunswick at Saint John, Box 5050, Saint John, New Brunswick E2L 4L5, Canada

Barry Glick

Chief Operations Officer, G & G Consultants, 106 Acorn Drive, Scotia, New York 12302-4702, USA

Claire Goggin

Centre for Criminal Justice Studies, Department of Psychology, University of New Brunswick at Saint John, Box 5050, Saint John, New Brunswick E2L 4L5, Canada

Arnold P. Goldstein

Centre for Research on Aggression, Syracuse University, 805 S. Crouse Avenue, Syracuse, New York 13244-2280, USA

Scott W. Henggeler

Family Services Research Center, Department of Psychiatry and Behavioral Sciences, Medical University of South Carolina, 67 President Street, Suite CPP/243, Box 250861, Charleston, SC 29425, USA

Clive R. Hollin

Centre for Applied Psychology, University of Leicester, Leicester LE1 7RH, UK

Alan W. Leschied

Faculty of Education, University of Western Ontario, 1137 Western Road, London, Ontario N6G 1G7, Canada

Friedrich Lösel

Institut für Psychologie, Bismarckstrasse I, Universität Erlangen-Nürnberg, D-91054 Erlangen, Germany

James McGuire

Department of Clinical Psychology, The University of Liverpool, Whelan Building, Liverpool L69 3GB, UK

Laurence Motiuk

Director General, Research Branch, Correctional Service of Canada, 340 Laurier Avenue W., Ottawa, Ontario K1A 0P9, Canada

Denise L. Preston

Research Branch, Correctional Service of Canada, c/o Collins Bay Institution, 455 Bath Road, Box 190, Kingston, Ontario K7L 4V9, Canada

Peter Raynor

Centre for Applied Social Studies, University of Wales Swansea, Singleton Park, Swansea SA2 8PP, UK

Sonja K. Schoenwald

Family Services Research Center, Department of Psychiatry and Behavioral Sciences, Medical University of South Carolina, 67 President Street, Suite CPP/243, Box 250861, Charleston, SC 29425, USA

Ralph C. Serin

Research Branch, Correctional Service of Canada, c/o Frontenac Institution, 455 Bath Road, Kingston, Ontario K7L 5E6, Canada

Paula Smith

Centre for Criminal Justice Studies, Department of Psychology, University of New Brunswick at Saint John, Box 5050, Saint John, New Brunswick E2L 4L5, Canada

Keller B. Strother

MST Services, 268 W. Coleman Blvd, Suite 2E, Mount Pleasant, SC 29464, USA

Gary D. Timbers

Director, Bringing It All Back Home Study Center, Appalachian State University, 204 Avery Avenue, Morganton, NC 28655, USA

Maurice Vanstone

Centre for Applied Social Studies, University of Wales, Singleton Park, Swansea, SA 2 8PP, UK.

Brandon C. Welsh

Department of Criminal Justice, University of Massachusetts at Lowell, 870 Broadway Street, Suite 2, Lowell, MA 01854-3044, USA

Montrose M. Wolf

Department of Human Development & Family Life, University of Kansas, 4001 Dole Blvd, Lawrence, KS 66045-2133, USA

SERIES EDITORS' PREFACE

ABOUT THE SERIES

At the time of writing it is clear that we live in a time, certainly in the UK and other parts of Europe, if perhaps less so in other parts of the world, when there is renewed enthusiasm for constructive approaches to working with offenders to prevent crime. What do we mean by this statement and what basis do we have for making it?

First, by "constructive approaches to working with offenders" we mean bringing the use of effective methods and techniques of behaviour change into work with offenders. Indeed, this might pass as a definition of forensic clinical psychology. Thus, our focus is application of theory and research in order to develop practice aimed at bringing about a change in the offender's functioning. The word *constructive* is important and can be set against approaches to behaviour change that seek to operate by destructive means. Such destructive approaches are typically based on the principles of deter- rence and punishment, seeking to suppress the offender's actions through fear and intimidation. A constructive approach, on the other hand, seeks to bring about changes in an offender's functioning that will produce, say, enhanced possibilities of employment, greater levels of self-control, better family functioning or increased awareness of the pain of victims.

A constructive approach faces the criticism of being a "soft" response to damage caused by offenders, neither inflicting pain and punishment nor delivering retribution. This point raises a serious question for those involved in working with offenders. Should advocates of constructive approaches oppose retribution as a goal of the criminal justice system as incompatible with treatment and rehabilitation? Alternatively, should

constructive work with offenders take place within a system given to retribution? We believe that this issue merits serious debate.

However, to return to our starting point, history shows that criminal
justice systems are littered with many attempts at constructive work with
offenders, not all of which have been successful. In raising the spectre of
success, the second part of our opening sentence now merits attention: that
is, "constructive approaches to working with offenders *to prevent crime*". In
order to achieve the goal of preventing crime, interventions must focus on
the right targets for behaviour change. In addressing this crucial point,
Andrews and Bonta (1994) have formulated the *need principle*:

> Many offenders, especially high-risk offenders, have a variety of needs. They
> need places to live and work and/or they need to stop taking drugs. Some have
> poor self-esteem, chronic headaches or cavities in their teeth. These are all
> "needs". The need principle draws our attention to the distinction between
> *criminogenic* and *noncriminogenic* needs. Criminogenic needs are a subset of
> an offender's risk level. They are dynamic attributes of an offender that,
> when changed, are associated with changes in the probability of recidivism.
> Non- criminogenic needs are also dynamic and changeable, but these changes
> are not necessarily associated with the probability of recidivism. (p. 176)

Thus, successful work with offenders can be judged in terms of bringing
about change in noncriminogenic need *or* in terms of bringing about
change in criminogenic need. While the former is important and, indeed,
may be a necessary precursor to offence-focused work, it is changing criminogenic need that, we argue, should be the touchstone of working with
offenders.

While, as noted above, the history of work with offenders is not replete
with success, the research base developed since the early 1990s, particularly
the meta-analyses (e.g. Lösel, 1995), now strongly supports the position that
effective work with offenders to prevent further offending is possible. The
parameters of such evidence-based practice have become well established
and widely disseminated under the banner of *What Works* (McGuire, 1995).

It is important to state that we are not advocating that there is only one
approach to preventing crime. Clearly there are many approaches, with
different theoretical underpinnings, that can be applied. Nonetheless, a
tangible momentum has grown in the wake of the *What Works* movement
as academics, practitioners and policy makers seek to capitalize on the possibilities that this research raises for preventing crime. The task now facing
many service agencies lies in turning the research into effective practice.

Our aim in developing this Series in Forensic Clinical Psychology is to
produce texts that review research and draw on clinical expertise to advance
effective work with offenders. We are both committed to the ideal of
evidence-based practice and we will encourage contributors to the Series

to follow this approach. Thus, the books published in the Series will not be practice manuals or "cook books": they will offer readers authoritative and critical information through which forensic clinical practice can develop. We are both enthusiastic about the contribution to effective practice that this Series can make and look forward to it developing in the years to come.

ABOUT THIS BOOK

It is a fact of life that researchers can produce as much high-quality research as they wish, but, unless there are those who can span the ravine between research and practice, the books and journal articles are only so many words on paper. The truth of this harsh fact is particularly apparent when considering the field of working with offenders. The rapid development throughout the 1990s of evidence-based programs to reduce offending, in both prisons and in the community, did not happen by accident. As events unfolded, a number of committed researchers were willing to take messages from research out into the field, challenging not only the notion that nothing works but also calling in question the effectiveness of much current practice. The assumption is often made that the conceptual struggle is with those who are sceptical about the effects of intervention. However, there are many of us who would rather face legions of sceptics than have to try and convince hardened professionals that they need to change their practice!

In the early stages of delivering the messages from research, researchers are often involved in conference and seminar presentations to service agencies, such as prisons and probation services. For researchers, this is usually a reasonably comfortable task: most researchers see presentation of research as part of their role, and they have the skills necessary for this type of work. However, the acid test for researchers emerges when the agencies begin to be convinced and want to buy into the research: the researcher then faces the hard question: So, how do we make this happen in practice? This question moves the debate into a new arena, the implementation of research findings. As anyone knows who has worked in the field, implementation of new practice is the biggest challenge of all. The researcher who treads in the deep waters of implementation needs a daunting range of attributes spanning policy formulation, developing treatment procedures, tact and diplomacy (lots!), management awareness, training skills, political awareness, practice skills, and committee and consultancy skills. With successful implementation comes the need for evaluation: which rather suggests that implementation is something researchers should take very seriously!

The editors of this book have, to their credit, seen clearly the issues of implementation as they are emerging at present. They have gathered a distinguished group of contributors who can speak to the relevant issues. It is illuminating to read the work of those people who are genuinely shaping their field, and to see the creativity and understanding that they bring to bear on very real issues. There is a great deal to be taken from this book by researchers, policy-makers, managers and practitioners: in time to come, we hope this text is seen as a landmark publication in bridging the divide between research and practice.

June 2001   Clive Hollin and Mary McMurran

References

Andrews, D. A., & Bonta, J. (1994). *The Psychology of Criminal Conduct*. Cincinnati, OH: Anderson Publishing Co.

Lösel, F. (1995). Increasing consensus in the evaluation of offender rehabilitation? Lessons from recent research synthesis. *Psychology, Crime and Law*, **2**, 19–39.

McGuire, J. (Ed.). (1995). *What Works: Reducing Reoffending*. Chichester. John Wiley.

PREFACE

The impetus for this book grew from the disparate viewpoints of research and practice. Ultimately, these converged to spur the development of this book. *Researchers* in the field of corrections in the 1990's were inundated with information from meta-analytic studies and at conferences delineating the key ingredients of effective correctional practice. Books published in the mid-1990s, in both adult corrections (Hollin, 1996; McGuire, 1995) and youth corrections (Glick & Goldstein, 1995; Hollin & Howells, 1996), focused almost exclusively on "what works". What was needed was a book that would capitalise on this important knowledge base and take it one critical step further by confronting and overcoming the "real world" challenges of program replication and program implementation.

Practitioners have always had to operationalise critical program-related concepts (e.g. treatment integrity) that have been only described superficially in most academic studies, and to cope with the day-to-day "push–pull" of correctional practice. They have had to balance what the research literature has to offer against the demands of administrators, policymakers and funders—not to mention the "counter control" of offenders. Moreover, those working with offenders have lacked an effective guidebook on how to cope with the pragmatic organizational and systemic issues which impact on their implementation of "state of the art" programs in the field.

Overall, what has been missing in the corrections field is a means to reconcile the perspectives of researchers and practitioners and thereby narrow the gap between what we *desire* from our rehabilitation programs and what we actually *deliver*. Thus, the idea for this book was born out of our commitment to provide a reference volume for both researchers and practitioners, which would review and report on the experience worldwide of *effective implementation* of offender rehabilitation programs that work. We believe that the utilization and extension of knowledge, what is popularly referred to as *technology transfer*, is the next level of systemic intervention in criminal justice. This volume is the first to be concerned with that transfer of knowledge. Prominent researchers and practitioners in the criminal justice field contribute their knowledge of what it takes to implement effective correctional practices with *ecological integrity*.

In order to accomplish our purpose, we have organized this volume into three parts. After an introductory chapter, Part I discusses key issues in correctional effectiveness. Part II details implementation issues arising in specific programs for youth and adults in corrections. Part III takes a much broader view by reviewing the experiences of those implementing, evaluating and consulting to correctional programs across multiple sites.

Personal thanks follow:

To Dean Fixsen and Karen Blase who have been pioneers in the field of program replication and model dissemination. Their own work developing the Teaching-Family Model has epitomized a multilevel, integrated and dynamic systems approach to treatment implementation. To Merice Walker Boswell, mentor, for teaching me so much about the value of a low profile and "positive persistence" in program delivery. To Leonard Harris, my best friend, for his faith in me and what this book represents. To the managers and staff of St Lawrence Youth Association, for their support of the Teaching-Family Model, and to Mary Lynn Cousins-Brame, for her exceptional efforts in implementing the model. — G.B.

To the many skilled and dedicated clinicians and researchers of the London Family Court who provided knowledge and friendship beyond their wildest imaginings. To the leaders in Canadian criminal justice research who not only mentored, but also befriended a somewhat naive clinical psychologist over two decades ago and reminded me that the literatures of other disciplines were also relevant to understanding the issues in juvenile justice. Most notably, the leadership of Don Andrews, Paul Gendreau, Peter Jaffe and Jim Bonta have been inspirational. — A.L.

References

Glick, B., & Goldstein, A. P. (Eds). (1995). *Managing Delinquency Programs that Work*. Latham, MD: American Correctional Association.

Hollin, C. R. (Ed.). (1996). *Working with Offenders: Psychological Practice in Offender Rehabilitation*. Chichester: John Wiley.

Hollin, C. R., & Howells, K. (Eds). (1996). *Clinical Approaches to Working with Young Offenders*. Chichester: John Wiley.

McGuire, J. (Ed.). (1995). *What Works: Reducing Reoffending*. Chichester: John Wiley.

INTRODUCTION

Chapter 1

IMPLEMENTATION ISSUES

Alan W. Leschied,[1,*] Gary A. Bernfeld[†] and David P. Farrington[‡]

* University of Western Ontario, London, Ontario, Canada
† Behavioral Science Technology Program, St Lawrence College, Kingston, Ontario, Canada
‡ Institute of Criminology, University of Cambridge, Cambridge, UK

TECHNOLOGY TRANSFER IN THE HUMAN SERVICE FIELD

The transfer of knowledge in the social and human services from what has largely been an academic-based knowledge to applied settings is challenging not only to correctional professionals but also to practitioners in a variety of human service settings. The literature chronicles numerous examples of programs that were either well conceived and poorly implemented or well implemented but poorly sustained (Bauman, Stein & Ireys, 1991). Of course, there is also the suspicion that the failure to implement or sustain programs that have demonstrated effectiveness in research may be tied to the more insidious, cynical intentions of some policy and program "experts". This has more to do with the unwillingness of such administrators to disavow the knowledge base in a given area and indeed purposefully undermine the integrity of that knowledge. Andrews and Bonta (1998) refer to this intentional undermining as *knowledge destruction*, a fact identified in both the

---

[1] Portions of this chapter written by the first author appeared in a compendium produced through Correctional Services Canada.

Offender Rehabilitation in Practice. Edited by G. A. Bernfeld, D. P. Farrington and A. W. Leschied.
© 2001 John Wiley & Sons, Ltd.

young offender (Leschied, Jaffe, Andrews & Gendreau, 1989) and substance abuse literature (Gendreau, 1996). Techniques of knowledge destruction are characterized by the seeming sophistication of argument in using scientific principles to negate scientific fact. Often, the use of such techniques reveals the negative beliefs and attitudes on the part of these commentators. Reductionism is the essence and dismissal is the intent. In the beginning, a careful reading of what is known about successful programs is paramount to successfully planned program implementation.

In an excellent review of the lessons learned from the literature on successful program implementation Lisbeth Shorr (1989) noted that the implementation of programs is "shaped by powerful forces" that are not easily modified even by "new knowledge". Indeed, Shorr's summary of factors necessary in successful implementation include the necessity of a climate that is "created by skilled, committed professionals respectful and trusting of the clients they serve ... *regardless* of the precepts, demands and boundaries set by professionalism and bureaucracies" (p. 257). The necessity of providing caring programs that are coherent and easy to use, providing continuity and circumventing the traditions of professional and bureaucratic limitations were absolutely the prerogative of such effective programs. Paul Gendreau (1996), of course, would add that a senior advocate in an organization who is willing to champion the cause of such a program is an essential ingredient as well.

"Powerful forces" as Shorr calls them are certainly at work in the corrections field when it comes to transferring knowledge to practice on a broad scale. Political beliefs that have shaped correctional practice have in many cases been antagonistic to the lessons learned from the literature on effective corrections. Deterrence, sanctions and punishment-based correctional practices and policies have been pre-eminent in the last two decades. This is despite what Palmer (1996) amongst others indicates has been a failure of such programs to demonstrate reductions in offending. Yet, juxtaposed to this emphasis on punishment reflected in correctional policy has been the extraordinary growth in knowledge in the area of effective treatment.

THE NECESSITY OF A KNOWLEDGE-BASED APPROACH

Cullen et al. (1998) cite data suggesting that there continue to be many, both within and outside the corrections profession, who have failed to recognize the growing literature on effective treatment with offender populations. Despite this disappointing lack of awareness, the literature continues to grow, documenting not only progress with regard to the accumulation of evidence of effective interventions, but also summaries from numerous meta-analyses that now speak to the *patterns* of effectiveness being documented *across* studies. Numerous researchers and practitioners now speak about the need for examining "technology transfer"; the application of what research has suggested can be effective and translation of that knowledge into routine correctional practice. This chapter focuses on the factors related to implementation of programs that attempt to comply with the principles of effective service. Though few in number, there are now studies that report on evaluations that *monitor* the *implementation* of programs at both the practitioner level—referred to as *treatment adherence*—and the broader program, service and system level—referred to as *program compliance*.

Coupled with the move to monitor and measure adherence is the growing emphasis on *dissemination* of information regarding effective programs. Training is pivotal, combining both the communication of program findings along with the kinds of support and consultation required to ensure the effective replication of those programs. Some of the more well-articulated interventions such as Multi-Systemic Therapy—see Chapter 5—have developed, along with field input and support, detailed practitioner and supervisor manuals that can assist successful dissemination, although it must be acknowledged that such higher level dissemination efforts that are also being evaluated are still relatively rare in the human services and corrections fields.

Fixsen, Blase, Timbers and Wolfe—see Chapter 7—summarize over 15 years of replication of the Teaching-Family Model across a continuum of residential and in-home programs for delinquents and other troubled youth by suggesting that the critical elements of implementation are now largely known. These include well-integrated clinical, administrative, evaluative and supervisory systems to ensure treatment integrity and quality.

The present chapter presents current findings related to program implementation and the replication of successful programs. Major findings from the meta-analyses are provided in the context of their significance to implementation issues. Implementation issues that relate to both community and residential programs are provided along with the organizational requirements that are necessary to support successful implementation efforts. Finally, there is discussion of the policy relevance in corrections of successful implementation and the future of research efforts in this area.

OVERVIEW OF MAJOR FINDINGS FROM THE META-ANALYSES

In the mid and late 1970s reviews of the program literature in corrections contributed to an extraordinary discussion that became the touchstone to a generation of corrections professionals. The *nothing works debate*, as it is been popularly known, not only became a matter for social scientists to consider but also played into the hands of policy makers and politicians in criminal justice. Depending upon their particular political leaning, decision makers used the results of such reviews to either proclaim the failure of rehabilitation, thereby perhaps unwittingly heralding the expanded use of "get tough" measures, or used them to develop the growing science of prediction and treatment in the corrections field. Followers of the debate will now be familiar with the names of Robert Martinson (1976) in the USA and in Canada, Jalal Shamsie (1979) whose titles of qualitative reviews of the literature so provocatively proclaimed that "Nothing worked" and that "Our treatments do not work: Where do we go from here?". And, with each provocation, there was a Paul Gendreau and Robert Ross (1979) or Ted Palmer (1996) who suggested that a more careful reading of the outcome literature would provide "bibliotherapy for cynics".

Two decades have now passed, and with more sophistication in providing *quantitative reviews* of the prediction and outcome literature, meta-analyses have assisted in developing a *science of criminal conduct*. Such a science draws not only on linking factors that help in the understanding of *criminogenic risk levels* of certain individuals—nature and strength—but also on the literature regarding treatments or systems of service delivery that can promote effective outcomes in correctional practice. The following subsection highlights some of the major findings from the meta-analyses that relate to implementation.

Contributions from the meta-analyses

There have been a number of contributions to the meta-analyses on correctional treatment. Perhaps the most well known are those authored by Don Andrews et al. (1990) and by Mark Lipsey (Lipsey 1995; Lipsey and Wilson, 1993). Technical understanding of the approach taken by these authors will not be provided here. Suffice to say that the quality and nature of the meta-analyses that are reported reflect the quality and number of the studies in the field. Hence, the nature and quality of knowledge could not have been achieved and reported on by Andrews et al. (1990) and Lipsey were it not for the efforts of so many who contributed to that knowledge base. Indeed, Leschied and Cunningham (1999) report that the accumulation of published accounts of outcome studies in the youth corrections field had *more than tripled* in the past 10 years (1989–1998) when compared to the years prior to 1988.

Major assessment issues

Both cross-sectional and longitudinal studies have identified factors that link past or current conditions that place individuals at increasing risk for criminogenic involvement. Andrews and Bonta (1998) summarize that these studies support a *social–psychological understanding* of criminogenic risk; that is, individuals may cognitively process certain conditions in their environment that develop or reward certain styles or content of thinking that are reflected in antisocial behavior. Those system variables that influence risk to a greater extent include families of origin, peer associates and school or working conditions. Data has also supported the link between antisocial behavior and substance use in the understanding of crime cycles (Huizinga, Menard and Elliott, 1989). Measures of those factors that contribute most significantly and seem to be attracting the greatest attention in the literature include multifactorial indicators as measured by the Level of Service Inventory (Andrews and Bonta, 1998), criminal sentiments (Simourd & Van de Ven, 1999) and psychopathy (Hare, 1991).

Accurate and relevant assessment of criminogenic risk is tied to the major outcomes from the meta-analyses on effective treatment. While Lipsey has identified the major *general* contributors to successful correctional programs the principal contribution of Andrews et al. (1990) rests in the refining of understanding regarding the appropriate targets of intervention. While Lipsey's results were encouraging regarding the average effect sizes supporting reductions of 10–30 per cent in reoffending within particular types of programming (i.e. behavioral over psychodynamic), Andrews et al. (1990) showed that certain program components targeted to specific criminogenic risk factors—referred to as clinical relevance—could improve outcomes by an even greater extent. Hence, Andrews et al. (1990) articulated the *risk principle of case classification* as a critical component of effective service thereby linking assessment with service delivery in the overall approach to effective correctional treatment. These findings therefore suggest that assessments of appropriate risk relevant to criminal justice involvement are a necessary and fundamental part of successful program implementation.

TREATMENT IMPLEMENTATION/INTEGRITY AS A "FIELD" IN ITS OWN RIGHT

With advances in the empirical understanding of assessment and treatment of offender populations, the next challenge appears to be the dissemination and application of the known principles of effective correctional treatment. While having a much briefer history, there is a growing literature on the dissemination and support for translating successful programs to different jurisdictions and service delivery systems. This section will highlight some of the more salient findings from that literature.

Hundert (1999), in describing the challenges and potential for losing good ideas as programs are disseminated, uses the "Bermuda Triangle" as a fitting analogy to describe implementation. Bauman et al. (1991) suggest there are at least three levels of development in the implementation of programs in the human services field including (a) building a generative knowledge base, (b) developing new programs and (c) disseminating effective programs for others to use. McCarthy (1989), for example, identified critical structural and systemic supports for planned organizational change across a large service delivery system. This summary identifies seven critical elements to dissemination:

- the decision at the senior level of government that a *sustained effort* at service delivery is needed;
- the need to actively foster *multilevel ownership* of innovation;
- *seeding* the service delivery system with several pilot programs or to foster interest and demonstrate efficacy;
- ensuring that the *centres of excellence* are given *long-term fiscal support* and are led by competent champions of innovation;
- the recognition that *leadership* from the "top" must be provided and maintained over time in order to neutralize the forces of counter-control which are expected to develop;
- building *community investment* in the innovation, so that its longevity is not limited to the initial supporters;
- *top to bottom training* of staff to foster their familiarity with and support of the innovation.

While Hundert, McCarthy and others have identified the seemingly over-whelming challenge of dissemination and implementation, enough is now known to begin to look at implementation within a structural, organiza-tional framework. The following section sets forth a multilevel systems perspective in looking at a comprehensible model of understanding human service program implementation around which the balance of this book is organized.

A MULTILEVEL SYSTEMS PERSPECTIVE

This section provides a rationale and working framework within which most of this book is organized. Bernfeld, Blase and Fixsen (1990) examined the delivery of human services within the context of a systems perspective. Their rationale for adopting such a perspective was that competing variables in multilevel systems often account for program failure, so that the identifica-tion and manipulation of these implementation variables is a prerequisite for program success. They contend that these variables operate at multiple levels and interact in a reciprocal and dynamic manner. Bernfeld et al. propose a "behavioural systems perspective", which integrates the optimal qualities of systems (macro) and behavioural (micro) models. This model fosters a broader and deeper examination of implementation variables and enables the system as a whole to use feedback in a self-corrective manner.

According to Bernfeld et al., implementation variables can be delineated at the client, program, organization and societal levels of analysis. Examples from the literature are provided to underscore the need for a *multilevel systems perspective* in treating behavioral disorders of adolescents:

- *Client level*—the importance of an ecobehavioral viewpoint (e.g. Cantrell & Cantrell, 1985) in which problems (and/or solutions) rarely exist solely in one member of an ecological unit (e.g. the youth), but are interactional in nature; hence the need to treat the youth's "social ecology".
- *Program level*—the impact of process or implementation variables, such as staff selection, training and supervision, on outcome. "Organizational behavior management" (e.g. Jung & Bernfeld, 1987) provides a conceptual and procedural base for managers to understand and influence treatment implementation.
- *Organizational level*—key "cultural" and "socio-political" factors that operate within organizations (e.g. Hoge & Andrews, 1986).
- *Societal level*—the adoption of behavioral innovations is linked to a variety of factors (Stolz, 1981), the strongest of which seems to be personal relationships with senior administrators and policymakers.

The above examples illustrate the scope of a systems perspective and direct us to its implications for other areas of study. The implementation of "best practices" in the correctional field is a function of the ability of policy makers, program administrators and service deliverers to translate knowledge and theory into practice with *integrity*, while ensuring *quality assurance*. A key to such an endeavor is to utilize a multilevel systems perspective. To paraphrase Burchard (1987), those in the corrections field should adopt a more *ecological* perspective (Rodgers-Warren & Warren, 1977) on service implementation, and "expand their vision beyond traditional therapeutic interventions under 'given' environmental circumstances" (Burchard, p. 594). It is only through such a broader and deeper systems perspective that we can narrow the gap between what we *desire* from our correctional services and what we actually *deliver*.

GENERAL CONSIDERATIONS FOR SUCCESSFUL IMPLEMENTATION

As with any change strategy in human service, the complexities of factors that need to be addressed in promoting a shift in correctional practice may seem daunting if not absolutely overwhelming to an initiator of program change. Ellickson and Petersilia (1983) identified six principal organizational considerations that were necessary in initiating program implementation in corrections:

i. Sincere motivation at implementation.
ii. Support at the top of leadership and each group whose cooperation is required for full implementation.
iii. Staff competence.
iv. A surplus of benefits over costs.
v. Clarity of goals and procedures.
vi. Clear lines of authority.

In addition, program shifts for implementation in corrections requires the support of both legal and non-legal stakeholders in the community. What may make sense from a program perspective may be seen by the courts as in conflict with the rule of law. For example, if justice is seen as too individualized (e.g. sanctions are not seen as proportionate given the nature of the offending) the rule of law may be perceived as undermined because of the inequity of the severity and nature of the sanction. Clarity in the purpose and role of the courts and other law-related forums needs to be seen as complementary to the role and purpose of correctional programs. A progressive example of this type of thinking can be found in the evolution of the declaration of principle in the Young Offenders Act in Canada that, since revisions to the Act in 1989, has considered the goal of community safety as a coincidental pursuit in addressing the needs and circumstances of the young offender.

CONTEXTUAL ISSUES IN SUCCESSFUL IMPLEMENTATION

Experience in North America over the past two decades has reflected the trend towards incarceration as the correctional policy of choice. Trends in the support for incarceration, coupled with the legacy of the "nothing works" conclusions of reviewers of correctional programs in the early and mid-1970s, created considerable challenges to implement programs that were not predicated simply on adding to the incarceration rate. In many respects, findings from program reviews suggesting that the community was the preferred context in which to deliver effective programs flew in the face of the "get tough" school of corrections policy. Hence, development of intensive probation supervision programs, with minimal evidence suggested the ability to influence offending rates, involved tough sells. There are two important factors to be considered. The first is to have an awareness of the extant literature on effective practice; to be aware of what is possible in delivering a successful program, and not to oversell the effects of even successful programs. While the general outcome literature is now reporting reductions in offending ranging from 20 to 40 per cent (Andrews et. al., 1990; Lipsey & Wilson, 1998), there are some areas of correctional practice where data has not supported claims of effectiveness. One such area is related to outcomes with psychopathic individuals. Lösel (1998) suggests that, while there are some promising approaches in treating this population, the chapter on effective treatment with psychopaths should be the shortest chapter in any correctional practice book.

The second critical consideration in promoting program implementation is knowledge of the willingness of policy makers, correctional professionals and the immediate community to accept a shift in policy. Petersilia (cited in Harris & Smith, 1996) suggests:

> Unless a community recognizes or accepts the premise that a change in corrections is needed, is affordable, and does not conflict with its sentiments regarding just punishment, an innovative project has little hope of surviving much less succeeding. (p. 194)

Community versus residential context for treatment

While there seem to be some minor variations in interpretation of the effects of the immediate context to support implementation of programs, as a general statement, community contexts seem more able to support effective outcomes when compared to programs delivered in residential contexts (Andrews, 1998). Henggeler, Schoenwald, Bourduin, Rowland and Cunningham (1998) argue that treating high risk youth in the community is a more ecologically valid approach to both assessing and treating high risk youth since it allows for an increased opportunity to work directly with the systems that are both influencing and being influenced by the behaviour of their families and peers. Hoge, Leschied and Andrews (1993), in a study on the components in young offender programs, found that factors of effective correctional practice were more likely to be identified in community programs than in residential programs.

EMPIRICAL FINDINGS RELATED TO IMPLEMENTATION: TREATMENT ADHERENCE AND PROGRAM COMPLIANCE

The evolution of research development in the corrections field has only recently emphasized the importance of providing outcome evaluation as a standard in service delivery. Indeed, one of the somewhat surprising findings reported in Andrews et al. (1990) is the fact that programs that were being evaluated *by those charged with their implementation* were actually characterized through their outcomes as more effective than those that were not being as closely monitored. Hence it would seem that evaluation could also be characterized as a factor in successful implementation. Monitoring for program implementation, however, has not met with the same level of development. The following subsections (Treatment adherence and Program compliance) will highlight two examples of implementation evaluation which serve to assist in understanding programs that are relatively successful in identifying effective implementation strategies.

Treatment adherence

For any experienced corrections professional, it will come as no surprise that implementation, while critical, is only a part of any success story. The real challenge arises in trying to (1) implement a program consistent with the components reflecting an effective strategy—referred to as program integrity (Andrews, Gordon, Hill, Kurkowski & Hoge, 1993), and (2) support those factors that can sustain a program after it has shown itself to be effective.

What are those factors that influence sustainability and help programs remain true to the factors critical for success?

Multi-Systemic Therapy (MST)

Scott Henggeler and his associates—see Chapter 5—at the Medical University of South Carolina have turned their attention not only to program contents that are effective with high-risk youth but also to those factors that can sustain an effective program over the longer term.

A brief overview of MST suggests that a therapeutic focus on certain systemic factors within the lives of highly conflicted youth (i.e. that share a present, solution, strength-based focus) will be rewarded with significant reductions in youth criminal activity. Results from Henggeler, Melton, Brondino, Scherer and Hanley (1997) suggested that while some treatment gains were sustained in some youths, others were not. Further analysis by the authors suggested that program sustainability was tied to the presence of certain therapist/program characteristics that in turn characterized specific components of the MST model. The conclusion of this study suggested that, to achieve sustainability of positive outcomes from intervention, adequate and ongoing training and consultation were necessary. Furthermore, these authors developed the Therapist Adherence Measure (TAM) which consists of 26 items that ask family members to rate their therapist on factors that would reflect consistency of the intervention with the principles of MST. Computer scoring with TAM allows for a relatively short turnaround time to provide a quantified summary to the therapist and their supervisor regarding how consistently the intervention was provided on a case-by-case basis. Data suggests that therapist adherence is positively correlated with client outcomes. The development of similar adherence measures particular to a given intervention is possible given clearly identified and well-articulated aspects of the nature of the intervention and type of service delivery.

Program compliance

While studies such as those with MST examine treatment adherence at the therapist level, another line of investigation recommends evaluating a program's ability to comply with preset conditions that *evidence has suggested* are consistent with the overall components of effective programs.

The Correctional Program Assessment Inventory (CPAI)

The CPAI (Gendreau & Andrews, 1996) is an inventory—see Gendreau, Goggin and Smith in Chapter 12—developed out of the meta-analysis literature on effective programs. It consists of 75 items covering six components critical to the understanding of what constitutes an effective program, along with two areas that are considered integral to effective programs, namely emphasis on evaluation and ethical considerations. The components consist of: program implementation, client preservice assessment, program characteristics, staff characteristics, evaluation and other (i.e. ethical considerations). All of the components and the questions asked of programs consist of factors influenced by the reviews of the effective corrections literature. Table 1.1 summarizes the six components of the CPAI.

In a large-scale review of young offender programs in one jurisdiction, Hoge et al. (1993) reviewed over one hundred programs measured by the extent and nature of components on the CPAI. The results of this study were telling. Data reflected the range of program components that were available and where they tended to reside. Table 1.2 summarizes the scale scores of the CPAI as a function of the location of the programs (i.e. custody, probation, etc.). These results suggest that the presence of programs with higher scores on the important scales from the CPAI tended to be in the community (characterized as Community Support Teams), as opposed to those in custody. Further analysis, using a measure such as the CPAI, can identify training and staff needs, movement of service from residential to community

Table 1.1 Summary of the CPAI components

Scale description

1. Program implementation: surveys the conditions under which the program was introduced.
2. Preservice assessment: surveys applications of the principle of risk, need and responsivity.
3. Program characteristics: assesses targeting of criminogenic factors and the use of cognitive behavioral techniques.
4. Therapeutic integrity: surveys service delivery, emphasizing intensity and matching conditions.
5. Relapse prevention: surveys extent to which programs focus on post-release programs.
6. Staff characteristics: surveys staff and training issues.
7. Evaluation: examines the extent to which the system emphasizes/encourages research and evaluation activities.
8. Other: assesses emphasis on ethical concerns and security of program funding.

Table 1.2 Mean total treatment scores—CPAI—of four Young Offender Service Sector programs

	Probation ($N = 18$)	Open custody ($N = 57$)	Secure custody ($N = 8$)	Community support team ($N = 9$)
Total treatment	0.21	0.26	0.29	0.51

Taken from Hoge, Leschied and Andrews (1993).

approaches by capitalizing on the strengths of certain programs. While the authors would agree that measures such as the CPAI should not be held as a "gold standard", nonetheless, such a measure holds promise in assessing programs on a broad scale.

ISSUES IN DISSEMINATION AND TRAINING

As programs generally, and correctional programs in particular, move to higher levels of accountability, the movement towards standards of practice and compliance reviews will be encouraged. Indeed, in the next 2 years Correctional Services Canada (CSC) will be moving towards adopting a set of standards to guide the content and delivery of programs. The increasing challenge therefore will be to move the developing knowledge to the field in order to implement effective correctional practices.

Access to that knowledge is an ongoing challenge, both to those who are partners in developing it, and also to those practitioners who are trying to access it. The tradition of developing knowledge only to have it published in relatively obscure academic journals read by few will, arguably, not move the field dramatically in developing innovative strategies. Indeed, this tradition of distancing knowledge from the field, by viewing publication as the end of knowledge development rather than the beginning, may be an answer to Cullen et al.'s (1998) query as to why so few in the corrections field lack familiarity with knowledge in the area of effective corrections.

A major challenge in corrections therefore will be to look to innovative ways to communicate what is known in order to support change at the policy and practitioner level. Increasing the availability of knowledge is perhaps the single largest challenge in this area. Four innovations in communication in corrections are worth noting as examples.

1. RCJNet is a list serve website that communicates to numerous corrections processionals about knowledge in the corrections field. Currently managed by Irving Kulik of CSC, the service provides website links, summaries of recent justice documents or summaries of research that may be of interest. Using the latest technology, RCJNet serves as a clearinghouse for current corrections information. The National Criminal Justice Reference Service (NCJRS) in Washington, DC serves a similar purpose in the USA in making current documents available online for widespread dissemination. (WEBSITES: RCJNet-L@post. queensu.ca; http://ojjdp.ncjrs.org/site.html)

2. The US National Institute of Justice (USNIJ) has initiated a distance education program providing learning opportunities to correctional professionals through a system of centres connected through satellite-linked communications systems. From a single source unlimited numbers of practitioners and policy makers, across wide geographic areas, can interact with the leaders in the field in hearing of new program or policy ideas. (WEBSITE: www.ojp.usdoj.gov/nij/)

3. The London Family Court Clinic, along with Multi-Systemic Therapy Services Incorporated in Charleston, South Carolina, has developed an interactive website that links MST teams across North America and Europe. Practitioners using MST are able to communicate with one another with respect to promising therapeutic approaches or clinical issues that may arise in the course of service delivery. Recently, the development of an MST clinical team in Norway was able to link to the Ontario teams. Collegial supervision takes on new meaning in this era of expanding technology! (WEBSITE: www.lfcc.on.ca; www.sc.edu/ ifis/MSTfact.html)

4.   The Toronto-based Institute for Anti-Social and Violent Youth (IAVY) directed by Jalal Shamsie has, for close on 25 years, provided an extracting and commentary service on articles of particular interest to the young offender field (*Youth Update*). Such services help to focus and summarize information of particular currency and relevance to the field by reviewing articles from major journals. (WEBSITE: www.iay.org)

SUMMARY

Implementation of programs in such a politically charged context as corrections is a challenging prospect. What corrections professionals have going for them, however, is a knowledge base that supports certain programs and policies over others with the goal of increasing community safety and lessening human misery. This chapter has highlighted the major issues in implementation as being:

1.   An acknowledgement of the literature on "what works" for effective corrections and policy practices. This literature highlights appropriate assessment strategies that increase the potential for interventions to be clinically relevant to factors that influence criminogenic risk.
2.   Identification of contextual factors that can influence the probability that program innovation will be successfully introduced. These factors include leadership support for implementation, staff competence and goal clarification for the reasons behind implementation.
3.   Specific contextual factors influence successful implementation. Current knowledge suggests that different factors influence successful *community-based* implementation versus *residential-based* implementation.
4.   Measures have been developed to assess and monitor the degree of success in program implementation. These include measures for both treatment adherence and program compliance.
5.   Training and dissemination are now considered the great challenges facing implementation in the corrections field. The nothing-works debate is now recognized as serving an importance purpose in focusing efforts in developing the current extent of knowledge on effective practice. However, as many have cited, the nothing-works debate is now over. Arguably what could shape the next generation of corrections professionals is the challenge of communicating the knowledge on effective strategies to practitioners. Using current technology, clearinghouse extracting services, the Internet and interactive communication

technology we can communicate that knowledge to those who make decisions both for policy and for practice.

Finally, as Shorr (1991) stated almost a decade ago,

> ... It is essential in order to institutionalize these effective interventions, to find better ways of maintaining accountability and achieving credibility by becoming a part of the shift toward outcome accountability, outcome-focussed assessment. (p. 3)

Once we have the knowledge, choose to implement those things that have shown themselves to be effective, and communicate those findings to the field, the obligation remains to evaluate the effects of those interventions towards which we have directed our knowledge.

Lastly, as work continues to document effective strategies in reducing offending, larger scale dissemination efforts need to be evaluated and refined. The first author's experience in supporting MST dissemination and development of programs in Ontario, across four geographically diverse sites, has supported the belief that large-scale efforts with cooperation across sites enlisting the support of the programs' initiators is possible. However, what remains to be evaluated is how such efforts can be sustained with what degree of effort in ongoing training and consultation. This question will in part be addressed in the National Institute of Justice study currently in progress using MST dissemination as a test of ongoing support for implementation.

CONCLUSION

The implementation of "best practices" in the correctional field is a function of the ability of policy makers, program administrators and service deliverers to translate knowledge and theory into practice *with integrity*. This chapter has summarized some of the major findings, largely from correctional meta-analyses, that can help guide the acceptance of effective interventions with offender populations. In addition, the somewhat smaller literature on the evaluation of treatment implementation and adherence has also been summarized. Within this outline is the structure of the *multi-level systems perspective* that provides a context for the known factors that are critical in successful implementation at the client, program, organizational and societal levels.

References

Andrews, D. A. (1998). *The Importance of the Appropriate Management of Risk and Reintegration Potential*, Presentation at the Beyond Prisons Conference, Queen's University and Correctional Services Canada, 16 March 1998.

Andrews, D. A., & Bonta, J. (1998). *The Psychology of Criminal Conduct*, 2nd ed. Cincinnati, OH: Anderson Publishing Co.

Andrews, D. A., Gordon, D. A., Hill, J., Kurkowski, K. P., & Hoge, R. D. (1993). Program integrity, methodology, and treatment characteristics: A meta-analysis of effects of family intervention with young offenders. Unpublished manuscript.

Andrews, D. A., Zinger, I., Hoge, R. D., Bonta, J., Gendreau, P., & Cullen, F. (1990). Does correctional treatment work? A clinically-relevant and psychologically-informed meta-analysis. *Criminology*, **28**, 369–404.

Bauman, L. J., Stein, R. E. K., & Reys, H. T. (1991). Reinventing fidelity: The transfer of social technology among settings. *American Journal of Community Psychology*, **19**(4), 619–639.

Bernfeld, G. A., Blase, K. A., & Fixsen, D. L. (1990). Towards a unified perspective on human service delivery systems: Application of the Teaching-Family Model. In R. J. McMahon & R. De V. Peters (Eds), *Behavior Disorders of Adolescents: Research, Intervention and Policy in Clinical and School Settings*, pp. 191–205. New York: Plenum.

Burchard, J. D. (1987). Social and political challenges to behavioral programs with delinquents and criminals. In E. K. Morris & C. J. Braukmann (Eds), *Behavioral Approaches to Crime and Delinquency*, pp. 577–594. New York: Plenum.

Cantrell, M. L., & Cantrell, R. P. (1985). Assessment of the natural environment. *Education and Treatment of Children*, **8**, 275–295.

Cullen, F. T., Wright, J. P., Brown, S., Moon, M. M., Blankenship, M. B., & Applegate, B. K. (1998). Attitudes toward prevention. *Crime and Delinquency*, **44**(2), 187–204.

Ellickson, P., & Petersilia, J. (1983). *Implementing New Ideas in Criminal Justice*. Santa Monica CA: The Rand Corporation.

Gendreau, P., & Andrews, D. A. (1996). *Correctional Program Assessment Inventory*. St John, New Brunswick: University of New Brunswick.

Gendreau, P., & Ross, R. R. (1979). Effective correctional treatment: Bibliotherapy for cynics. *Crime and Delinquency*, **21**, 463–489.

Hare, R. (1991). *The Hare Psychopathy Checklist—Revised*. Toronto, Ontario: Multi Health Systems.

Harris, P., & Smith, S. (1996). Developing community corrections: An Implementation perspective. In A. T. Harland (Ed.), *Choosing Correctional Options that Work: Defining the Demand and Evaluating the Supply*, pp. 183–222. Thousand Oaks, CA: Sage.

Henggeler, S. W., Melton, G. B., Brondino, M. J., Scherer, D. G., & Hanley, J. H. (1997). Multisystemic therapy with violent and chronic juvenile offenders and their families: The role of treatment fidelity and successful dissemination. *Journal of Consulting and Clinical Psychology*, **65**(5), 821–833.

Henggeler, S. W., Schoenwald, S. K., Bourduin, C. M., Rowland, M. D., & Cunningham, P. B. (1998) *Multisystemic Treatment of Antisocial Behaviour in Children and Adolescents*. New York: The Guilford Press.

Hoge, R. D., & Andrews, D. A. (1986). A model for conceptualizing interventions in social service agencies. *Canadian Psychology*, **27**, 332–341.

Hoge, R. D., Leschied, A. W., & Andrews, D. A. (1993). *An Investigation of Young Offender Services in the Province of Ontario*, A report of the repeat offender project. Toronto, Ontario: Ministry of Community and Social Services.

Huizinga, D. H., Menard, S., & Elliott, D. S. (1989). Delinquency and drug use: Temporal and developmental patterns. *Justice Quarterly*, **6**(3), 419–455.

Hundert, J. (1999). Bringing applied behaviour analysis out of the trenches. *The ONTABA Analyst*, **5**(3), 1–2 and 5.

Jung, C. H., & Bernfeld, G. A. (1987). Enhancing the effectiveness of child care services through organizational behavior management. *Journal of Child Care*, **3**, 73–85.

Leschied, A. W., Jaffe, P. G., Gendreau, P., & Andrews, D. A. (1989). Treatment issues and young offenders. In R. Corrado, N. Bala, M. Leblanc, & R. Linden (Eds), *Juvenile Justice in Canada: A Theoretical and Analytical Assessment*. Vancouver, BC: Butterworth Publications.

Leschied, A. W., & Cunningham, A. (1999). Clinical trials of multisystemic therapy in Ontario: Rationale and current status of a community-based alternative for high risk young offenders. *Forum on Corrections Research*, pp. 25–29.

Lipsey, M. (1995). What do we learn from 400 research studies on the effectiveness of treatment with juvenile delinquents. In J. McGuire (Ed.), *What Works: Reducing Reoffending*, pp. 63–78. Chichester: John Wiley.

Lipsey, M. W., & Wilson, D. B. (1998). Effective interventions for serious juvenile offenders: A synthesis of research. In R. Loeber, & D. P. Farrington (Eds), *Serious and Violent Offenders: Risk Factors and Successful Interventions*, pp. 313–366. Thousand Oaks, CA: Sage.

Lösel, F. (1998). Treatment and management of psychopaths. In D. J. Cooke, A. Forth, & R. D. Hare (Eds), *Psychopathy: Theory, Research and Implications for Society*, pp. 303–354. The Hague: Kluwer Academic.

Martinson, R. (1979). What works: Questions and answers about prison reform. *The Public Interest*, **35**, 22–54.

McCarthy, P. (1989). *The Delaware Family Preservation Project: Implementing Planned Organizational Change*, Paper presented at the Third Annual Empowering Families Conference, Charlotte, NC, November 1989.

Palmer, T. (1996). Programmatic and nonprogrammatic aspects of successful implementation. In A. T. Harland (Ed.), *Choosing Correctional Options that Work: Defining the Demand and Evaluating the Supply*, pp. 131–182. Thousand Oaks, CA: Sage.

Rodgers-Warren, A., & Warren, S. F. (1977). *Ecobehavioral Perspectives in Behavioural Analysis*. Baltimore: University Park Press.

Shamsie, J. (1979). Our treatments do not work. Where do we go from here? *Canadian Journal of Psychiatry*.

Shorr, L. B. (1989). *Within Our Reach: Breaking the Cycle of Disadvantage*. New York: Doubleday.

Shorr, L. B. (1991). *Successful Programs: From Moving Models to Moving Mountains*, Paper presented at the Empowering Families Conference, St Louis, Missouri, 7 December.

Simourd, D., & Van de Ven, J. (1999). Assessment of criminal attitudes: Criterion-related validity of the criminal sentiments scale-modified and pride in delinquency scale. *Criminal Justice and Behaviour*, **26**(1), 90–106.

Stolz, S. B. (1981) Adoption of innovations from applied behavioral research: "Does anybody care?" *Journal of Applied Behavioral Analysis*, **14**, 491–505.

PART I: KEY ISSUES IN CORRECTIONAL EFFECTIVENESS

PROLOGUE

In his chapter James McGuire highlights the current emphasis in correctional interventions on evidence-based practice and systematic reviews of evaluations. He also reviews meta-analyses that have proved that many correctional interventions are effective in reducing recidivism. The most effective programs are community-based and include risk/needs assessment, cognitive–behavioral techniques and a multi-modal approach. McGuire concludes with a discussion of how these principles have been used in the accreditation of English prison programs.

Brandon Welsh and David Farrington review attempts to compare the financial costs and benefits of correctional intervention programs. They describe the steps involved in an economic (cost-benefit) analysis. Despite extensive searches of the literature, they could only find seven existing cost-benefit analyses of correctional interventions. Importantly, in all cases the financial benefits exceeded the financial costs, with benefit : cost ratios ranging from 1.13 to 7.14. This was in spite of the fact that financial benefits were underestimated in all studies because of the omission of intangible costs to victims (e.g. pain and suffering). Welsh and Farrington advocate more cost-benefit analyses. Also, since the quality of any economic analysis depends on the quality of the underlying evaluation design, they recommend more use of randomized experiments in evaluating correctional interventions.

In the final chapter of this part Friedrich Lösel provides an overview of the *quality* of research and evaluations that influence the implementation of correctional programs. While acknowledging that the corrections field is in better shape than most human service areas with respect to a "field relevant" knowledge base, Professor Lösel outlines areas where knowledge is necessary to promote continued successful program implementation. These recommendations include: improving research designs with field trials that use contrast groups that make outcome comparisons more meaningful; differentiating offender characteristics within samples that assist in answering the question "effective with respect to *whom*"?; developing more sensitive outcome measures that identify offender changes that relate to reductions in recidivism; and inclusion of cost-benefit analysis in outcome evaluations as part of the standard for evaluating correctional effectiveness.

Chapter 2

WHAT WORKS IN CORRECTIONAL INTERVENTION? EVIDENCE AND PRACTICAL IMPLICATIONS

JAMES MCGUIRE

Department of Clinical Psychology, University of Liverpool, Liverpool, UK

The present moment is in many senses a fortunate one in which to be writing about evaluation of correctional services. There is currently a significant growth of interest in evaluation of interventions across many fields, particularly in public services such as health and education. In criminal justice agencies the contemporary era of interest in outcomes is traced by many to widely cited research reviews published during the 1970s. While those reviews drew predominantly negative conclusions, the expanding use of meta-analysis as a technique of research review during the 1980s and thereafter has radically altered our state of knowledge in this field as in others. The application of meta-analytic review, for example, by Glass, McGaw and Smith (1981) to outcome evaluation in education and psychotherapy created a trend which today has widespread ramifications not only in the domain of research activity but also in practice and the formation of public policy.

At present there is a convergence of interest in the outcomes of interventions designed to reduce the frequency or severity of a broad spectrum of

Offender Rehabilitation in Practice. Edited by G. A. Bernfeld, D. P. Farrington and A. W. Leschied.
© 2001 John Wiley & Sons, Ltd.

social problems. To begin this chapter, that convergence will be depicted in outline as a means of setting the scene for what follows. The bulk of the chapter will then be divided into two main sections. First, the current position with regard to our knowledge of correctional interventions will be summarized. Second, some developments in practice and policy which are at least in part a consequence of these findings will be described and discussed.

The approach adopted in the chapter will parallel that taken elsewhere in this book. While it is essential to have an understanding and knowledge-base concerning effective interventions or "treatments" at the individual client level, this information must be integrated with a model of processes on other levels if it is to be appropriately and effectively deployed. Such a *behavioural systems perspective* obliges us to consider four aspects of innovation, and evaluation of effectiveness: *client, programme, organisational* and societal (Bernfeld, Blase & Fixsen, 1990). Furthermore, it is essential to view these system components as engaged in dynamic interaction over time.

EVIDENCE BASED PRACTICE

It is impossible to trace a single origin of the currently widespread expectation that interventions to solve human problems should be founded on a firm evidence base, and that the resultant services should be extensively evaluated to determine their impact and effectiveness. Academics, practitioners and politicians alike appear to have awoken, particularly during the last quarter of the 20th century, to the need to evaluate systems of services and their effects. This is not to say that there was never any attempt to do so prior to that period. Evaluative research was conducted, but its connections with fundamental research informing the rationale for interventions on the one hand, and with public policy considerations on the other, were perhaps less explicitly articulated than they are today.

For politicians the process was driven by concerns, with varying degrees of relationship to underlying ideologies, to reduce government spending and taxation and to obtain high efficiency and "value for money". The application of econometrics approaches, cost-benefit analyses and latterly also "league tables" of performance, date from the same period (at least in the UK). But in the field of health, medical practitioners themselves had already become concerned with the outcomes of their interventions. There was a growing sense that though large volumes of research results were available, their cumulative benefit was limited. For research findings to constitute real advances in knowledge they have to be systematically reviewed and integrated. Unless this happens it is difficult to link findings to meaningful changes in practice. The medical epidemiologist Cochrane (1979) provided a significant impetus to changing this process when he spoke of the marked need to examine whether medicine and related health research fields could genuinely claim to have sound empirical foundations, when no systematic record existed of the effectiveness of different interventions. When, some years later, Mulrow (1987) examined a series of review articles published in medical journals over a 12-month period (June 1985 to June 1986), she found major shortcomings in the manner in which reviews were conducted and reported.

It was in response to comments and findings such as these that the Cochrane Collaboration was created in 1993. This is an international network of researchers and reviewers coordinated through 15 separate sites in Europe, North and South America, Australia and South Africa. Its self-appointed task is to locate, evaluate and integrate the results of well-designed intervention studies (usually randomized controlled trials or RCTs). By 1999 the available set of outcome studies, assembled as the Cochrane Database of Systematic Reviews, contained more than a quarter of a million entries. These have been made accessible to researchers and other users through the Cochrane Library, accessible via the Internet and regularly updated.

More recently still, this development has led to a parallel innovation focused not on health but on the study of educational and social interventions including those in correctional services. The result was the creation of the Campbell Collaboration which had its inaugural international gathering in February 2000 and held its first full scientific conference in April 2001. Even prior to its formal launch the Collaboration had (as of July 1999) assembled a database of 10,000 entries, entitled the Social, Psychological, Educational and Criminological Trials Register (the SPECTR database; Petrosino, Boruch, Rounding, McDonald & Chalmers, 1999).

In summary then: across many fields of endeavour there is now a standard philosophy, encapsulated in the phrase *evidence-based practice*, that is regarded as a cornerstone of the process of consolidating and synthesizing scientific knowledge. It has become a virtual prerequisite of the design and delivery of services and of consultation between researchers, practitioners and policy makers. This also serves as a benchmark for identifying unanswered questions and for signalling the necessary next steps for research investigations.

RESEARCH ON "CORRECTIONAL TREATMENT"

Interventions designed to reduce crime are sometimes depicted as residing on one of three levels: *primary*, *secondary* and *tertiary* (Guerra, Tolan & Hammond, 1994). The first, sometimes called *developmental prevention*, entails provision of services to families and children in environments, such as socio-economically deprived neighbourhoods, with the aim of reducing not only long-term difficulties including delinquency but also mental health problems and substance abuse (Yoshikawa, 1994). *Secondary prevention* is focused on known at-risk groups (e.g. individuals who have conduct disorders) in attempts to avert subsequent involvement in juvenile offending (Kaufman, 1985). *Tertiary prevention* is addressed to adjudicated offenders, those already convicted of crimes, with the objective of reducing rates of recidivism (Gendreau & Andrews, 1990). It is only this third level of preventive efforts that is the focus of the present chapter.

In the field of corrections the issue of effective interventions at the tertiary level began to be intensely debated from approximately the mid-1970s when, almost simultaneously, research reviews were conducted in both Europe and North America. The primary objective of most evaluative research in this field has fairly consistently been to discover methods of reducing offender recidivism. In the United Kingdom, Brody (1976) reviewed 100 studies of the impact of different types of court sentences and other interventions which attempted to evaluate this outcome. The attempt to arrive at clear conclusions was hampered by the poor quality of much of the research that had been undertaken, but the available findings appeared to point towards very little if any notable impact in terms of reduced rates of reoffending. Perhaps more widely known, in the United States a review of 231 treatment studies was published by Lipton, Martinson and Wilks (1975; Martinson, 1974). In the latter paper Martinson argued that "treatment", by which he meant any added ingredient in criminal justice agencies (such as provision of counselling, education, vocational training or psychological therapy), could not be shown to add anything of value to the available network of criminal justice sentences, sanctions or other formalized legal procedures.

In the wake of these exceedingly pessimistic conclusions a number of fairly critical rejoinders appeared (e.g. Palmer, 1975). The strongest challenge, issued by Ross and Gendreau (1980) comprised an edited book containing reports on effective services in which there was evidence of reductions in recidivism, demonstrating clearly the extent to which more positive evidence had been ignored. Ironically, in a subsequent publication of his own, the thrust of the initially reported negative findings was reversed by Martinson himself (1979). Despite the very large volume of positive evidence now available in this field the issue of treatment effectiveness continues to be disputed, and this remains a field in which it can be difficult to discern the boundaries between empirical evidence and underlying attitudes and values that may be operating.

However, the systematic study of criminal sentencing and of the treatment of offenders has been virtually transformed over recent years by the appearance of numerous review studies based on meta-analysis. Since its initial use in the field of corrections in 1985 meta-analysis has been employed in a

Table 2.1 Meta-analytic reviews of interventions with offenders

Source author (date)	Number of outcomes	Mean effect size
Garrett (1985)	121	+0.18
Gensheimer et al. (1986)	31	+0.26
Mayer et al. (1986)	17	+0.33
Gottschalk et al. (1987a)	61	+0.22
Gottschalk et al. (1987b)	14	+0.25
Lösel and Koferl (1989)	16	+0.11
Whitehead and Lab (1989)	50	+0.13
Andrews et al. (1990)	154	+0.10
Izzo & Ross (1990)	46	Cog > non-cog, 2.5:1[a]
Roberts & Camasso (1991)	46	0.06–0.81[b]
Lipsey (1992)	397	+0.10
Gendreau & Goggin (1996)	138	0.00
Pearson et al. (1997)	846	—[b]
Lipsey & Wilson (1998)	200	0.12/0.22[c]
Redondo et al. (1999)	57	+0.15
Dowden & Andrews (1999)	229	+0.09
Andrews & Dowden (1999)	24	—[b]
Dowden & Andrews (2000)	52	+0.07

[a] Findings were expressed as a ratio of effects of two different types of programme.
[b] No mean effect size was reported.
[c] Mean effect sizes for institutional and community-based programmes, respectively.

number of reviews of treatment-outcome studies with offenders (Lösel, 1995). A series of 18 meta-analyses of tertiary-level offender treatment has recently been reviewed by McGuire (2001). Some basic information concerning these reviews is given in Table 2.1.

Table 2.1 displays the main findings from these reviews in chronological order of appearance, showing the number of outcomes subsumed in each, and the mean effect size where reported. Findings of meta-analyses can be expressed in a number of ways, but two types of statistics tend to predominate in the reviews published in this field (Rosenthal, 1994). One is the use of correlation coefficients, usually Pearson's r or phi (ϕ), depicting the strength of the relationship between the independent variable (membership of treatment or control samples) and the dependent variable (outcome in terms of success or failure with regard to recidivism). The other is the Cohen's d statistic which is a measure of the extent of change in the means of experimental and control groups, expressed as a function of the pooled sample variance. In computing either of these statistics a number of adjustments may be made (e.g. to take account of variations in sample sizes in the different studies subsumed). Where this procedure was used the weighted effect sizes so obtained are the ones quoted in the table.

Some information will now be given concerning the meta-analytic reviews summarized including the designated scope of each.

Garrett (1985). The first meta-analytic review in this area was a survey of 111 outcome studies conducted in the period 1960–1984, describing residential treatment programmes for juvenile offenders. Cumulatively, 13,055 individuals were involved in the studies, with a mean age of 15.8. Ten of the studies examined the effects of more than one treatment, producing a total of 121 effect sizes.

Gensheimer, Mayer, Gottschalk and Davidson (1986). These authors reviewed 44 studies of diversion schemes for young offenders (mean age 14.6 years). Of these studies 31 involved comparisons between experimental and control groups with a combined sample size of 10,210; other studies entailed pre-post comparisons only.

Mayer, Gensheimer, Davidson and Gottschalk (1986). A review of studies of the effects of interventions based on social learning principles. A set of 34 studies yielded 39 effect sizes, but only 17 were controlled experimental studies with recidivism as an outcome variable.

Gottschalk, Davidson, Gensheimer and Mayer (1987a). This review addressed the impact of community-based programmes for young offenders. From an initial pool of 643 research studies 163 were extracted. Of these, 61 studies with a cumulative sample size of 11,463 included recidivism as an outcome variable.

Gottschalk, Davidson, Mayer and Gensheimer (1987b). The focus of this meta-analysis was on behavioural programmes for young offenders. From the same database as employed in the preceding review 25 studies were identified yielding 30 tests of treatment effects. However, only 14 addressed recidivism as the outcome variable.

Lösel and Koferl (1989). This study investigated the impact of German "socio-therapeutic" prison regimes for serious, recidivistic, mainly adult offenders. Patterns of effects were studied amongst 16 studies evaluating 11 prisons operating such regimes. A main focus of the review was the association between regime characteristics and recidivism outcomes.

Whitehead and Lab (1989). A review of juvenile offender treatment studies published in the period 1975–1984. This incorporated 50 studies, the majority dealing with diversion programmes. A wide range of effect sizes was noted with strict limits being set regarding what was considered to be a significant finding.

Andrews et al. (1990). In this review a series of 154 outcome effects from studies with both adult and juvenile offenders was analysed in a number of ways. Most importantly, studies were classified according to the extent to which the respective interventions adhered to "principles of correctional intervention" derived from earlier research. The pattern of findings supported the hypothesis that services which applied the principles of "human service" (risk, need and responsivity) produced larger effect sizes than those that did not do so.

Izzo and Ross (1990). A review designed to compare programmes for juvenile offenders with and without cognitive-training elements. Rather than computing a mean effect size the authors reported the ratio of relative effectiveness of the two types of programme.

Roberts and Camasso (1991). This was a review of evaluations of 46 treatment programmes for young offenders published between 1980 and 1990. The mean age of the samples studied was 15.1 years; some interventions were targeted on offenders in the 9–12 age range and entailed primary prevention in the sense defined earlier in this chapter.

Lipsey (1992, 1995). To date, this is the largest published meta-analytic review, encompassing 443 studies of treatment of offenders in the age range 12–21. Of these studies 397 focused on recidivism as an outcome variable; 65 per cent of the studies obtained positive findings.

Gendreau and Goggin (1996). A review of a different type, integrating results from 138 outcome studies focused on intermediate punishment or "smart sentencing": the use of enhanced punishment, surveillance, random drug testing, intensive probation supervision and other criminal sanctions or court-mandated procedures.

Pearson, Lipton and Cleland (1997). This report, given as a conference presentation, is part of a larger but as yet unpublished review, known as the CDATE (Correctional Drug Abuse Treatment Effectiveness) project. When completed this will be the most comprehensive meta-analysis available, including both published and unpublished primary studies, covering all age groups and on a worldwide scale, and also including studies of substance abuse treatments.

Lipsey and Wilson (1998). A review of studies of treatment of serious, persistent young offenders (age range 14–17). The authors located 117 studies of community-based interventions (mean effect size +0.22) and 83 based in institutions (mean effect size +0.12). Approximately half of the studies were RCTs.

Redondo, Sánchez-Meca and Garrido (1999). An integrative survey of studies conducted in European countries between 1980 and 1993. The 49 studies included were based on a total sample of 7,728 participants, covering a wide age range, and generating a total of 57 effect sizes.

Dowden and Andrews (1999). A study of outcomes of interventions with young offenders; 134 primary studies provided 229 tests of the effectiveness of treatment. The mean effect size was +0.09; effect sizes ranged from −0.43 to +0.83.

Andrews and Dowden (1999). A review undertaken to test the hypothesis that principles of "human service" (risk, need and responsivity) which have emerged from meta-analyses on studies of male offenders applied to female offenders also. A set of 26 studies yielded 45 tests, 24 on samples composed exclusively of female offenders.

Dowden and Andrews (2000). A review of studies focused on reduction of violent recidivism; 34 studies were located yielding 52 tests; 70 per cent of the comparisons were based on adult offender samples.

Whilst several of the foregoing reviews have study samples that overlap to some extent, the total number of independent outcomes nevertheless exceeds 2,000. The majority of the meta-analyses, and the primary studies on which they are based, originate from North America, and are focused on interventions with younger offenders (predominantly juveniles in the age range 14–17 and young adults aged 18–21). However, there are several that incorporate studies of adults across a wider age range. There are indications that effect sizes for adult populations tend to be somewhat lower than those obtained with juvenile offender samples (Cleland, Pearson, Lipton & Yee, 1997). The overwhelming majority of the primary study samples consisted of male offenders. The recent review by Dowden and Andrews (1999) was designed to counterbalance this and explore whether similar patterns would emerge from studies with women offenders.

FINDINGS OF META-ANALYSES: PRINCIPAL TRENDS

On the basis of findings such as those shown in Table 2.1 it is difficult to sustain the view that "nothing works" to reduce offender recidivism. The mean effect sizes for treatment over control groups are uniformly positive. The patterns of effects obtained through meta-analysis are not always easy to interpret, and Lösel (1995) has cautioned against some of the pitfalls. It is vital to take account of the possible impact of the quality and rigour of research designs as it is known that effect sizes are typically lower amongst experimental studies involving randomization and other controls on extraneous variables. Perhaps unsurprisingly, the quality of design in the primary studies varies considerably. Most reviews report aspects of this and in some (e.g. Lipsey, 1992; Pearson, Lipton, & Cleland, 1997), schemes were developed for coding this in the analyses. Such a system has also been introduced in other studies using traditional narrative or tabulation approaches (e.g. MacKenzie, 1997).

In all of the reviews reported to date, however, broadly similar trends have emerged. Overall, as has been concluded by Lösel (1995), the net effect of treatment whilst positive is comparatively modest. At a mean ϕ coefficient estimated by Lösel to be in the region of 0.1 it is considerably lower, for example, than that obtained for outcomes of psychotherapy for mental health problems (Lambert & Bergin, 1994; Lipsey & Wilson, 1993). While this may appear disappointing, and in statistical terms is non-significant, even this level of reduction would be regarded by many observers as worth securing. Moreover, when set alongside other meta-analytic effect sizes and judged in terms of practical significance it compares reasonably well. For example, it is larger than the effect size obtained for the outcomes of some medical interventions, such as the use of aspirin to reduce the risk of a myocardial infarction. It is not far below the effect size for heart bypass surgery to reduce the risk of coronary disease, on which considerable sums are invested (Rosenthal, 1994; and see McGuire, 2001).

It should also be borne in mind that within the meta-analytic findings there are some interventions which do not reduce recidivism at all. On the contrary, they are associated with *increases* in it. This is the case for those which employ intensified criminal sanctioning (Andrews et al., 1990) or "deterrence" (Lipsey, 1992, 1995; Lipsey & Wilson, 1998). If these studies were excluded from the meta-analyses the mean effect for other types of treatment would be somewhat higher. Counter to the intuitions of many lay commentators on criminal justice there is little evidence that punitive sanctions effectively deter criminal acts amongst adjudicated offenders: their effect as judged by large-scale reviews is either neutral or in some instances negative.

At the other end of the scale, there are more constructive types of interventions that have a correspondingly significant effect in *reducing* rates of reoffending. Some programmes have been found to reduce recidivism by on average between 25 and 30 per cent. Predominantly, these interventions employ behavioural and/or cognitive skills training methods, or elements of them combined in specified ways.

GUIDELINES FOR EFFECTIVE INTERVENTIONS

The above meta-analytic studies have been the subject of extensive discussion in the criminal justice field. On the basis of them several reviewers have argued that it is possible to identify with confidence those features of programmes which contribute to higher levels of effectiveness (Andrews, 1995; Gendreau, 1996a, b; Hollin, 1999; Palmer, 1992). The publication of several edited collections of reviews has helped to reinforce this point (Harland, 1996; McGuire, 1995; Ross, Antonowicz & Dhaliwal, 1995). A review commissioned by the US National Institute of Justice examined these types of interventions alongside other approaches to crime prevention (Sherman et al., 1997). Still other reviewers have considered the role the findings might play in practical policies for offender services (Nuttall, Goldblatt & Lewis 1998; Vennard, Sugg, & Hedderman, 1997).

There is now a consensus that the probability of achieving positive outcomes can be maximized by combining a number of elements in offender programmes. Those components making for greater impact are distinct from the legal sanction or sentence imposed on individuals (McGuire, 1998). This overturns the claim made by Martinson (1974), outlined earlier, that treatment adds nothing to the network of criminal justice services. Additionally, three of the meta-analyses indicate that, on balance, community-based interventions have larger effect sizes than those delivered in institutions (Andrews et al., 1990; Lipsey & Wilson, 1998; Redondo, Sánchez-Meca & Garrido, 1997).

However, there are important interaction effects to be noted in this respect. Poorly designed, inappropriate forms of interventions emerge as ineffective regardless of the criminal justice setting in which they are delivered. Better designed services are of maximum benefit when provided in a non-custodial setting. Furthermore, even well-designed intervention programmes may have nil and possibly even negative effects if the quality of delivery is poor. This highlights the importance of the relationship between programme and organizational dimensions as defined by Bernfeld et al. (1990). There are no known treatment or training materials that will achieve their goals in the absence of trained and committed staff with adequate resources and managerial support.

On the basis of the available reviews it is possible to forward tentative guidelines for effective programmes of intervention designed to reduce recidivism. The following features have been identified as contributing to what Wexler (1998) has called "likely-to-succeed" interventions. They typically include these elements:

1. Those programmes and services that work best are founded on an explicit and well-articulated model of the causes of crime and criminal acts. This should be conceptually clear and based on sound, systematic empirical evidence.
2. There is a recognition of the importance of assessment of risk of re-offending based on criminal history and other variables, and allocation of offenders to different levels of supervision or service in accordance with this information.
3. It is vital to conduct assessment of criminogenic needs or dynamic risk factors—such as attitudes, the influence of criminal companions, skills deficits, substance dependency or self-control problems—that are known to be linked to offending behaviour and that may fluctuate over time.
4. The most effective interventions involve application of methods that correspond to the active, focused and participatory learning and change styles encountered in many offenders, alongside an acknowledged need to adapt services to individual differences in this regard.
5. Effective methods are characterized by clear objectives, and require

skilled and structured engagement by staff in tasks which are readily accepted as relevant to individual offenders' needs.

6. The most consistent positive effects are obtained through application of cognitive–behavioural models, comprising a collection of theoretically interrelated methods which focus on the dynamic interactions between individuals' thoughts, feelings and behaviour at the time of an offence.

7. There is a need for services to be delivered by personnel who have appropriate training and adequate resources; who adhere to their appointed objectives, adopt suitable methods and undertake systematic evaluation of individuals' progress and of the outcomes of their services overall. These elements constitute what is known as *programme integrity* (Hollin, 1995).

Where studies have been identified which combine several of these features, the impact on future recidivism has been found to be very substantial. Andrews and his colleagues (1990) presented evidence that incorporating several of the above ingredients within an offender programme (labelled by them the principles of *risk*, *criminogenic need* and *responsivity*) can lead to reductions in recidivism greater than 50 per cent. With further elements added, effect sizes are commensurately increased. Multimodal and systemic programs, in which several aspects of the environment of young offenders have been targets for intervention, have yielded the largest effect sizes to date. For example, Borduin, Mann, Cone and Henggeler (1995) have reported the outcome of *multi-systemic therapy* in which recidivism of serious young offenders was reduced by a factor in excess of 70 per cent over a follow-up period of 4 years (see also Henggeler, Schoenwald, Borduin, Rowland & Cunningham, 1998).

On the basis of a recently published review, it can be tentatively suggested that correctional interventions of the type discussed here may also be relatively cost-effective (Welsh & Farrington, 2000). Although to date there have been relatively few studies using econometric evaluations, the benefit-cost ratios of seven studies reviewed by these authors ranged from 1.13 : 1 to over 7 : 1 (see Chapter 3).

IMPACT OF RESEARCH FINDINGS

The findings on reduction of recidivism summarized above have begun to have an impact on the direction of both practice and policy with offenders in a number of countries. It is in considering such applications (actual or proposed) that the need to focus in parallel upon several aspects of programme implementation becomes apparent. This recapitulates the point emphasized earlier: that programmes should be planned with reference to those who will participate in them, and in the organizational and societal context in which they are delivered (Bernfeld et al., 1990; Harris & Smith, 1996). Recently Gendreau, Goggin and Smith (1999) have outlined a framework and enunciated key principles to be observed when attempting to transfer the findings of research in this field to wider scale implementation in criminal justice services.

During 1996 the prison service (England and Wales) embarked on a major initiative to increase the number of prison establishments providing programmes and activities designed to reduce rates of recidivism following release. As with many other agencies, the process of management in the prison service has been linked to the use of *Key Performance Indicators* (KPIs) which are measures of the achievement of core objectives of the service. In 1996 the provision of programmes designed to reduce recidivism was established as an indicator of this kind (KPI-7). Two independent specialist panels were appointed; one for accrediting programmes for sex offenders, the other dealing with general offending behaviour programmes. The panels published sets of criteria for evaluating the design and delivery of prison-based interventions.

Programmes designed to meet these criteria, and which have been accredited as doing so by the consultative panels, are now in use in more than 50 of England and Wales's 150 penal institutions. The introduction of these processes into the prison service in England and Wales from 1996 onwards has been described in more detail by Lipton, Thornton, McGuire, Porporino and Hollin (2001). Similar developments have occurred in the Scottish Prison Services and in Correctional Services of Canada. It may be that such initiatives will also be pursued by prison services in several other countries.

To sustain an initiative of this kind is a substantial undertaking, and has involved the deployment of significant additional resources. It has entailed an extensive programme of staff training events, creation of a system of monitoring and audit and associated mechanisms for administration and information management, both within individual prisons and on a service-wide scale. For example, all sessions of cognitive-skills programmes are videotaped for scrutiny (on a sampling basis) by external assessors. Procedures have been put in place for the systematic evaluation of programmes in respect of both short-term effects on intervening variables, and long-term impact on criminal recidivism.

The research findings outlined earlier have also had a marked impact on community agencies for offenders, principally the probation service (and, more recently, youth justice services also). During 1997–1998 in England and Wales the Probation Inspectorate, which monitors the working standards of probation nationally, conducted a focused or "thematic" inspection to examine the extent to which probation staff employ practices based on research evidence. The main report on this work (Underdown, 1998) proposed a series of new initiatives to extend the usage of evidence-based practice in probation work. This subsequently led to the selection of a number of programmes designated as *Pathfinder* projects that were earmarked for further development. In late 1999 a new accreditation process was established to operate jointly for prison and probation services. It is envisaged that programmes satisfactorily meeting accreditation criteria will be delivered at a large number of sites and that by the end of 2001 more than 20,000 offenders will have attended such programmes.

For a programme to be accredited for use in prison or prison settings a proposal must be submitted to the *Joint Prison Probation Accreditation Panel*, which, like its predecessor in the prison service, consists of independent experts and consultants. A submission should include copies of all relevant materials—such as a description of the programme's theoretical rationale and evidence base, session manuals, staff training manuals, assessment and evaluation measures, and ideally some preliminary indications of effectiveness. These are then judged against a pre-agreed set of *accreditation criteria* that define the minimal requirements for approval of a programme (Home Office Probation Unit, 1999). The criteria are shown in Table 2.2.

With regard to each criterion, a programme may score 0 (*not met*) 1 (*partially met*), or 2 (*fully met*). Some of the criteria (items 1, 2, 7, 9, 10 and 11 in Table 2.2) are *mandatory*; in other words, it is essential that the requirements be fully met. To be accredited a program must achieve a minimum score of 19/22 points, including full marks on all mandatory items.

In addition to programme accreditation each location in correctional services (such as an individual prison, probation office or other unit) must also satisfactorily meet criteria for *site accreditation*. This is part of a process of certifying programme and treatment integrity at that site. Systems for collecting information on quality of delivery (programme integrity) must also be in place, and the data so collected made available for an annual *site audit*. Audit reports are then scrutinized both by correctional agency staff and by members of the independent accreditation panel.

FUTURE DEVELOPMENTS AND QUESTIONS

Many of the programmes which are currently being implemented in both prison and probation settings employ methods of cognitive training initially piloted and evaluated in Canada (e.g. Robinson, 1995). However, there are several approaches to working with offenders that are potentially "likely-to-succeed". In respect of these much more research is required. In any case, researchers are still at an early stage in evaluating what the real impact of the

Table 2.2   Home Office Joint Prison–Probation Accreditation Panel: Criteria for accreditation of programmes.

1.   *Model of change*. There should be a clear, evidence-based theoretical model underpinning the programme which explains how it is proposed that it will have an impact on factors linked to offending behaviour.

2.   *Dynamic risk factors*. Programme materials should identify factors linked to offending, specified in the model, and which if changed will lead to a reduction in risk of reoffending, and the programme contents should reflect these objectives.

3.   *Range of targets*. Multimodal programmes with a range of treatment targets have yielded the largest effect sizes in research reviews. Programme manuals specify an appropriate range of targets and the nature of their interrelationships.

4.   *Effective methods*. The methods of change utilized in the programme should have empirical support concerning effectiveness and be coordinated in an appropriate way.

5.   *Skills orientated*. Programmes targeting skills that will enable offenders to avoid criminal activities have yielded higher effect sizes in outcome studies. The skills targeted by the programme should have explicit links to risk of reoffending and its reduction.

6.   *Intensity, sequencing, duration*. The overall amount of programming (numbers of contact hours), the mode of delivery of sessions and total programme duration should be appropriate in the light of available evidence, the programme's objectives and contents, and the risk level of the targeted offender groups.

7.   *Selection of offenders*. The population of offenders for whom the programme is designed should be explicitly and clearly specified. There should be agreed and realistic procedures for targeting and selection, and for exclusion of inappropriate referrals.

8.   *Engagement and participation*. This criterion refers to the principle of responsivity. Information should be provided concerning how this will be addressed, and how offenders will be encouraged and motivated to take part in and adhere to the programme.

9.   *Case management*. In prison settings, offenders are allocated a personal officer with responsibility for overseeing their individual sentence plans. On probation they are supervised by a case manager. To be effective, programmes should be interlinked with these processes, and guidelines provided for implementation within services.

10.   *Ongoing monitoring*. In order to safeguard the integrity of a programme and the treatment methods used, procedures should be in place for collection of monitoring quality-of-delivery data, and systems established for review of this and for taking action on the basis of it.

11.   *Evaluation*. Finally, programme materials should include assessment and evaluation measures and a framework for evaluation of its overall delivery, short-term and long-term impact.

current policy initiatives may be. Existing studies should be replicated, but in addition many other research questions remain unanswered.

For example, the process of risk–needs assessment must be informed by longer term validation research and far more needs to be known that might guide practitioners toward better informed selection of individuals for the most appropriate forms of intervention. In addition, research work with offender groups has been focused almost exclusively on young white males (the researchers, in most cases, being slightly older white males). Whilst some studies have been conducted in the United States that have included African American samples (e.g. Goldstein, Glick, Carthan & Blancero, 1994), there is still comparatively little published that would enable us to extrapolate conclusions of existing studies to work with members of other ethnic groups, or with women offenders.

Several key aspects of service delivery are at the moment only poorly understood. For example, what is the most appropriate time to offer participation in programmes to individuals in custodial settings? Similarly, is there an optimal time for pacing or delivery of programmes in the community? Finally, with the exception of programmes for sex offenders (see Marshall, Anderson & Fernandez, 1999), there are still comparatively few well-established examples of interventions specially devised for work on specific types of offence. That situation is, however, gradually changing. There are published evaluations of programmes focused on a variety of offence patterns such as violence (e.g. Henning & Frueh, 1996; and for a range of illustrations see Ross et al., 1995). As work proceeds on the development and dissemination of a sizeable portfolio of offence-focused programmes, much more data will become available concerning both their effectiveness and their limitations.

References

Andrews, D. A. (1995). The psychology of criminal conduct and effective treatment. In J. McGuire (ed.), *What Works: Reducing Re-offending: Guidelines from Research and Practice*. Chichester: John Wiley.

Andrews, D. A., & Dowden, C. (1999). A meta-analytic investigation into effective correctional intervention for female offenders. *Forum on Corrections Research*, **11**, 18–20.

Andrews, D. A., Zinger, I., Hoge, R. D., Bonta, J., Gendreau, P., & Cullen, F. T. (1990). Does correctional treatment work? A clinically relevant and psychologically informed meta- analysis. *Criminology*, **28**, 369–404.

Bernfeld, G. A., Blase, K. A., & Fixsen, D. L. (1990). Towards a unified perspective on human service delivery systems: application of the teaching-family model. In R. J. McMahon, & R. De V. Peters (Eds), *Behavioral Disorders of Adolescence*. New York: Plenum.

Borduin, C. M., Mann, B. J., Cone, L. T., & Hengeler, S. W. (1995). Multi-systemic treatment of serious juvenile offenders: Long-term prevention of criminality and violence. *Journal of Consulting and Clinical Psychology*, **63**, 569–578.

Brody, S. (1976). *The Effectiveness of Sentencing*, Home Office Research Study No. 35. London: HMSO.

Cleland, C. M., Pearson, F. S., Lipton, D. S., & Yee, D. (1997) *Does Age Make a Difference? A Meta-analytic Approach to Reductions in Criminal Offending for Juveniles and Adults*, Paper presented at the Annual Meeting of the American Society of Criminology, San Diego, CA, November.

Cochrane, A. L. (1979). 1931–1971: A critical review, with particular reference to the medical profession. In *Medicines for the Year 2000*. London: Office of Health Economics.

Dowden, C., & Andrews, D. A. (1999). What works in young offender treatment: a meta- analysis. *Forum on Corrections Research*, **11**, 21–24.

Dowden, C., & Andrews, D. A. (2000). Effective correctional treatment and violent reoffending: A meta-analysis. *Canadian Journal of Criminology*, **42**, 449–467.

Garrett, C. G. (1985). Effects of residential treatment on adjudicated delinquents: A meta- analysis. *Journal of Research in Crime and Delinquency*, **22**, 287–308.

Gendreau, P. (1996a). Offender rehabilitation: What we know and what needs to be done. *Criminal Justice and Behavior*, **23**, 144–161.

Gendreau, P. (1996b). The principles of effective intervention with offenders. In A. T. Harland (Ed.), *Choosing Correctional Options that Work: Defining the Demand and Evaluating the Supply*. Thousand Oaks, CA: Sage.

Gendreau, P., & Andrews, D. A. (1990). Tertiary prevention: what the meta-analyses of the offender treatment literature tell us about 'what works'. *Canadian Journal of Criminology*, **32**, 173–184.

Gendreau, P., & Goggin, C. (1996) Principles of effective correctional programming. *Forum on Corrections Research*, **8**, 38–41.

Gendreau, P., Goggin, C., & Smith, P. (1999). The forgotten issue in effective correctional treatment: Program implementation. *International Journal of Offender Therapy and Comparative Criminology*, **43**, 180–187.

Gensheimer, L. K., Mayer, J. P., Gottshalk, R., & Davidson, W. S. (1986). Diverting youth from the juvenile justice system: A meta-analysis of intervention efficacy. In S. A. Apter, & A. P. Goldstein (Eds), *Youth Violence: Programs and Prospects*, Elmsford, NJ: Pergamon.

Glass, G. V., McGaw, B., & Smith, M. L. (1981). *Meta-analysis in Social Research*. Newbury Park, CA: Sage.

Goldstein, A. P., Glick, B., Carthan, W., & Blancero, D. A. (1994). *The Pro-Social Gang: Implementing Aggression Replacement Training*. Thousand Oaks, CA: Sage.

Gottschalk, R., Davidson, W. S., Gensheimer, L. K., & Mayer, J. P. (1987a). Community-based interventions. In H. C. Quay (Ed.), *Handbook of Juvenile Delinquency*. New York: John Wiley.

Gottschalk, R., Davidson, W. S., Mayer, J., & Gensheimer, L. K. (1987b). Behavioral approaches with juvenile offenders: A meta-analysis of long-term treatment efficacy. In E. K. Morris, & C. J. Braukmann (Eds), *Behavioural Approaches to Crime and Delinquency*. New York: Plenum.

Guerra, N. G., Tolan, P. H., & Hammond, W. R. (1994). Prevention and treatment of adolescent violence. In L. D. Eron, J. H. Gentry, & P. Schlegel (Eds), *Reason to Hope: A Psychosocial Perspective on Violence and Youth*. Washington, DC: American Psychological Association.

Harland, A. T. (Ed.) (1996). *Choosing Correctional Options that Work: Defining the Demand and Evaluating the Supply*. Thousand Oaks, CA: Sage.

Harris, P., & Smith, S. (1996). Developing community corrections: an implementation perspective. In A. T. Harland (Ed.), *Choosing Correctional Options that Work: Defining the Demand and Evaluating the Supply*. Thousand Oaks, CA: Sage.

Henggeler, S. W., Schoenwald, S. K., Borduin, C. M., Rowland, M. D., & Cunningham, P. B. (1998). *Multisystemic Treatment of Antisocial Behavior in Children and Adolescents*. New York: Guilford Press.

Henning, K. R., & Frueh, B. C. (1996). Cognitive-behavioral treatment of incarcerated offenders: An evaluation of the Vermont Department of Corrections' Cognitive Self-Change Program. *Criminal Justice and Behavior, 23*, 523–542.

Hollin, C. R. (1995). The meaning and implications of programme integrity. In J. McGuire (Ed.), *What Works: Reducing Reoffending: Guidelines from Research and Practice*. Chichester: John Wiley.

Hollin, C. R. (1999). Treatment programmes for offenders: Meta-analysis, "What Works", and beyond. *International Journal of Law and Psychiatry, 22*, 361–371.

Home Office Probation Unit (1999). *What Works Initiative: Crime Reduction Programme. Joint Prison and Probation Accreditation Criteria*. London: Home Office.

Izzo, R. L., & Ross, R. R. (1990). Meta-analysis of rehabilitation programmes for juvenile delinquents. *Criminal Justice and Behavior, 17*, 134–142.

Kaufman, P. (1985). *Meta-analysis of Juvenile Delinquency Prevention Programs*, Unpublished Master's Thesis, Claremont Graduate School.

Lambert, M. J., & Bergin, A. E. (1994). The effectiveness of psychotherapy. In A. E. Bergin & S. L. Garfield (Eds), *Handbook of Psychotherapy and Behavior Change*. New York: John Wiley.

Lipsey, M. W. (1992). Juvenile delinquency treatment: A meta-analytic inquiry into the variability of effects. In T. Cook, D. Cooper, H. Corday, H. Hartman, L. Hedges, R. Light, T. Louis, & F. Mosteller (Eds), *Meta-analysis for Explanation: A Casebook*. New York: Russell Sage Foundation.

Lipsey, M. W. (1995). What do we learn from 400 studies on the effectiveness of treatment with juvenile delinquents? In J. McGuire (Ed.), *What Works: Reducing Re-offending: Guidelines from Research and Practice*. Chichester: John Wiley.

Lipsey, M. W., & Wilson, D. B. (1993). The efficacy of psychological, educational, and behavioral treatment: Confirmation from meta-analysis. *American Psychologist, 48*, 1181–1209.

Lipsey, M. W., & Wilson, D. B. (1998). Effective intervention for serious juvenile offenders: A synthesis of research. In R. Loeber and D. P. Farrington (Eds), *Serious and Violent Juvenile Offenders: Risk Factors and Successful Interventions*. Thousand Oaks, CA: Sage.

Lipton, D. S., Martinson, R., & Wilks, J. (1975). *The Effectiveness of Correctional Treatment: A Survey of Treatment Evaluation Studies*. New York: Praeger.

Lipton, D. S., Thornton, D., McGuire, J., Porporino, F., & Hollin, C. R., (2000) Program accreditation and correctional treatment. *Substance Use and Misuse, 35*, 1705–1734.

Lösel, F. (1995). The efficacy of correctional treatment: A review and synthesis of meta-evaluations. In J. McGuire (Ed.), *What Works: Reducing Re-offending: Guidelines from Research and Practice*. Chichester: John Wiley.

Lösel, F., & Koferl, P. (1989). Evaluation research on correctional treatment in West Germany: A meta-analysis. In H. Wegener, F. Lösel, & J. Haisch (Eds), *Criminal Behaviour and the Justice System: Psychological Perspectives*. New York: Springer-Verlag.

Mackenzie, D. L. (1997). Criminal justice and crime prevention. In L. W. Sherman, D. Gottfredson, D. L. Mackenzie, J. Eck, P. Reuter, & S. Bushway (Eds), *Preventing Crime: What Works, What Doesn't, What's Promising*. Washington, DC: Office of Justice Programs.

Marshall, W. L., Anderson, D., & Fernandez, Y. (1999). *Cognitive Behavioural Treatment of Sexual Offenders*. Chichester: John Wiley.

Martinson, R. (1974). What works? Questions and answers about prison reform. *The Public Interest*, **10**, 22–54.

Martinson, R. (1979). New findings, new views: A note of caution regarding sentencing reform. *Hofstra Law Review*, **7**, 243–258.

Mayer, J. P., Gensheimer, L. K., Davidson, W. S., & Gottschalk, R. (1986). Social learning treatment within juvenile justice: A meta-analysis of impact in the natural environment. In S. A. Apter, & A. P. Goldstein (Eds), *Youth Violence: Programs and Prospects*, Elmsford, NJ: Pergamon.

McGuire, J. (Ed.) (1995). *What Works: Reducing Re-offending: Guidelines from Research and Practice*. Chichester: John Wiley.

McGuire, J. (1998). Memorandum of evidence. *Alternatives to Custodial Sentences*, Third report of the House of Commons Home Affairs Committee. London: HMSO.

McGuire, J. (2001). Criminal sanctions versus psychologically-based interventions with offenders: A comparative empirical analysis. *Psychology, Crime & Law* (in press).

Mulrow, C. D. (1987). The medical review article: State of the science. *Annals of Internal Medicine*, **106**, 485–488.

Nuttall, C., Goldblatt, P., & Lewis, C. (1998). *Reducing Offending: An Assessment of Research Evidence on Ways of Dealing with Offending Behavior*, Home Office Research Study No. 187. London: Home Office.

Palmer, T. (1975). Martinson re-visited. *Journal of Research in Crime and Delinquency*, **12**, 133–152.

Palmer, T. (1992). *The Re-Emergence of Correctional Intervention*. Newbury Park, CA: Sage.

Pearson, F. S., Lipton, D. S., & Cleland, C. M. (1997). *Rehabilitative Programs in Adult Corrections: CDATE Meta-analyses*, Paper presented at the Annual Meeting of the American Society of Criminology, San Diego, CA, November.

Petrosino, A. J., Boruch, R. F., Rounding, C., McDonald, S., & Chalmers, I. (1999). *A Social, Psychological, Educational and Criminological Trials Register (SPECTR) to Facilitate the Preparation and Maintenance of Systematic Reviews of Social and Educational Interventions*, background paper for the Cochrane Collaboration Meeting, School of Public Policy, University College London, July.

Redondo, S., Sánchez-Meca, J., & Garrido, V. (1999). The influence of treatment programmes on the recidivism of juvenile and adult offenders: An European meta-analytic review. *Psychology, Crime amd Law*, **5**, 251–278.

Roberts, A. R., Camasso, M. J. (1991). The effect of juvenile offender treatment programs on recidivism: a meta-analysis of 46 studies. *Notre Dame Journal of Law, Ethics and Public Policy*, **5**, 421–441.

Robinson, D. (1995). *The Impact of Cognitive Skills Training on Post-release Recidivism among Canadian Federal Offenders*. Ottawa: Correctional Services of Canada.

Rosenthal, R. (1994). Parametric measures of effect size. In H. Cooper and L. V. Hedges (Eds), *Handbook of Research Synthesis*. New York: Russell Sage Foundation.

Ross, R. R., Antonowicz, D. H., & Dhaliwal, G. K. (Eds) (1995). *Going Straight: Effective Delinquency Prevention and Offender Rehabilitation*. Ottawa: Air Training and Publications.

Ross, R. R., & Gendreau, P. (Eds) (1980). *Effective Correctional Treatment*. Toronto: Butterworths.

Sherman, L., Gottfredson, D., McKenzie, D., Eck, J., Reuter, P., & Bushway, S. (1997). *Preventing Crime: What Works, What Doesn't, What's Promising*. Washington, DC: Office of Justice Programs.

Underdown, A. (1998). *Strategies for Effective Offender Supervision: Report of the HMIP What Works Project*. London: Home Office.

Vennard, J., Sugg, D., & Hedderman, C. (1997). *Changing Offenders' Attitudes and Behaviour: What Works?*, Home Office Research Study No. 171. London: HMSO.

Welsh, B. C., & Farrington, D. P. (2000) Correctional intervention programs and cost benefit analysis. *Criminal Justice and Behavior*, **27**, 115–133.

Wexler, D. B. (1998). How the law can use What Works: A therapeutic jurisprudence look at recent research on rehabilitation. *Behavioral Sciences and the Law*, **15**, 368–369.

Whitehead, J. T., & Lab, S. P. (1989). A meta-analysis of juvenile correctional treatment. *Journal of Research in Crime and Delinquency*, **26**, 276–295.

Yoshikawa, H. (1994). Prevention as cumulative protection: Effects of early family support and education on chronic delinquency and its risks. *Psychological Bulletin*, **115**, 28–54.

Chapter 3

EVALUATING THE ECONOMIC EFFICIENCY OF CORRECTIONAL INTERVENTION PROGRAMS

Brandon C. Welsh* and David P. Farrington[†]

* Department of Criminal Justice, University of Massachusetts at Lowell, Lowell, Massachusetts, USA
[†] Institute of Criminology, University of Cambridge, Cambridge, UK

In the wake of rising criminal justice costs, government spending reviews and crime rates the public considers unacceptable (in most industrialized countries), issues of economic efficiency, cost savings and accountability of crime prevention programs have received increased attention in political, policy, and, more recently, academic circles. Correctional intervention programs have not been immune from this attention, with administrators increasingly called upon to show that effective programs have also produced a monetary gain (e.g. for government) or cost less than other forms of intervention.

Recent, leading empirical reviews of the literature on correctional intervention programs (Lipsey, 1995; Lipsey & Wilson, 1998; MacKenzie, 1997) demonstrate that many types of interventions are effective in reducing recidivism. But what does the research evidence tell us about the economic efficiency or monetary value of correctional intervention programs? This is the main focus of this chapter.

Offender Rehabilitation in Practice. Edited by G. A. Bernfeld, D. P. Farrington and A. W. Leschied.
© 2001 John Wiley & Sons, Ltd.

Evaluation studies of correctional intervention programs have been included in the present review if they met three criteria. First, the program was focused on reducing reoffending in the community. Second, the outcome evaluation was based on a "real life" program. That is, program outcomes were neither assessed using statistical modeling techniques alone nor hypothesized on the basis of case study data, but rather employed research designs with the capacity to control for threats to internal and external validity, such as experimental and quasi-experimental designs. This was important, because we used the "scientific methods scale" developed by Sherman et al. (1997, see below) to assess the methodological quality of the studies. Third, a benefit–cost analysis was performed that had either calculated or permitted the calculation of a benefit–cost ratio for the purpose of assessing the program's economic efficiency. Studies that did not perform a benefit–cost analysis were included if they presented sufficient benefit and cost data to enable an assessment of economic efficiency.

We employed four search strategies to locate studies meeting our criteria. First, we searched the Social Sciences Citation Index (1981–1998) of the Institute for Scientific Information (ISI) database on the Internet-accessible Bibliographic Databases (BIDS) service. Second, we searched the most recent issues of major European and North American criminological journals to cover any time lag in the updating of the ISI database. Third, we examined the bibliographies of leading narrative and empirical (e.g. meta-analytic) reviews of the literature on the effectiveness of correctional intervention programs. Fourth, we contacted leading academics and researchers in the fields of correctional intervention and welfare economics in an effort to identify unpublished or in-press studies.

Only seven published studies meeting our criteria for inclusion could be identified. In our search for benefit–cost studies of correctional intervention programs we identified a few studies that may or may not have met our criteria for inclusion, but we were unsuccessful in obtaining copies. For the most part, these consisted of reports dating from the 1970s and 1980s by different branches of the United States federal government and non-governmental organizations in the United States. For example, Zedlewski (1992) cited a benefit–cost analysis study of prison and alternative sanctions prepared for the National Institute of Justice, and Weimer and Friedman (1979) cited three studies published by the Commission on Correctional Facilities and Services of the American Bar Association.

Interestingly, we found that, unlike other crime prevention strategies (for community prevention, see Welsh & Farrington, 2000; for developmental prevention, see Welsh, 2001; for situational prevention, see Welsh & Farrington, 1999), a great deal has been published on the application of economic evaluation techniques to correctional intervention. However, for the most part, these studies have consisted of statistical modeling exercises and analyses of hypothetical examples of correctional practices (e.g. Greenwood et al., 1994; Hofler & Witte, 1979), and cost and cost-effectiveness analyses (e.g. Bloom & Singer, 1979; Knapp, Robertson & McIvor, 1992; Schoenwald, Ward, Henggeler, Pickerel & Patel, 1996). Statistical modeling exercises have not been included because they are not real-life programs, and cost and cost-effectiveness analysis studies have not been included because they do not provide an assessment of economic benefits, only of costs (see p. 48).

The chapter has been organized into six parts. The first part presents a brief description of correctional intervention. The second part introduces the technique of economic analysis and discusses key methodological features of benefit–cost analysis. The third part summarizes key features of the seven correctional intervention programs. The fourth part summarizes the benefit-cost findings of the seven programs. The fifth part reviews in detail a selected study. The sixth part provides a conclusion and discussion, focusing on priorities for future research and policy development.

CORRECTIONAL INTERVENTION

MacKenzie (1997, p. 9-1) classified correctional programs focused on reducing reoffending in the community into six categories, which are by no means mutually exclusive:

(1) incapacitation: "depriving the offender of the capacity to commit crimes usually through detention in prison or capital punishment";

(2) deterrence: "punishment that is so repugnant that neither the punished offender (specific deterrence) nor others (general deterrence) will commit the crime in the future [because of fear of punishment]" (e.g. shock probation, fines);

(3) rehabilitation: "treatment directed toward changing the offender and thereby preventing future criminal behavior of the treated individual" (e.g. cognitive skills training, academic programs);

(4) community restraints: "surveillance and supervision of offenders in the community in order to reduce their capacity and/or opportunity for criminal activities" (e.g. intensive supervision, house arrest, electronic monitoring);

(5) structure, discipline and challenge: "physically and/or mentally stressful experiences to change the offenders in a positive way or deter them from later crime (specific deterrence) (e.g. boot camps, wilderness programs); and

(6) combining rehabilitation and restraint: "to insure that offenders make changes that are associated with a reduction in future criminal behavior (e.g. drug treatment with urine testing).

In the academic literature, correctional intervention is often distinguished from punishment, as in MacKenzie's (1997) classification scheme. The present review did not locate any studies meeting our criteria for inclusion that were focused solely on punishment. Correctional intervention attempts to modify offender behavior through some combination of treatment and external controls (Palmer, 1992). Treatment, according to Palmer (1992, p. 3), attempts to "affect the individual's future behavior, attitudes toward self, and interactions with others by focusing on such factors and conditions as the individual's adjustment techniques, interests, skills, personal limitations, and/or life circumstances." In this chapter, correctional intervention is mainly concerned with offender treatment.

BENEFIT–COST ANALYSIS

An economic analysis (e.g. benefit–cost analysis, cost-effectiveness analysis) can be described as a tool that allows choices to be made between alternative uses of resources or alternative distributions of services (Knapp, 1997, p. 11). Many criteria are used in economic analysis. The most common is efficiency (achieving maximum outcomes from minimum inputs), which is the focus of this chapter. Our specific focus on economic efficiency, however, is not meant to imply that correctional intervention programs should only be continued if benefits outweigh costs. There are many important non-economic criteria on which correctional intervention programs should be judged.

Our interest was in the economic costs *and* benefits of correctional intervention programs. Of the two main techniques of economic analysis— benefit–cost and cost-effectiveness analysis—only benefit–cost analysis enables an assessment of both costs and benefits. A cost-effectiveness analysis can be referred to as an incomplete benefit–cost analysis, because no attempt is made to estimate the monetary value of program effects produced (benefits or disbenefits), only resources used (costs). For example, a cost-effectiveness analysis can specify how many crimes were prevented per $1,000 spent on a program. Another way to think about how benefit–cost and cost-effectiveness analysis differ is that "cost-effectiveness analysis may help one decide among competing program models, but it cannot show that the total effect was worth the cost of the program" (Weinrott, Jones & Howard, 1982, p. 179), unlike benefit–cost analysis.

A benefit–cost analysis is a step-by-step process that follows a standard set of procedures. Six main steps comprise a benefit–cost analysis:

(1)   define the scope of the analysis;
(2)   obtain estimates of program effects;
(3)   estimate the monetary value of costs and benefits;
(4)   calculate present value and assess profitability;
(5)   describe the distribution of costs and benefits (an assessment of who gains and who loses, e.g., program participant, government/taxpayer, crime victim); and
(6)   conduct sensitivity analyses (Barnett, 1993, pp. 143–148).

Each of these steps is summarized below. For more information on these steps see Barnett (1993, 1996) and Barnett and Escobar (1987, 1990), as applied in the context of early childhood intervention programs. As well, for methodological features of benefit–cost analysis in general see the excellent text by Layard and Glaister (1994), and the volume by Welsh et al. (2001).

Define the scope of analysis

This step can be divided into two parts: first, defining the alternatives to be compared (e.g. participation in a program versus non-participation) and, second, identifying the limits of the comparison (Barnett, 1993, p. 144). A determination is made at this stage about the perspective the economic analysis will take. The "public" (government/taxpayer and crime victim) and "society" (government/taxpayer, crime victim and program partici-pant) are the two most common perspectives used in economic analysis. The decision about which perspective to take has important implications for evaluating the program, particularly if it is being funded by public money. That is, if conclusions are to be drawn about the monetary benefits or costs of a program to the public, the benefits or costs must be those that the public will either receive or incur. In reporting on the benefit–cost findings of the reviewed studies, we have used, as far as possible, the perspective of the public.

Another important element at this stage is the decision about what program outcomes are to be measured. Administrative issues (e.g. resources, time) or parameters of the study may limit the number of outcomes that can be measured. The best approach is to attempt to estimate all of the relevant outcomes and, later, to estimate their monetary value independently (see the step on estimating monetary value).

Estimate program effects

Determining that a program prevented crimes requires an estimate of how many crimes would have been committed in the absence of the program, and a disentangling of program effects on crime from all the other possible influences on crime. Program effects can be measured in different ways, with differing degrees of statistical power.

In practical terms, a benefit–cost analysis or any other type of economic analysis is an extension of an outcome evaluation, and is only as defensible as the evaluation upon which it is based. Weimer and Friedman (1979, p. 264) recommend that benefit–cost analyses be limited to programs that have been evaluated with an "experimental or strong quasi-experimental design". The most convincing method of evaluating correctional or other intervention programs is the randomized experiment (Farrington, 1983), which is often referred to as the "gold standard" of evaluation designs. The key feature of randomized experiments is that the experimental and control groups are equated before the experimental intervention on all possible extraneous variables (within the limits of statistical fluctuation). As a rule of thumb at least 50 units in each category are needed (Farrington, 1997). Non-randomized experiments and before–after designs without a control group are less convincing methods of evaluating correctional intervention programs.

To assess the methodological quality of the studies we used the "scientific methods scale" developed by Sherman et al. (1997). This is as follows, with level 1 being the lowest and level 5 the highest:

1. Correlational evidence: low offending correlates with the program at a single point in time.
2. Non-equivalent control group or one-group pre-post design:
    (a) program group compared with non-equivalent control group;
    (b) program group measured before and after intervention (with no control group).
3. Equivalent control group design: program group compared with comparable control group, including pre-post and experimental-control comparisons.
4. Control of extraneous variables: program group compared with control group, with control of extraneous influences on the outcome (e.g. by matching, prediction scores or statistical controls).
5. Randomized experiment: units assigned at random to program and control groups.

This methodological rating scale is concerned with the overall internal validity of evaluations; external validity, or the "generalizability of internally valid results" (Sherman et al., 1998, p. 3), was not addressed as part of the scientific methods scale. The scientific methods scale was important to the present research, because, as noted above, a benefit–cost analysis is only as strong as the evaluation design upon which it is based. Ideally, studies included in the present review would have been restricted to benefit–cost analyses of programs with high-quality evaluation designs (level 3 or higher), but the small number of existing analyses militated against this.

Estimate monetary value

The estimation of the monetary value of program resources used (costs) and effects produced (benefits) is the most important step in an economic analysis. As described by Barnett (1993, p. 145), "This step makes it possible to put all program consequences on an equal footing, so program costs, various positive outcomes, and any negative outcomes can be aggregated to provide a single measure of the program's impact on society and on particular sub-groups of society."

It is also the step which distinguishes a benefit–cost analysis from a cost-effectiveness analysis. (The cost-effectiveness analysis does not attempt to estimate the monetary value of program effects.) Estimating the monetary value of costs is considered to be less complex than benefits, but no less important. Each is dealt with below.

The most crucial issue involved in carrying out benefit–cost studies of correctional intervention programs and crime prevention programs in general is deciding about what program resources used and effects produced should have dollar figures attached. No prescribed formula exists for what to include (or exclude). Prest and Turvey (1965, p. 683) note that benefit–cost analysis "implies the enumeration and evaluation of all the relevant costs and benefits." Estimating the monetary value of program benefits requires a great deal of ingenuity on the part of the evaluator. Unlike program costs, which can most often be broken down into operating (e.g. overhead, administration) and capital (e.g. rental of facilities), program benefits are disparate and involve a number of assumptions in order to arrive at reasonable estimates of monetary value. In some ways, estimating the monetary value of the benefits of correctional intervention programs is limited (beyond the limits imposed by the underlying evaluation) only by the ingenuity of the evaluator and the resources available to the evaluator.

Another important issue which must be considered at this stage is the distinction between real and notional or putative monetary benefits. Often, crime prevention programs claim that real monetary benefits were achieved. Real monetary benefits can only be achieved if the program results in a direct reduction in some real item of expenditure (e.g. personnel, equipment). For example, a small-scale community-based treatment program for juvenile offenders will only produce real benefits after the point at which reductions in crime become large enough to permit the affected agencies (e.g. correctional service, police) to reduce the number of personnel, equipment or some other expenditure item. This, of course, does not imply that notional benefits of crime prevention programs should be ignored altogether. Identifying real benefits is a task in itself, and notional benefits may have the effect instead of suppressing expenditures, which may facilitate the re-allocation of resources to other pressing needs.

An important and closely related issue is the distinction between marginal and average costs and benefits. In the context of program resources used, "Marginal costs describe how the total cost of an operation changes as the unit of activity changes by a small amount", while "[a]verage costs are derived by simply dividing total costs by total workload in a given period of time" (Aos, 1998, p. 13). The main limitation of average costs, as noted by Aos (1998, p. 13) is, that "some of those costs . . . are fixed and do not change when workload changes." By using marginal cost estimates for correctional intervention programs in a custodial setting, for example, only the direct costs of an additional inmate (e.g. food, utilities) would be taken into account, while the most expensive prison operating budget item—personnel costs—would be excluded up to the point where the number of additional inmates required additional staff coverage.

Calculate present value and profitability

Present value is concerned with making all monetary costs and benefits of a program comparable over time. The time value of money is best understood by the following: "A dollar today is worth more than a dollar next year because today's dollar can be invested to yield a dollar plus interest next year" (Barnett & Escobar, 1987, p. 390). If a program's costs and benefits are confined to 1 year then the calculation of present value is unnecessary.

Two separate steps must be carried out to adjust for differences in the value of money over time. First, the effect of inflation is removed by "translating nominal dollars from each year into dollars of equal purchasing power, or *real dollars*." This is achieved by the application of a price index to the nominal monetary units, which more or less cancels out the effect of inflation. Second, the time value of money is taken into account "by calculating the *present value* of real dollars from each year" (Barnett, 1993, p. 146, emphases in original). For this to be achieved, real monetary units from different years must be discounted using an inflation-adjusted discount rate (between 3 and 7 per cent per annum in the United States) to their "common value at the beginning of a program" (Barnett & Escobar, 1987, p. 390). One of the limitations of not calculating present value is that benefits will be slightly larger than they should be. The reason for this is that the calculation of present value very often reduces future benefits more than present costs.

The second part of this step is an assessment of profitability or economic efficiency. We have used the benefit–cost ratio to measure the economic efficiency of programs rather than net value (benefits minus costs) for two principal reasons: (1) the benefit–cost ratio provides a single measurement of the benefit of a program that is derived from a one monetary unit (one dollar) investment or expenditure, and (2) for all comparisons, the benefit–cost ratio controls for the different time period of a program (e.g. a benefit–cost ratio of a program that used 1992 US dollars can reasonably be compared with the benefit–cost ratio of a program that used 1976 British pounds).

Describe the distribution

The fifth step involves describing the distribution of program costs and benefits; that is, who gained and who lost from the program. This is an assessment of equity or fairness in the distribution of program costs and benefits. Besides assessing the distribution of costs and benefits for program participants, a program may wish to assess the distribution among, for example, high- and low-income populations.

Conduct sensitivity analyses

This step is used to check the validity of and to test the effects of variations in assumptions made in an economic analysis. A typical sensitivity analysis involves, for example, the use of a range of discount rates in the calculation of present value. "Sensitivity analysis can be used to indicate the range of values within which assumptions can be safely ignored or the specific conditions that must be found or produced if a policy or program is to yield the desired results" (Barnett & Escobar, 1987, p. 391). Too often though this step, as with the one above, is left out. Only two programs reviewed here did this (Friedman, 1977; Holahan, 1974).

REVIEW OF STUDIES

Seven correctional intervention studies meeting the criteria for inclusion were identified. Table 3.1 summarizes key features of the seven studies.

Table 3.1 Summary of correctional intervention studies

Study authors, location	Age at intervention	Targeted offending behavior	Treatment setting	Duration and primary type of intervention	Sample size	Scientific methods score	Follow-up[a]	Treatment effects[b]	Benefit-cost ratio[c]
Holahan (1974), Washington, DC	18–25 years	Property offending in general	Community	3 months: pre-trial diversion with counselling, job training and remedial education	307 adults: T = 200 C = 107	3 (before-after, experimental-control)	12 months	Police arrests +	2.36
Friedman (1977), New York City	32 years (average; T only)	n.a.	Community	8 months (average): employment	229 adults: T = 120 C = 109[d]	5 (randomized experiment)	16 months (average)	Police arrests + Social service use + Employment + Health – Education –	1.13
Austin (1986), Illinois	19–40 years (87.9% of sample)	Criminal offending in general	Community	n.a.: early release	1,557 adults and youths: T = 1,202 C = 355	3 (before-after, experimental-control)	2.5 years	Police arrests +	2.82
Pearson (1988) and Pearson & Harper (1990), New Jersey	n.a.	Non-violent offending in general	Community, institution	18 months (average): employment, intensive supervision, incapacitation	686 adults: T = 554 C = 132	3 (before-after, experimental-control)	n.a.	Convictions + Institution time +	1.48

Study	Age	Offense	Setting	Intervention	Sample	Design	Follow-up[a]	Outcomes[b]	Benefit–cost ratio[c]
Gray & Olson (1989), Arizona	18–44 years (median = 23 years)	Burglary	Community, institution	n.a.: multiple services, deterrence, incapacitation, rehabilitation	112 adults	2 (before–after)	n.a.	n.a.	Probation = 1.70 Prison = 0.24 Jail = 0.17
Prentky & Burgess (1990), Massachusetts	n.a.	Child molestation	Institution (maximum security)	5.1 years (median): rehabilitation[e]	182 individuals: T = 129 (adults), C = 53	2 (before–after, experimental–control, retrospectively chosen C)	5 and 25 years	Victim-involved sexual offenses (15 charges) +	1.16
Gerstein et al. (1994), California	33.3 years (mean)	Criminal offending and substance abuse in general	Community, residential	2.8 months (mean): substance abuse (4 modalities)	3,055 adults	2 (before–after)	15 months (average)	Criminal activity + Substance abuse + Health + Social service use + Employment –	7.14

[a] The period of time in which program effects were evaluated after the intervention had ended.
[b] "0" = no treatment effects; "+" = desirable treatment effects; "–" = undesirable treatment effects.
[c] Expressed as a ratio of benefits to costs in dollars.
[d] This comprises the remaining sample after 2 years from the start of the program; no information was provided on the sample at the start of the intervention.
[e] No information was provided on the type of rehabilitation used.
Notes: T = treatment group; C = control group; n.a. = not available.

The studies were published between 1974 and 1994, and all were carried out in the United States. Interventions were provided to a wide age range of subjects. Targeted offending behaviors included burglary, child molestation and substance abuse. In six of the seven studies, the community was the setting for treatment; however, in three of these (Gerstein et al., 1994; Gray & Olson, 1989; Pearson, 1988), treatment was also administered in institutional or residential settings. The initial sample size at the start of treatment ranged from 112 to 3,055 subjects.

The type of primary treatment employed varied across the studies, including pre-trial diversion, employment and intensive supervision. Two of the studies (Austin, 1986; Gerstein et al., 1994) did not evaluate correctional treatment *per se*. In the study by Austin (1986), the decision to release offenders from prison prior to the expiration of the prison sentence may not be a correctional intervention, but it does represent an alternative to incarceration that has received some consideration. In the study by Gerstein et al. (1994), which evaluated alcohol and drug abuse prevention services throughout California, not all of the participating subjects were under the authority of the Department of Corrections at the time of treatment. We decided to include these two studies partly because of the paucity of benefit–cost research on correctional intervention. Few similarities were also shown in the duration of treatment, which ranged from 2.8 months to 5.1 years, for the five studies that reported this information.

Five of the seven studies used an experimental evaluation design to evaluate program effects, although one of these (Prentky & Burgess, 1990) used a non-equivalent (retrospectively selected) control group. The study by Friedman (1977), which was aimed at reintegrating former offenders and drug addicts into the community through the provision of paid employment and aftercare (e.g. methadone maintenance for ex-addicts), employed random assignment to experimental and control conditions. Across the seven studies, the mean score on the scientific methods scale was 2.86, with three studies (Gerstein et al., 1994; Gray & Olson, 1989; Prentky & Burgess, 1990) having a score of 2.

Gray & Olson (1989) did not present before–after changes in offending, nor did other published papers on this study (Gray, 1994; Gray, Larsen, Haynes & Olson, 1991; Haynes & Larsen, 1984). Each of the other six studies that reported treatment effects assessed recidivism and, in each case, the first rearrest or reconviction was the measure of recidivism used. The length of follow-up ranged from 12 months to 25 years, with two studies (Pearson, 1988; Gray & Olson, 1989) not reporting this information. Overall, treatment effects on recidivism were desirable. For example, Project Crossroads (Holahan, 1974), which provided first-time property offenders with a range of short-term (3 months) supportive services (e.g. counseling, job training, remedial education) in lieu of traditional criminal justice processing, achieved a 28.6 per cent reduction in the rate of recidivism 12 months post-treatment (26.0% for the treatment group versus 36.4% for the control group), and New Jersey's Intensive Supervision Program (Pearson, 1988; Pearson & Harper, 1990) produced lower conviction rates for the treatment compared to the control group (12% versus 23%) after an unspecified period of time. As illustrated in Table 3.1, desirable program effects were also found for other outcomes, such as employment, health and social service use, but two studies (Friedman, 1977; Gerstein et al., 1994) reported undesirable program effects in some of these areas.

SUMMARY OF BENEFIT–COST FINDINGS

Six of the studies carried out a benefit–cost analysis. The seventh study (Pearson, 1988), which is reviewed below, carried out a cost analysis, but published data that enabled us to calculate benefits and hence a benefit–cost ratio. Benefits realized by the correctional intervention programs included costs avoided to the criminal justice system and crime victims, increased employment earnings and savings to public health care and welfare. All seven studies showed a desirable benefit–cost ratio. One of these (Gray & Olson, 1989) calculated benefit–cost ratios for each of the three treatments being compared (one desirable and two undesirable; see Table 3.1). For the purposes of this discussion, only the desirable ratio, for probation, is considered, because probation more closely fits our concern with correctional (rehabilitative) intervention than does prison or jail (the other two treatments). For the seven studies the benefit–cost ratios ranged from a low of 1.13 to a high of 7.14, meaning that for each dollar spent on the programs, the public (government/taxpayer and crime victim) received in return $1.13 to $7.14 in various savings.

No significant patterns emerge from a comparison between key features of the seven studies and their benefit–cost ratios. Some findings are, however, noteworthy. The two studies with the largest sample sizes (Austin, 1986; Gerstein et al., 1994) produced the highest benefit–cost ratios: 2.82 and 7.14, respectively. However, the study with the largest sample size (Gerstein et al., 1994) used a comparatively weak evaluation design, relying on before–after measures with no control group. Also, a reduced sample size of unknown magnitude was used to estimate economic benefits. For the study by Austin (1986), which used an experimental–control design, the benefit–cost analysis was based on the treatment group only. This had the dual effect of reducing the sample size (from 1,557 to 1,202) and reducing confidence in the program's reported benefit–cost findings.

A notable feature of all studies is the omission of intangible costs to victims of crime (e.g. pain, suffering, lost quality of life, fear of future victimization) in the benefit–cost calculations. In five of the seven studies,[1] the monetary costs to crime victims were limited to tangible or out-of-pocket expenses, such as property loss and damage and medical expenses. To be fair to the authors, the majority acknowledged the difficulties involved in assessing and quantifying in monetary terms intangible costs to crime victims. These difficulties include: the lack of existing estimates of the intangible costs to victims of crime, which first appeared in the published literature in Cohen (1988), and the doubts of many researchers about the validity of these costs and/or the underlying theory used in their calculation (Zimring & Hawkins, 1995, p. 138).

The importance of assessing and quantifying intangible costs to crime victims in benefit–cost analyses was illustrated in Cohen's (1988) reanalysis of Austin's (1986) benefit–cost calculations. For example, Cohen estimated that the average rape cost $51,058 (in 1985 dollars), made up of three main components: direct losses, $4,617; pain, suffering and fear of injury, $43,561; and risk of death, $2,880. Adding the pain and suffering cost component to Austin's (1986) estimates of the direct losses incurred by crime victims, while maintaining the other costs, increased the total costs of the program[2] to approximately $110 million (Cohen, 1988, p. 550), a sixfold increase. This resulted in a reversal of the benefit–cost findings, from producing a dividend on public expenditure (a benefit–cost ratio of 2.82) to a loss or an undesirable benefit–cost ratio of 0.45 ($49 million divided by $110 million). Austin's findings have been retained, because in most of the studies insufficient data was provided to allow for any recalculation of costs or benefits.

It is noteworthy that four of the seven studies (Friedman, 1977; Gerstein et al., 1994; Holahan, 1974; Pearson, 1988) assessed and quantified in monetary terms outcomes other than recidivism. Education, employment, health, social service use and illicit substance use were the different kinds of outcomes monetized in these studies. In two of these four studies (Friedman, 1977; Pearson, 1988), benefits from improvements in these outcomes exceeded benefits from reduced recidivism. Although far from conclusive, this is an important finding because it suggests that correctional intervention programs have the potential to influence other important areas of an offender's life and produce, in some cases, substantial economic returns for publicly funded services such as health and welfare.

---

[1] One study (Friedman, 1977) did not explain the type of victim costs quantified, while the other (Pearson, 1988) did not assess or quantify victim costs.

[2] Costs of the program were made up of criminal justice reprocessing of recidivists (e.g. arrest, prosecution), parole supervision of early releases and direct costs to crime victims (caused by early releasees).

The following section reviews in detail the New Jersey Intensive Supervision Program (Pearson, 1988). We felt that it was important to review a study to illustrate key issues involved in assessing a program's monetary benefits and costs. We chose this study because it used a high-quality research design and it is one of the more recently published programs. Also, we (Welsh & Farrington, 2000) previously reviewed the study by Friedman (1977), which was the highest quality study of the seven.

NEW JERSEY INTENSIVE SUPERVISION PROGRAM

The New Jersey Intensive Supervision Program (ISP), started in 1983, was part of the new wave of much heralded (see e.g. Petersilia & Turner, 1993) correctional experiments (and policy developments) on intermediate sentencing alternatives to imprisonment and probation or parole for serious offenders, which took place in the United States throughout the 1980s. Under ISP, which operated in the community, offenders sentenced to prison were re-sentenced to the program by a specially designated panel of judges. Four main goals guided the New Jersey ISP: (1) to improve the use of scarce prison resources, (2) to be a cost-beneficial and cost-effective alternative to ordinary incarceration, (3) to prevent criminal behavior of program participants while in the community, and (4) to deliver appropriate, intermediate punishment in the community (Pearson & Harper, 1990, pp. 75–76).

Design and method

An experimental–control design with before–after measures was used to assess the effectiveness of the New Jersey ISP. Program participants were made up of non-violent felony offenders who were considered relatively low risk. The treatment group—those enrolled in ISP—consisted of 554 individuals. A comparable control group that served "ordinary terms of imprisonment" was drawn from a random sample of 500 similar offenders sentenced to prison prior to the start of the program and consisted of 132 individuals. The control group was termed CLOSE OTI, meaning a subset of the full sample serving ordinary terms of imprisonment. Pearson and Harper (1990) reported that discriminant function analyses showed that the two groups were matched closely on socio-demographic background variables and past official offending. No other details were provided on their profiles.

ISP participants had to spend on average 18 months in the program to be granted a successful completion. The program intervened on multiple levels. The following interventions were mandatory requirements for all participants: (1) serve a minimum of 2 months in prison, (2) receive intensive supervision (personal, curfew and urinalysis contacts), (3) actively seek or hold employment, (4) community service (a minimum of 16 hours per month) and (5) payment of fines, restitution, and other monetary consequences.

In addition, individual or group counseling was required by those with identified problems, such as substance abuse dependence, and each partici-pant was assigned a community sponsor to monitor progress and offer assistance and advice of a general nature. Failure to comply with program rules and conditions, many of which were tied to the interventions, resulted in return to prison. Data sources included official state crime statistics, court and corrections records, and employment records.

Results

Pearson and Harper (1990) reported summary findings for conviction rates and prison time for the ISP participants alone and for the comparison of ISP versus CLOSE OTI. Only the comparative findings are considered here.

After 2 years,[3] the treatment group showed statistically significantly lower conviction rates than the control group (12% versus 23%). Time spent in prison differed substantially between the two groups. At an unknown time interval following the completion of the program, presumably covering the same period of time for both groups, the treatment group had spent a median of 109 days in prison, while the controls had served a median of 308 days.

Economic analysis

A benefit–cost analysis was not performed. Rather, the authors (Pearson, 1988; Pearson & Harper, 1990) performed what could be described in economic terms as a cost analysis of the resources used (costs) by ISP relative to CLOSE OTI. However, the authors published data that enabled the calculation of monetary benefits, which allowed for a simple benefit–cost analysis of ISP.

Total benefits for ISP were estimated at $4,500 per person per year. The benefits, expressed as per person per year, break down as follows: $4,000 in increased employment earnings. This was calculated by subtracting the mean gross legitimate income of CLOSE OTI participants (approximately $4,000) from that of ISP (approximately $8,000); and $500 in community

---

[3] It was not clear from the data provided by the authors how many of the ISP members had, by this point in time, completed the program which had an average duration of 18 months.

service work performed by ISP participants. This was calculated by dividing the average yearly aggregate contribution ($200,000) by a caseload of 400 ISP participants, presumably the number enrolled over the course of 1 year. No data was provided on the monetary value of the control group's contribution, if any, to community service work.

Total costs for ISP were estimated at $3,031 per person per year. Program costs were calculated on the basis of the 2 year period indicated by the authors:

(1) ISP costs per person = [109 prison days at $59/day] + [449 ISP days at $15/day] = $13,166/2 years = $6,583 per year.
(2) CLOSE OTI costs per person = [308 prison days at $59/day] + [422 parole days at $2.5/day] = $19,227/2 years = $9,614 per year.
(3) Total costs per person per year for ISP = CLOSE OTI costs ($9,614) − ISP costs ($6,583) = $3,031.

Dividing total per person per year benefits ($4,500) by costs ($3,031) produced a desirable benefit–cost ratio of 1.48, which means that for each dollar spent on the New Jersey Intensive Supervision Program, $1.48 was returned to the public and program participants.

DISCUSSION AND CONCLUSION

The present review suggests that correctional intervention can be an economically efficient strategy for reducing reoffending in the community. Importantly though, this review was not able to provide evidence about what type of treatment represents the best value for public money or whether it is more economical to administer treatment in an institutional or community setting. It also was not possible to address the larger issue of concern to the field of corrections, which is whether treatment is more economically efficient than punishment. Some of the studies reviewed here relied on some combination of these two correctional aims. Disentangling their independent effects and costs and benefits was not a focus of the reviewed studies and could not be achieved, because of a lack of sufficient data. More benefit–cost research on correctional intervention programs is needed before these important issues can be addressed.

Most of the studies had large samples and reasonable follow-up periods. Out of the seven studies reviewed, four had a high-quality research design: an experimental–control design with before–after measures, making it possible to exclude threats to internal validity and ensure that it was the intervention that produced the observed effects. From the three less rigorous studies (Gerstein et al., 1994; Gray & Olson, 1989; Prentky & Burgess, 1990), the study by Gray and Olson (1989) is the most difficult to interpret. Because before–after measures were not presented there is no way of assessing the validity of the three reported benefit–cost ratios. Also, with a high attrition rate for the sample and no control group, there is a very high likelihood that the findings were influenced by variables other than the interventions. The use of before–after measures without a control group in one study (Gerstein et al., 1994) and the use of a non-equivalent (retrospectively selected) control group in another (Prentky & Burgess, 1990) also limit confidence that can be placed in reported treatment effects and benefit–cost findings.

In addition to the methodological problems associated with the research designs for some of the studies, this review has two other important limitations. First, it is necessarily based on a small number of studies. Locating only seven published benefit–cost studies was quite surprising, given the substantial literature on correctional effectiveness and, as noted above, the comparatively large body of economic evaluation research on correctional intervention. Since the leading review on the subject 20 years ago (Weimer & Friedman, 1979), not a great deal has changed in benefit–cost research on correctional intervention.

Second, despite the overall rigorous nature of the benefit–cost analyses of the programs, costs and benefits were not estimated comparably. Benefits tended to be estimated conservatively, while costs were often accounted for in full. The cost and benefit figures were invariably reported in such a way that did not allow us to compare studies according to standard criteria.

Advancing knowledge about the monetary value of correctional intervention programs should begin with policy makers and researchers playing a greater role to ensure that correctional intervention programs include, as part of the original research design, provision for an economic analysis, preferably a benefit–cost analysis. Prospective economic analyses have many advantages over retrospective ones. Researchers must also ensure that benefit–cost analyses are not only methodologically rigorous, but also comprehensive: all resources used (costs) and all relevant program effects (benefits) need to be valued.

As a top priority, future benefit–cost research on correctional intervention should be concerned with standardizing the measurement of benefits and costs. The development of a standard list of program benefits and costs would overcome some of the difficulties that presently face researchers in conducting benefit–cost analyses and would greatly facilitate comparisons of benefit–cost findings of different correctional intervention programs.

Greater use of experimental research designs, particularly randomized experiments, is needed. As an economic analysis is only as strong as the evaluation upon which it is based, the stronger the research design of the outcome evaluation, the more confidence that can be placed in the findings of the economic analysis.

Lastly, funding bodies must be prepared to finance benefit–cost research. Governmental agencies with responsibility for the treatment of offenders should commit a percentage of their research budgets to support benefit–cost analyses of a number of new and existing correctional intervention programs. With these improvements in research design, public money can be spent more responsibly, rationally and effectively to reduce crime.

References

Aos, S. (1998). *Costs and Benefits: Estimating the "Bottom Line" for Crime Prevention and Intervention Programs*, A description of the cost-benefit model, version 2.0, Unpublished paper, Olympia, WA: Washington State Institute for Public Policy.

Austin, J. (1986). Using early release to relieve prison crowding: A dilemma in public policy. *Crime and Delinquency*, **32**, 404–502.

Barnett, W. S. (1993). Cost-benefit analysis. In L. J. Schweinhart, H. V. Barnes, & D. P. Weikart (Eds), *Significant Benefits: The High/Scope Perry Preschool Study through Age 27*, pp. 142–173. Ypsilanti, MI: High/Scope Press.

Barnett, W. S. (1996). *Lives in the Balance: Age-27 Benefit-cost Analysis of the High/Scope Perry Preschool Program*. Ypsilanti, MI: High/Scope Press.

Barnett, W. S., & Escobar, C. M. (1987). The economics of early educational intervention: A review. *Review of Educational Research*, **57**, 387–414.

Barnett, W. S., & Escobar, C. M. (1990). Economic costs and benefits of early intervention. In S. J. Meisels & J. P. Shonkoff (Eds), *Handbook of Early Childhood Intervention*, pp. 560–582. Cambridge: Cambridge University Press.

Bloom, H. S., & Singer, N. M. (1979). Determining the cost-effectiveness of correctional programs: The case of Patuxent Institution. *Evaluation Quarterly*, **3**, 609–628.

Cohen, M. A. (1988). Pain, suffering, and jury awards: A study of the cost of crime to victims. *Law and Society Review*, **22**, 537–555.

Farrington, D. P. (1983). Randomized experiments on crime and justice. In M. Tonry & N. Morris (Eds), *Crime and Justice: A Review of Research*, Vol. 4 pp. 257–308. Chicago: University of Chicago Press.

Farrington, D. P. (1997). Evaluating a community crime prevention program. *Evaluation*, **3**, 157–173.

Friedman, L. S. (1977). An interim evaluation of the supported work experiment. *Policy Analysis*, **3**, 147–170.

Gerstein, D. R., Johnson, R. A., Harwood, H. J., Fountain, D., Suter, N., & Malloy, K. (1994). *Evaluating Recovery Services: The California Drug and Alcohol Treatment Assessment (CALDATA)*. Sacramento, CA: Department of Alcohol and Drug Programs.

Gray, T. (1994). Research note: Using cost-benefit analysis to measure rehabilitation and special deterrence. *Journal of Criminal Justice*, **22**, 569–575.

Gray, T., Larsen, C. R., Haynes, P., & Olson, K. W. (1991). Using cost-benefit analysis to evaluate correctional sentences. *Evaluation Review*, **15**, 471–481.

Gray, T., & Olson, K. W. (1989). A cost-benefit analysis of the sentencing decision for burglars. *Social Science Quarterly*, **70**, 708–722.

Greenwood, P. W., Rydell, C. P., Abrahamse, A. F., Caulkins, J. P., Chiesa, J., Model, K. E., & Klein, S. P. (1994). *Three Strikes and You're Out: Estimated Benefits and Costs of California's New Mandatory-Sentencing Law*. Santa Monica, CA: RAND.

Haynes, P., & Larsen, C. R. (1984). Financial consequences of incarceration and alternatives: Burglary. *Crime and Delinquency*, **30**, 529–550.

Hofler, R. A., & Witte, A. D. (1979). Benefit-cost analysis of the sentencing decision: The case of homicide. In C. M. Gray (Ed.), *The Costs of Crime*, pp. 165–186. Beverly Hills, CA: Sage.

Holahan, J. (1974). Measuring benefits from prison reform. In R. H. Haveman, A. C. Harberger, L. E. Lynn, W. A. Niskanen, R. Turvey & R. Zeckhauser (Eds), *Benefit–cost and Policy Analysis 1973: An Aldine Annual on Forecasting, Decision-making, and Evaluation*, pp. 491–516. Chicago: Aldine.

Knapp, M. (1997). Economic evaluations and interventions for children and adolescents with mental health problems. *Journal of Child Psychology and Psychiatry*, **38**, 3–25.

Knapp, M., Robertson, E., & McIvor, G. (1992). The comparative costs of community service and custody in Scotland. *Howard Journal*, **31**, 8–30.

Layard, R., & Glaister, S. (Eds) (1994). *Cost-Benefit Analysis*, 2nd ed. Cambridge: Cambridge University Press.

Lipsey, M. W. (1995). What do we learn from 400 research studies on the effectiveness of treatment with juvenile delinquents? In J. McGuire (Ed.), *What Works: Reducing Re-offending—Guidelines from Research and Practice*, pp. 63–78. Chichester: John Wiley.

Lipsey, M. W., & Wilson, D. B. (1998). Effective intervention for serious juvenile offenders: A synthesis of research. In R. Loeber & D. P. Farrington (Eds), *Serious and Violent Juvenile Offenders: Risk Factors and Successful Interventions*, pp. 313–345. Thousand Oaks, CA: Sage.

MacKenzie, D. L. (1997). Criminal justice and crime prevention. In L. W. Sherman, D. C. Gottfredson, D. L. MacKenzie, J. E. Eck, P. Reuter, & S. D. Bushway, *Preventing Crime: What Works, What Doesn't, What's Promising*, pp. 9-1–76. Washington, DC: National Institute of Justice, US Department of Justice.

Palmer, T. (1992). *The Re-emergence of Correctional Intervention*. Newbury Park, CA: Sage.

Pearson, F. S. (1988). Evaluation of New Jersey's intensive supervision program. *Crime and Delinquency*, **34**, 437–448.

Pearson, F. S., & Harper, A. G. (1990). Contingent intermediate sentences: New Jersey's intensive supervision program. *Crime and Delinquency*, **36**, 75–86.

Petersilia, J., & Turner, S. (1993). Intensive probation and parole. In M. Tonry (Ed.), *Crime and Justice: A Review of Research*, Vol. 17, pp. 281–335. Chicago: University of Chicago Press.

Prentky, R., & Burgess, A. W. (1990). Rehabilitation of child molesters: A cost-benefit analysis. *American Journal of Orthopsychiatry*, **60**, 108–117.

Prest, A. R., & Turvey, R. (1965). Cost-benefit analysis: A survey. *Economic Journal*, **75**, 683–735.

Schoenwald, S. K., Ward, D. M., Henggeler, S. W., Pickrel, S. G., & Patel, H. (1996). Multisystemic therapy treatment of substance abusing or dependent adolescent offenders: Costs of reducing incarceration, inpatient, and residential placement. *Journal of Child and Family Studies*, **5**, 431–444.

Sherman, L. W., Gottfredson, D. C., MacKenzie, D. L., Eck, J. E., Reuter, P., & Bushway, S. D. (1997). *Preventing Crime: What Works, What Doesn't, What's Promising*. Washington, DC: National Institute of Justice, US Department of Justice.

Sherman, L. W., Gottfredson, D. C., MacKenzie, D. L., Eck, J. E., Reuter, P., & Bushway, S. D. (1998). *Preventing Crime: What Works, What Doesn't, What's Promising*, Research in brief, July. Washington, DC: National Institute of Justice, US Department of Justice.

Weimer, D. L., & Friedman, L. S. (1979). Efficiency considerations in criminal rehabilitation research: Costs and consequences. In L. Sechrest, S. O. White, & E. D. Brown (Eds), *The Rehabilitation of Criminal Offenders: Problems and Prospects*, pp. 251–272. Washington, DC: National Academy of Sciences.

Weinrott, M. R., Jones, R. R., & Howard, J. R. (1982). Cost-effectiveness of teaching family programs for delinquents: Results of a national evaluation. *Evaluation Review*, **6**, 173–201.

Welsh, B. C., & Farrington, D. P. (1999). Value for money? A review of the costs and benefits of situational crime prevention. *British Journal of Criminology*, **39**, 345–368.

Welsh, B. C., & Farrington, D. P. (2000). Monetary costs and benefits of crime prevention programs. In M. Tonry (Ed.), *Crime and Justice: A Review of Research*, Vol. 27, pp. 305–361. Chicago: University of Chicago Press.

Welsh, B. C. (2001). Economic costs and benefits of primary prevention of delinquency and later offending: A review of the research. In D. P. Farrington & J. W. Coid (Eds), *Early Prevention of Adult Antisocial Behavior*. Cambridge: Cambridge University Press (in press).

Welsh, B. C., Farrington, D. P., & Sherman, L. W. (Eds) (2001). *Costs and Benefits of Preventing Crime*. Boulder, CO: Westview Press.

Zedlewski, E. W. (1992). *Costs and Benefits of Sanctions: A Synthesis of Recent Research*, Paper presented at the National Conference on Prosecution Strategies, San Diego, CA, June.

Zimring, F. E., & Hawkins, G. (1995). *Incapacitation: Penal Confinement and the Restraint of Crime*. New York: Oxford University Press.

Chapter 4

EVALUATING THE EFFECTIVENESS OF CORRECTIONAL PROGRAMS: BRIDGING THE GAP BETWEEN RESEARCH AND PRACTICE

FRIEDRICH LÖSEL

Institut für Psychologie I, Universität Erlangen-Nürnberg, Erlangen, Germany

INTRODUCTION

In the mid-1980s, we completed a report that contained a systematic review and meta-analysis of the available evaluation studies on social-therapeutic prisons in Germany (Lösel, Koferl, & Weber, 1987). In contrast to widespread opinions that offender rehabilitation has failed, this synthesis resulted in a slightly more positive conclusion. On the one hand, we recognized many methodological problems in the primary studies and a lack of well-controlled research. This conclusion was in line with what Lipton, Martinson and Wilks (1975) had found in their famous overview of the research in the English-speaking world. On the other hand, our meta-analysis revealed a small, but rather consistent effect size of approximately 10 percentage points more positive outcomes in the treatment groups than in the comparison groups. This effect was significant and not correlated with threats to

Offender Rehabilitation in Practice. Edited by G. A. Bernfeld, D. P. Farrington and A. W. Leschied.
© 2001 John Wiley & Sons, Ltd.

internal validity. A later update including more recent studies produced similar results (Lösel, 1995a).

Our cautiously positive evaluation of the efficacy of offender rehabilitation in Germany's social-therapeutic prisons was supported by broader research integrations and meta-analyses from both North America and other European countries (e.g. Andrews et al., 1990; Antonowicz & Ross, 1994; Dowden & Andrews, 1999; Garrett, 1985; Gendreau & Goggin, 1996; Gensheimer, Mayer, Gottschalk & Davidson, 1986; Gottschalk, Davidson, Gensheimer & Mayer, 1987; Izzo & Ross, 1990; Lipsey, 1992; Lipsey & Wilson, 1998; Palmer, 1992; Pearson, Lipton & Cleland, 1996; Petrosino, 1997; Redondo, Garrido & Sánchez-Meca, 1997; Redondo, Sánchez-Meca & Garrido, 1999; Roberts & Camasso, 1991; Sherman et al. 1997). Although some authors still favored the conclusion that "nothing works" in offender rehabilitation (e.g. Logan et al., 1991; Whitehead & Lab, 1989), the international scientific discussion had moved to a more differentiated perspective of "what works" (McGuire, 1995). Reports to the United States Congress (Sherman et al., 1997) or to the Council of Europe (Lösel, 1995b) also emphasized that some types of offender treatment are relatively effective or promising, whereas others are not.

The research syntheses from the 1980s and 1990s showed the following: the number of relatively well-controlled studies had increased, and, in some areas, many used a randomized design or matched control groups (e.g. Lipsey & Wilson, 1998). The aggregation of large numbers of studies through meta-analysis reduced or at least demonstrated the impact of threats to the internal or external validity of single studies. The mean effect sizes in all meta-analyses were positive and varied approximately between $r = 0.10 \pm 0.05$ (Lösel, 1995c, 1998). Nearly all research syntheses showed relatively consistent differences between modes of treatment: theoretically and empirically well-founded, multimodal, cognitive-behavioral and skill-oriented programs that address the offenders' risk, needs and responsivity had substantially larger effects than the overall mean (e.g. 0.20). Clearly structured therapeutic communities or social-therapeutic prisons and (in the case of ambulatory treatment for serious juvenile offenders) family-oriented programs were also promising. In contrast, traditional psychodynamic and non-directive therapy and counseling, low-structured milieu therapy and therapeutic communities, merely formal variations in punishment or diversion, deterrence, boot camps and measures of smarter punishment had relatively weak or no effects (e.g. Andrews et al., 1990; Gendreau & Goggin, 1996; Hollin, 1999; Lipsey, 1992; Lipsey & Wilson, 1998; Lösel, 1995c; Rawlings, 1999; Redondo et al., 1997, 1999; Sherman et al., 1997; see also Chapter 2 by James McGuire in this book).

These and other results led to guidelines for effective correctional programming (e.g. Andrews, 1995; Gendreau, 1995; Lösel, 1995a). Countries such as Canada, England and Scotland use such principles for program accreditation. These developments represent a clear progress toward quality management in service delivery. However, this should not mislead us into believing that effective offender treatment is now only a question of good implementation of proven programs. Looking closely at what we know about offender treatment, we often face a mixture of sound and replicated empirical research, weaker and inconsistent data, practical experiences and theoretical generalizations. This is particularly the case with respect to questions of differential indication: what mode of program for what type of offenders delivered by which personnel in which setting under which contextual circumstances shows what kind of effects?

The majority of controlled studies addresses juvenile delinquency where outcomes seem to be a little more positive (e.g. Pearson et al., 1996). However, even here, generalizations to practice may be questionable. A large portion of studies used follow-up periods of less than 1 year (Lipsey, 1992a) and various important types of treatment were investigated only in few experiments. For example, in a meta-analysis of 200 studies on the treatment of serious and violent juvenile offenders, the most effective interpersonal skills programs were evaluated only in three studies of non-institutionalized and three studies of institutionalized offenders (Lipsey & Wilson, 1998). In his integration of more than 400 studies on juvenile offender treatment, Lipsey (1992a) found only four controlled evaluations of employment programs. This was the most effective type of intervention in the juvenile justice system. In non-juvenile justice contexts, however, where more studies on vocational and employment programs are available, such interventions were least effective.

Problems of generalizability are even more obvious in the treatment of serious adult offenders and specific offender groups. In our own meta-analysis of German social-therapeutic prisons, for example, only one study used a randomized design (Lösel, 1995a). A second true experiment can now be added (Ortmann, 2000). Studies on therapeutic communities (TCs) in England revealed clinically relevant and encouraging results (e.g. Cullen, 1997; Dolan, 1997; Genders & Player, 1995). However, not one evaluation was truly experimental or had an otherwise fully comparable control group. Research on the treatment of psychopathic offenders showed similar deficits (Blackburn, 2000; Dolan & Coid, 1993; Lösel, 1998); however, this does not yet imply that psychopaths are basically untreatable (Lösel, 2000).

In the field of sex offenders, Alexander (1999) found 359 English-language articles published between 1943 and 1996. A total of 79 of these studies presented systematic outcome data. However, when comparable control groups were used as an inclusion criterion, Hall (1995) could only integrate 12 studies in his meta-analysis. The significant effect of hormonal treatment was based on only four studies, of which one had a negative effect size and one investigated the rarely used measure of castration. Evaluating prison- and non-prison-based treatment of sex offenders, Polizzi, Mackenzie and Hickman (1999) were left with only four studies scoring at least 4 points (minor differences in a non-equivalent comparison group) on the 5-point Maryland Scale of Methodological Rigor (Sherman et al., 1997). White, Bradley, Ferriter and Hatzipetrou (1998) applied the strict criteria of the Cochrane Collaboration and could integrate only three studies. Finally, in a review of German-language research on sex offender treatment, Lösel (2000) found only one study with a randomized design, which, nonetheless, lacked statistical power due to its small sample size.

These examples show that there are far fewer methodologically well-founded treatment studies on specific types of programs, offenders and settings than the general "what works" discussion would suggest. If we further take into account that studies with a higher quality of design tend to show smaller effects (Lipsey, 1992a; Lipsey & Wilson, 1998; Lösel, 1995c; Pearson et al., 1996), the need for more sound evaluation research becomes obvious. However, this is much easier to demand than to realize. It is also often questionable how far even good evaluation studies can be generalized to everyday treatment practice. With respect to juvenile offender treatment, Lipsey (1995) and Lipsey and Wilson (1998) found that program monitoring by the researcher resulted in larger effects. Dowden and Andrews (1999) reported a strong correlation between researcher involvement and the efficacy of programs for female offenders. These results probably indicate high treatment integrity that is achieved less frequently in everyday practice. Many controlled evaluation studies also apply exclusion criteria that are less viable in regular treatment. In Hall's (1995) meta-analysis of sex offender treatment, for example, most studies contained only two-thirds of the clients who were initially available.

To avoid misunderstanding, my intention is not to replicate the long-standing controversy about the priority of internal versus external validity in program evaluation. In line with Cook and Campbell (1979), I emphasize internal validity as a necessary condition of any generalization across subjects, time, outcomes and contexts (Lösel & Nowack, 1987). However, the above-mentioned and other examples indicate discrepancies between a large part of offender treatment research and the rehabilitation programs in daily practice. The situation seems to be similar in general psychosocial treatment. Here, experts questioned whether the relatively positive results of controlled psychotherapy research can be transferred to everyday practice (e.g. Donenberg, Lyons & Howard, 1999; Orlinsky, 1994; Weisz, Donenberg, Weiss & Han, 1995). As a consequence, the US National Institute of Mental Health recently started a big program of "real world" effectiveness research to move promising treatments into practice (Foxhall, 2000). Clinical utility research, for example, addresses not only effectiveness but also issues of access, transferability, sample specificity, and the uniqueness of each human condition (Beutler & Howard, 1998).

Because offender treatment evaluation is less based on university and analogue studies, the gap between research and practice may be smaller in our field. However, we also need a new generation of both relatively well-controlled and practice-oriented evaluation studies. Against this background, the present chapter addresses basic problems and possible solutions from the perspective of evaluation methodology as well as practical demands. It presents a brief discussion of the following issues:

(a)   the content of programs and control conditions;
(b)   the availability of control groups;
(c)   the dropout problem;
(d)   offender characteristics;
(e)   outcome measurement; and
(f)   the wider social context of treatment programs.

THE CONTENT OF PROGRAMS AND CONTROL CONDITIONS

The label "program" refers to a broad variety of interventions in offender rehabilitation. At the one pole we find programs with a fixed number of structured teaching modules that are based on detailed manuals for program staff and materials for the clients (e.g. Bettman, 2000; Ross & Ross, 1995). The other pole is formed by very complex "packages" of individual and group treatment, social regulations and processes, education and work programs, and so forth that are integrated in TCs and similar institutions (e.g. Cullen, 1997; Dolan, 1997). Many other programs vary between these poles. The various approaches are not equally suitable for systematic evaluation. If a program is very heterogeneous in its content, the treatment reliability (integrity) and the statistical power are questionable (Lösel & Wittmann, 1989; Weisburd, Petrosino & Mason, 1993). In contrast, relatively circumscribed and standardized programs normally lead to higher integrity. They provide us with clearer information about the causes of failure or success than very complex interventions do. Sherman et al. (1997) have given us a proper analogy for this problem: in medicine, we would evaluate only the effect of aspirin and not a whole hospital or pharmacy in general.

Unfortunately, we still do not have anything like aspirin for offender treatment. In practice, many offenders receive rather complex interventions, different combinations of programs or multiple services. Even pharmacological treatment such as cyproterone acetate for subgroups of sexual offenders or serotonin reuptake inhibitors for some violent offenders are rarely applied without psychosocial interventions as well. Thus, the question of efficacy in offender rehabilitation is often similar to multiple medication or to differences between clinics (e.g. in postoperative mortality). Evaluation is also complicated by other issues:

(a) We often only know the concept of a program and not what was really delivered to the clients (Lösel & Wittmann, 1989).
(b) Program labels from traditional "schools" of psychotherapy may exaggerate differences and underscore practical similarities (e.g. Pfäfflin, 1999).
(c) Various indicators of treatment delivery such as total duration or contact hours per week show independent and contradictory relations with effect size (e.g. Lipsey & Wilson, 1998).
(d) Psychotherapy research suggests that process variables such as cooperation, therapeutic bond, mutual affirmation, client openness or suitability may be more important for efficacy than specific techniques (Orlinsky, Grawe & Parks, 1994).
(e) In accordance with this, types of program are only one source of outcome variance among others, such as offender variables, design features or general program characteristics (e.g. Lipsey & Wilson, 1998; Redondo et al., 1997).
(f) Institutional conditions, such as training and supervision of qualified staff; attitudes and involvement of the personnel; or cooperation, support and other characteristics of the organizational climate are also relevant for effective programing (e.g. Andrews & Dowden, 1999; Antonowicz & Ross, 1994; Gendreau, Goggin & Smith, 1999; Hollin, 1995; Lipsey & Wilson, 1998; Lösel, 1993; Moos, 1975; Spencer, 1999).

In consequence, we need many more process analyses of treatment delivery in practice. Such studies should assess the dimensionality of treatment and investigate dose-response relationships. For example, Moos (1974) has demonstrated that climate variables, such as cohesion, openness and norm orientation, are relevant in correctional institutions. Ortmann (2000) assessed simple indicators of program delivery, release preparation and organizational features. He demonstrated differences in favor of therapeutic institutions as well as correlations between these factors and treatment efficacy. Lösel and Bliesener (1989) analyzed time budgets of prison psychologists. The differences in rehabilitation activities and organizational development were in line with the basic therapeutic orientation and other organizational characteristics. Results on schools (Rutter, Maughan, Mortimore & Ouston, 1979) and institutions of residential care (Lösel & Bliesener, 1994) also suggest that the psychosocial dimensions of the institution must be assessed in a systematic way. In sanction and treatment environments, such an assessment may include data on safety, opportunities, contacts, therapeutic orientations, coerciveness, discipline, continuity of care and so forth (e.g. Mulvey, 2000).

We must also bear in mind that untreated control or comparison groups do not spend the time during treatment in a vacuum. Because they do not receive "nothing", it is very important to know what "non-treatment" or "treatment as usual" means. In evaluations of institutional treatment, for example, conditions for control groups from regular prisons are similar to those of the treated groups in various ways: they are also exposed to the effects of loss of freedom and a prison subculture; they participate in work programs; they can take advantage of schooling and other training provisions; sometimes they receive counseling or crisis intervention through social services; they may obtain day passes, holidays or work outside; and they are prepared for release and often monitored in a similar way by probation officers in the community. Depending on which influences arise from these conditions, comparison with the treated group will involve only gradual differences rather than a program-versus-nothing dichotomy. The factual differences between program and control conditions may sometimes be small. Unfavorable institutional conditions can also have detrimental influences, whereas a good regime may compensate for the lack of a specific program.

That the effect of a program depends on outcomes in the control group just as much as on the program itself can be seen in evaluations of the social-therapeutic prisons in two German cities (Dünkel & Geng, 1994; Egg, 1990). Both studies produced highly similar recidivism rates using various official criteria (e.g. Lösel & Egg, 1997). In Berlin, however, outcomes in the comparison groups from regular prisons were worse than in Erlangen, with the result that only the Berlin study had a significant treatment effect. Hall's (1995) meta-analysis of sexual offender treatment reveals a similar tendency toward larger effects in studies with relatively negative outcomes in the control group. It may seem ironic, but the more rehabilitative elements we find in regular prisons, the harder it becomes to confirm effects of a treatment program. Vice versa, treatment effects are easiest to confirm when the "normal" state response to offenders is particularly ineffective. Perhaps, some international differences in programming and evaluation may be related to this issue. The consequence for methodologically sound and practice-related evaluations is a description of the program, the organization and the social context—not just for the treatment group but also for controls.

AVAILABILITY OF CONTROL GROUPS

A powerful study on the effect of offender treatment should use a randomized design or a quasi-experimental design with comparable untreated groups. However, the Introduction to this chapter has shown that these standards are often not attained when we are dealing with programs for serious and adult offenders. It is not that researchers have been unaware of the methodological deficits, but that practical constraints frequently did not permit an optimal design. For example, it is harder to form control groups when evaluating a complete institution rather than a clearly delimited program that is applied within an institution. This is the case in complex programs, such as TCs, social-therapeutic prisons or forensic clinics. Here, placement follows specific criteria, and equivalent control groups often cannot be formed for legal and therapeutic reasons. For example, mentally disordered offenders need various interventions for reasons of institutional management. The situation is similar to that for acutely depressive or suicidal patients who cannot be left "untreated". In these fields, we can compare different forms of treatment (e.g. drug therapy versus cognitive behavior therapy). However, as mentioned above, in offender treatment we rarely use treatments without a psychosocial component. Comparisons between basically different programs are difficult to realize within the same institution. Multi-center comparisons are rare because of legal, organizational, financial, psychological or other obstacles. Designs with waiting-list control groups are also difficult to use in offender treatment. On the one hand, intensive programs may already take up most of the time of incarceration, and, on the other hand, several years of follow-up are needed to assess recidivism adequately.

Naturally, we should strive toward randomized designs as far as possible, although major threats to validity may still emerge in true experiments (e.g. through dropouts, small sample sizes, diffusion of treatment, experimental rivalry, demoralization of untreated controls, etc.). At the same time, we should accept that evaluation in practice cannot follow one royal path. It is a complex process of integrating various bits of information through which the system learns about itself (Cronbach et al., 1980). Campbell and Stanley (1963) have already emphasized that every experiment is imperfect. In accordance with these pioneers of evaluation, offender treatment studies should implement the best design the situation makes possible. It is important to note, however, that such a flexible use of reasonable designs is still based on the methodology of quasi-experimentation (for a "softer" position, see e.g. Pawson & Tilley, 1994).

One strategy—practice-oriented evaluation—should establish common and structured data files on offender risk and later recidivism. Empirically validated instruments such as the LSI-R (Andrews & Bonta, 1995) or the VRAG (Quinsey, Harris, Rice & Cormier, 1998) may be used as core measures. When the system is applied uniformly in various institutions, the formation of relatively equivalent comparison groups can be facilitated. It is also possible to derive typical base rates of recidivism in specific offender populations. If treated clients reveal a failure rate that is clearly below the typical range of outcome, whereas selection, attrition and other serious threats to validity are in a normal range, even a *post-hoc* comparison may become a useful piece of information. A systematic documentation of offenders also permits more statistical controls that may be used to rule out the alternative explanations.

Although there may be problems of rivalry or coordination, we should more frequently design multi-center comparisons. A further approach is to separate complex programs into distinct modules that can be subjected to controlled evaluation within an institution (Lösel, 1995b). Attempts should also be made to gain information on the efficacy of programs through a systematic grading of their intensity or dosage. If there is a consistent dose–effect relationship, even an otherwise non-interpretable single group pretest–posttest design may reveal usable information. As Carlson and Schmidt (1999) have shown, the latter designs should not be excluded. That they often yield larger mean effects than control group designs seems not to be due to methodological weakness but to differences in the equations for calculating effect sizes.

In specific cases, regression–discontinuity designs, interrupted time series and cohort designs are also conceivable in offender treatment evaluation. Surprisingly, such designs are rarely used in our field. Cohort studies, for example, can reduce the problems with one-shot evaluations of new programs. Programs need time to ripen along with practical experiences and scientific progress. This could be tested by regular analyses of institutional cohorts. Quasi-experimental, aggregated case study approaches (Howard, Orlinsky & Lueger, 1994) may also be applied in offender treatment. Finally, evaluators should bear in mind that, on all levels of methodological rigor, a design is more useful when the underlying theories of causation, programming and change are well elaborated (Chen, 1989).

THE DROPOUT PROBLEM

Almost all evaluation studies on offender treatment have substantial dropout rates. In favorable cases, these are below 10 per cent; in the least favorable, almost one-half. Approximately one-quarter is fairly typical. In part, these clients leave voluntarily because they had had other expectations, found treatment too strenuous or no longer believed that participation would lead to early release or other advantages. Clients are also requested to leave because of, for example, a lack of cooperation, violence, drug use and other institutional misconduct. Complex long-term programs sometimes include a trial phase lasting several months in which treatment is broken off particularly frequently (Lösel & Egg, 1997).

The dropout problem is important for both methodological and clinical reasons. Program completers represent a positive selection of clients, whereas dropouts often have much higher recidivism rates (e.g. Hanson & Bussière, 1998; Lösel et al., 1987). If dropout phenomena are not similar in the control group, an originally randomized design or a well-controlled quasi-experimental design may fall apart. If data analysis allocates dropouts to the treated group, this often results in only low or no differences from untreated groups. However, such evaluations are unfair to program deliverers, because non-completers have not been exposed to the whole program. In conclusion, the best way to perform a methodologically adequate data analysis is to present results separately for the different groups and then perform different conservative or optimistic estimates of effects (if enough information on dropouts and control clients is available).

That dropouts often exhibit higher failure rates than untreated offenders may be traced back to individual characteristics. However, it is also necessary to consider dropout risks that have more to do with the program, the institution or the social context. For example, intake criteria may be too unspecific, or insufficient information is provided on the program. An empirically based offender intake assessment is particularly important (e.g. Andrews & Bonta, 1998; Hoge & Andrews, 1996). This should clarify the specific risks and needs of the offender and not be too narrow with respect to treatment motivation. The latter may be very complex and include, for example, real mental suffering, instrumental intentions, self-efficacy expectations, experiences of forced choice and ambivalences (e.g. Dahle, 1995). An assessment of such motivational patterns must be related to motivation enhancement techniques in the program (e.g. Bettman, 2000). It is also necessary to test whether the program design is sufficiently differentiated and flexible to handle individual idiosyncrasies or transient motivation problems in clients. In highly structured programs, switching between group and individual treatment, opportunities to make up for omissions or absences, or temporary transfers within the institution are just some of the provisions that may help to stop difficult offenders from dropping out. Finally, staff must always critically examine how far there are tendencies to exclude unfavorable cases because they may impair the social climate in the program and lead to more failures in outcome data.

Even with a relatively valid intake assessment and program modules designed to encourage treatment motivation, it is impossible to prevent all dropouts. Therefore, evaluations should address organizational and individual processes after the early termination. Dolde (1996), for example, found that some dropouts did not reoffend more often than the group with regular treatment. If such results could be replicated with larger samples, they may indicate processes of flexible handling, constructive reassignment and non-stigmatization in the respective institutions. Individual differences in subcultural identification, active coping and self-stigmatization may also be relevant for such untypically positive developments in treatment dropouts. More research is needed to understand how benefits can be gained from uncompleted treatments through the flexible management of failures. On the organizational level, decision makers must be aware that dropping out of a certain program, at a certain time, and under certain circumstances should not lead to a self-fulfilling prophecy of being generally unresponsive to treatment. On the side of the offenders, it is necessary to encourage an adequate processing of treatment dropout that avoids the typical external attributions, unrealistic expectations regarding self-efficacy or defeatist identifications with the criminal role.

DIFFERENTIATED OFFENDER CHARACTERISTICS

Many controlled evaluations are based on very roughly described offender categories, such as age, gender, ethnic group, types of offense and offense history. However, even these data cannot be taken for granted. For example, Lipsey and Wilson (1998) found that gender was not reported in 8 per cent of studies; age, in 9 per cent; ethnic group, in 24 per cent; and indications of aggressive offense history, in 16 per cent. Vague information is probably one of the reasons why offender characteristics explain between 1 and 40 per cent of variance in effect sizes (e.g. Lipsey, 1992a; Lipsey & Wilson, 1998; Redondo et al., 1997; 1999).

Evaluations which address differential treatment indications must be based on relatively detailed offender data. Practitioners normally combine structured instruments (e.g. Andrews & Bonta, 1995; Hare, 1991; Quinsey et al., 1998) and clinical approaches to assess offense characteristics, criminal history, non-criminal development, social functioning, interpersonal relationships, personality traits and psychiatric syndromes (e.g. Dolan & Coid, 1993; McMurran & Hodge, 1994). However, these clinically relevant differences between offenders are not yet sufficiently included in controlled evaluations. This is probably due to the aggregated outcome measurement (see below), the problem of statistical power in small subsamples and a lack of comparable diagnoses across time and sites.

Although previous offending is among the best predictors of later recidivism (Gendreau, Little & Goggin, 1996), criminal history is only a vague indicator for a specific kind of treatment. The same holds for offense types. The label "sexual offender", for example, is applied to a very heterogeneous group of offenders who often commit other offenses as well (Beier, 1995; Hanson & Bussière, 1998). Offense history is particularly useful for differential indication if it reveals markers for an underlying responsiveness to treatment and change process. Persistent property offenders, for example, seem to gain less from treatment than violent or sexual offenders (Lipsey & Wilson, 1998; Ortmann, 2000). Probably, these results reflect differences in the etiology and maintainance of the problem behavior (e.g. deviant socialization and crime as routine activity versus conflict and personality-related influences). Similarly, subtypes of sexual offense may be indicators of different motivations and degrees of disorder. For example, in child molestors, the risk of recidivism is lower when victims are female and not strangers, and offenders show no sexual disorder/paraphilia (Hanson & Bussière, 1998).

A detailed assessment of the offender's risks and needs should refer to functional issues of responsivity to treatment. For example, psychopaths as indicated by the PCL-R (Hare, 1991) have a high risk of violent and general reoffending (Hart, 1998; Hemphill, Hare & Wong, 1998). Whereas the score on the second factor (impulsive-antisocial lifestyle) is a good predictor of reoffending, the relational and emotional characteristics of the first factor are more relevant for treatment. They reveal that psychopaths lack the functional prerequisites for psychotherapeutic processes and thus are most difficult to manage or treat (Lösel, 1998). Inappropriate programs may even make these clients more problematic (Rice et al., 1992). Criminal history alone would not yet suggest this, because higher risk is not necessarily associated with low treatment efficacy. In contrast, effect sizes are somewhat larger in high-risk than in low-risk groups (Dowden & Andrews, 1999; Lipsey & Wilson, 1998). However, we should not overgeneralize this message, because it depends on the range of risks that are included in the respective data. From a clinical as well as methodological perspective, an inverted U-shaped relationship between risk level and treatment efficacy is most plausible (Lösel, 1996): in cases of very low risk, "natural" protective mechanisms normally counteract reoffending and lead to desistance from criminality over the course of development (e.g. Lösel & Bender, in press). Due to such influences, the recidivism rate in low-risk control groups is also relatively low and thus leads to small program effects. In cases of very high risk, such as psychopathic offenders, however, even sound programs may promote only very limited behavioral changes and small effect sizes. Recent studies support the inverted U-shaped function (e.g. McGuire, Thornton, in press). Practice-oriented evaluations must refer also to comorbidities in offenders. These are rather frequent in forensic treatment. For example, only 3 per cent of the inmates of Henderson Hospital (UK) scored within a single cluster of personality disorder (Dolan, 1997). Although it is not yet clear whether this covariation is due to a poor discriminant validity or an overlap in etiologically different syndromes (Lilienfeld, 1994), it shows the need for differentiated program evaluation. The same holds for alcoholism and substance abuse. For example, Woody, McLellan, Luborsky and O'Brien (1985) found that clients with opiate dependence, major depression and antisocial personality disorder or with the first two or only the first one of these syndromes had better treatment results than those with opiate dependence and antisocial personality disorder. Comorbidities between externalizing problems and internalizing problems, such as anxiety, depression or psychophysiological disorders are also not infrequent (e.g. Dolan & Coid, 1993; Loeber, Farrington, Stouthamer-Loeber & Van Kammen, 1998). Although there is some overlap in the explanatory factors for both problem syndromes (McCord & Ensminger, 1997; Loeber et al., 1998), such comorbidities may reflect different causal mechanisms (Rutter, 1997) and differences in the above-mentioned processes of motivation, cooperation and bonding in treatment (Orlinsky et al., 1994). Thus, for example, outcomes will differ between clients with purely externalizing or mixed problems, primary and secondary psychopaths, or undercontrolled and overcontrolled violent offenders (Blackburn, 1993). Therefore, on the one hand, studies should more explicitly address specified offender groups. On the other hand, practice should use comparable assessment instruments that enable data integrations and evaluations across time and various sites.

OUTCOME MEASUREMENT

Official data on reoffending and reconviction are particularly important outcome measures for practice and policy making. However, for good reasons, evaluations also include other criteria, such as self-reports of delinquency (mainly for less serious offenses), measures of personality and attitudes, social skills, behavior within the institution or other indicators of adaptation (e.g. at school, at work, in the community). Although the choice of outcome criteria is a central issue, the reliability, validity and sensitivity of the measures used was not demonstrated in most evaluations of juvenile offender treatment (Lipsey, 1992b). Whereas a multi-setting–multi-informant approach has proved to be essential for the assessment of problem behavior (Achenbach et al., 1987; LeBlanc, 1998), offender treatment evaluation frequently limits itself to one data source.

This is particularly the case for official recidivism. Undetected offenses, selection processes and other problems limit its validity for criminal behavior (Barbaree, 1997; Lösel et al., 1987; Palmer, 1992; Lloyd, Mair & Hough, 1994). Depending on the structure of the justice system, it may also vary in its sensitivity. Lipsey and Wilson (1998), for example, found that studies using police contact (arrest) showed larger effects than those that measured recidivism through court contact, parole violation or institutionalization. Such discrepancies can even appear within one single study. For example, in an evaluation of a program for serious juvenile offenders, Lösel and Pomplun (1998) used three indicators of recidivism:

(1) any new entry in the German Federal Central Register (including registrations for petty offenses);
(2) all new entries except dismissal, educational court order, or other minor sanctions and
(3) new entries with an unconditional prison sentence.

The mean follow-up period was 4 years. Results showed that the treatment and comparison group did not differ significantly in terms of the first two criteria. However, when the third criterion (indicating the most serious type of recidivism) was applied, there was a significant difference in favor of the program group. In conclusion, methodologically sound and practice-oriented evaluations of offender treatment should not just include one measure of official reoffending but a differentiated set of indicators that are sensitive enough to avoid artifacts.

This is also the case for the length of follow-up. As a general trend, we find larger effects in studies with shorter follow-up periods (Lösel, 1995c). Frequently, recidivism of treated groups is delayed during the first year after release and comes closer to the control group when the survival curves typically stabilize after 4–5 years. In sexual offenders, the risk of recidivism is even more expanded over time (Beier, 1995). The consequences of such results for evaluation practice are not as simple as they might seem at first glance. Obviously, we should not only use short follow-up periods, as is mostly the case in juvenile offender treatment. However, the longer the follow-up period the less we need to measure the specific impact of the program. Its effect becomes more and more confounded with natural developmental factors in the community and programs of aftercare (if applied). Furthermore, expanded follow-up periods often lead to high attrition rates. Last but not least, prospective designs with long follow-up periods are not only costly but also evaluate old programs that may already have been modified (see above). For these and other reasons, short follow-up times are not inadequate. However, they should be used only as a starting point in a continuous update of outcome data over a longer period.

A change from one-shot program evaluations to multiple measurements goes beyond official data on recidivism. Intermediate criteria, such as attitudes, personality measures or institutional adaptation, tend to show higher effect sizes than measures of criminal behavior with a longer follow-up period (Feldman, 1989; Lösel, 1995c). In principle, larger effects can be anticipated the more the outcome variable is proximal to treatment (Lipsey, 1992b). However, in evaluation practice, we are often confronted with inconsistencies or indirect relations between different types of outcome data.

For example, Ortmann (2000) found no systematic relation between intermediate personality measures and recidivism. Lösel and Koferl (1989) reported no differences in effect sizes between psychological outcome at the end of treatment and reoffending several years later. Hanson and Wallace-Capretta (2000) demonstrated that some factors commonly believed to inhibit domestic violence showed no meaningful relationship with recidivism. According to Lipsey (1992b), effect sizes in psychological measures and academic performance did not correlate with those in delinquency, but with school participation that was, in turn, correlated with recidivism. On the one hand, such discrepancies may be due to using inadequate or unreliable intermediate variables instead of proven risks factors (Andrews & Bonta, 1998). On the other hand, intermediate measures can be so restricted to the specific program contents that transfer becomes questionable (e.g. Beelmann, Pfingsten & Lösel, 1994; Lösel & Wittmann, 1989).

In general, effect criteria should reflect symmetry between treatment and outcome (see Lösel & Wittmann, 1989; Wittmann, 1985): the success of a rather specific intervention is not tested adequately with very broad outcome measures and vice versa. Dynamic assessments should form a systematic chain of proximal to distal outcome. This may, for example, include measures of treatment motivation and institutional adaptation, program performance, social information processing, crime-related attitudes, social skills, work behavior, social relations, substance use, self-control in risk situations and criminal behavior (e.g. Andrews & Bonta, 1998; Bettman, 2000; Hanson & Harris, 2000). Response curves can be used to evaluate individual changes and, when appropriate, can be aggregated to measure outcome on the group level (Krause, Howard & Lutz, 1998).

However, even within a well-developed chain of outcome measures, we may obtain inconsistent results. This is because the typical bivariate correlations between risk factors and offending are small (e.g. Gendreau et al., 1996; Hawkins et al., 1998). Evaluators should also bear in mind that systematic chains of outcome measures are not generalizable across all offender groups. For example, whereas institutional misbehavior is a predictor of recidivism in general (e.g. Bonta & Motiuk, 1992; Monahan, 1989), it is less indicative of sexual reoffending in child molesters.

THE COMMUNITY CONTEXT

Dynamic risk assessments emphasize not only characteristics before and during the intervention but also the social environment to which the offender returns (e.g. Hanson & Harris, 2000; Monahan, 1989). Thus, the efficacy of a program may depend heavily on the wider context and particularly on the community within which the treated offender lives. The respective influences can be structured into three main areas:

(a) professional services of aftercare and relapse prevention;
(b) "natural" protective or risk mechanism factors in the microsocial context of the client; and
(c) general features of the neighborhood and community. Program delivery as well as evaluation need to address these issues in the following three subsections.

(a) Aftercare and relapse prevention services

Even very intensive rehabilitation programs are only a small part of the variety of developmental factors that impact on the client's thinking and behavior. Therefore, it is necessary to deliver services that consolidate the competencies acquired during treatment, to provide control over risks and to cope with the crises that may arise. Although systematic measures of aftercare and relapse prevention are particularly emphasized for the treatment of drug-addicted and sexual delinquents (Annis, 1986; Laws, 1999), they seem to be relevant for violent, personality-disordered and other serious offenders as well (e.g. Lösel, 1998; Serin, 1995). Studies have shown larger effects not only for combinations with rather specific treatment programs but also with complex interventions. For example, institutional treatment within a structured therapeutic community was more effective when followed by an ambulatory TC program (Wexler, 1997). However, if the aftercare and relapse prevention program is not an integral part of the treatment under focus, we often do not know what happens to clients when they return to their natural context. Therefore, a careful evaluation of differential treatment effects should assess the characteristics of the services provided to offenders after the intervention or control phase. This may include not only type and intensity of services but also cooperation routines between the institutions, probation officers and other staff involved. According to practical experiences, these multi-agency networks are very important for preventing recidivism (e.g. Roberts, 1995; Spencer, 1999). However, they are rarely addressed in controlled treatment evaluations.

(b) Natural protective factors

Even without any treatment program, a subgroup of high-risk offenders desists from criminal behavior. In these cases, natural protective mechanisms improve non-deviant social bonds and skills that make delinquent behavior less attractive. Although our knowledge on such processes is still rudimentary, various personal and social resources have repeatedly shown a protective function against antisociality (Lösel & Bender, in press): for example, bonds to non-deviant family members or other reference persons; acceptance and supervision in education; cognitive competencies and planning for the future; an easy temperament; school achievement and bonds to school; non-deviant peer groups; work motivation, vocational skills and employment; and a supportive and prosocial intimate partner. Protective social and vocational relations seem to be particularly relevant for positive turning points in criminal careers (Sampson & Laub, 1993; Werner & Smith, 1992). Because such factors moderate the effects of interventions (e.g. Hammerschick et al., 1997; Spiess, 1986), they need to be assessed in treatment evaluations. Natural protective factors should also be included more systematically in program planning and delivery (e.g. Lösel, 2000; Spencer, 1999).

(c) Community characteristics

Individual and microsocial risk and protective factors interact with neighborhood and community features (Lynam et al., in press; Sampson, Raudenbush & Earls, 1997; Wikström & Loeber, in press). Although it is not yet clear how much variance in criminal behavior is explained by the latter characteristics, the wider context forms an important framing condition for offending (e.g. Farrington, Sampson & Wikström, 1993).

Therefore, community features, such as concentration of poverty, unemployment, multiproblem families, violence, drug use and other deficits in "social capital", must be taken into account in treatment evaluation. If, for example, a program promotes vocational skills and work motivation, it may be particularly successful in communities with low unemployment rates (Sherman et al., 1998). In other contexts, the acquired skills will be less protective against reoffending. Counterproductive influences may result from neighborhoods with high criminality and violence. In a community in which peers and neighbors model and reinforce deviant behavior it is more difficult to preserve program effects than in a social context with less negative influences (Sherman, et al., 1997; Thornberry, 1998). As a consequence, program evaluation should include at least some key characteristics of the community to which the treated clients return. Such aggregated data can be used not only to explain differential effects but may also contribute to integrated local programs of crime prevention (Catalano, Arthur, Hawkins, Berglund & Olson, 1998).

CONCLUSION AND PERSPECTIVES

During the last 15 years there is growing evidence that some modes of offender treatment work and others are promising. However, various examples have shown that there is still a lack of methodologically sound evaluations, particularly of complex programs and multiple services for specific adult and serious offender groups and of the service delivery in everyday practice. Therefore, guidelines for good practice emphasize not only principles such as risk level, criminogenic need, skill orientation, responsivity, program intensity and continuity of care but also ongoing monitoring and evaluation (see e.g. the criteria of the accreditation panels of Correctional Service Canada). Regular evaluation of program delivery in practice can give us answers to the question: What mode of treatment for what type of offender under which institutional circumstances and in which social context shows what kind of effects? However, this goal can only be reached if evaluation studies are bridging gaps between treatment research and practice.

This chapter has shown that we need much more process data about the content of program delivery, staff characteristics and dimensions of the institutional regime. It is also necessary to assess the control group conditions in a similar way. The problems of non-equivalent control groups cannot be solved by demands for randomized experiments alone. They must be addressed through various evaluation designs with sufficient methodological quality. Common assessment instruments across various sites can play a central role for increasing both internal and external validity. Dynamic risk and need assessment should include data on comorbidities as well as functional characteristics of responsivity to treatment. The dropout problem also must be tackled more effectively. Adequate assessment procedures, program modules on motivation and flexible procedures of case management are suggested here. Outcome evaluation should not rely primarily on one-shot studies but refer to a theoretically based chain of various change measures including longer follow-up periods. Last but not least, practice-oriented evaluations must put the program in its wider social context. This can be attained by assessing data on services of aftercare and relapse prevention, natural protective factors and community characteristics.

Methodologically sound and practice-oriented evaluations should be designed and monitored in cooperation with local university departments or other independent researchers. Regular external supervision from accreditation panels or similar institutions is also recommended. The scientific bases for evaluation should be derived from both (quasi-) experimental intervention research and developmental research on criminal behavior (Farrington, Ohlin & Wilson, 1986). The results of individual studies should be continously integrated and updated through meta-analyses on specific types of offenders, programs, institutions and social contexts. Such systematic data can form the basis for a rational crime policy. In contrast, the tendencies toward pure punishment, selective incapacitation and increased incarceration rates (Haney & Zimbardo, 1999; Tonry, 1998) seem to be much less based on empirical research (Sherman et al., 1997).

For political and economic reasons, evaluations must include a realistic discussion of effect sizes. According to the criteria of Cohen (1988), the typical effects of successful offender treatment programs are still small ($0.10 < r < 0.30$). However, small effects are practically relevant when an intervention is effective under unfavorable conditions or no better alternative is yet available (Prentice & Miller, 1992). Small effects may be also rather substantial (e.g. approximately 10–30 per cent more successes than in the control group). As cost-benefit analyses of offender treatment have shown, such effect sizes can pay off from an economic perspective (e.g. Prentky & Burgess, 1992; Welsh & Farrington, 1999; see also Chapter 3 by Brandon Welsh and David Farrington in this book). When, furthermore, we take suffering victims and public safety in account, it is worthwhile to invest money in more methodologically sound evaluations of offender treatment in everyday practice.

References

Alexander, M. A. (1999). Sexual offender treatment efficacy revisited. *Sexual Abuse: A Journal of Research and Treatment*, **11**, 101–116.

Andrews, D. (1995). The psychology of criminal conduct and effective treatment. In J. McGuire (Ed.), *What Works: Reducing Reoffending*, pp. 35–62. Chichester: John Wiley.

Andrews, D. A., & Bonta, J. (1995). *LSI-R: The Level of Service Inventory—Revised*. Toronto: Multi-Health.

Andrews, D. A., & Bonta, J. (1998). *The Psychology of Criminal Conduct*, 2nd ed. Cincinatti, OH: Anderson Publishing Co.

Andrews, D. A., & Dowden, C. (1999). A meta-analytic investigation into effective correctional intervention for female offenders. *Forum on Corrections Research*, **11**(3), 18–21.

Andrews, D. A., Zinger, I., Hoge, R. D., Bonta, J., Gendreau, P., & Cullen, F. T. (1990). Does correctional treatment work? A clinically relevant and psychologically informed meta-analysis. *Criminology*, **28**, 369–404.

Annis, H. (1986). A relapse prevention model for treatment of alcoholics. In W. E. Miller & N. Heather (Eds), *Treating Addictive Behaviors*, pp. 407–435. New York: Plenum.

Antonowicz, D., & Ross, R. R. (1994). Essential components of successful rehabilitation programs for offenders. *International Journal of Offender Therapy and Comparative Criminology*, **38**, 97–104.

Barbaree, H. E. (1997). Evaluating treatment efficacy with sexual offenders: The insensitivity of recidivism studies to treatment effects. *Sexual Abuse: A Journal of Research and Treatment*, **9**, 111–128.

Beelmann, A., Pfingsten, U., & Lösel, F. (1994). Effects of training social competence in children: A meta-analysis of recent evaluation studies. *Journal of Clinical Child Psychology*, **23**, 260–271.

Beier, K. M. (1995). *Dissexualität im Lebenslängsschnitt*. Berlin: Springer Wiley.

Bettman, M. (2000). *Violence Prevention Program: Accreditation Case File*. Ottawa: Correctional Service Canada.

Beutler, L. E., & Howard, K. I. (1998). Clinical utility research: an introduction. *Journal of Clinical Psychology*, **54**, 297–301.

Blackburn, R. (1993). *The Psychology of Criminal Conduct*. Chichester: John Wiley.

Blackburn, R. (2000). Treatment or incapacitation? Implications of research on personality disorders for the management of dangerous offenders. *Legal and Criminological Psychology*, **5**, 1–21.

Bonta, J., & Motiuk, L. L. (1992). Inmate classification. *Journal of Criminal Justice*, **20**, 343–353.

Campbell, D. T., & Stanley, J. C. (1963). *Experimental and Quasi-experimental Designs for Research*. Chicago: Rand McNally.

Carlson, K. D., & Schmidt, F. L. (1999). Impact of experimental design on effect size: Findings from the research literature. *Journal of Applied Psychology*, **84**, 851–862.

Catalano, R. F., Arthur, M. W., Hawkins, J. D., Berglund, L., & Olson, J. J. (1998). Comprehensive community- and school-based interventions to prevent antisocial behavior. In R. Loeber & D. P. Farrington (Eds), *Serious and Violent Offenders: Risk Factors and Successful Interventions*, pp. 248–283. Thousand Oaks, CA: Sage.

Chen, H. T. (1989). Theory-driven Evaluations. Newbury Park, CA: Sage.

Cohen, J. (1988). *Statistical Power Analysis for the Behavioral Sciences*, 2nd ed. New York: Academic.

Cook, T. D., & Campbell, D. T. (1979). *Quasi-experimentation. Design and Analysis Issues for Field Settings*. Chicago: Rand McNally.

Cronbach, L. J., Ambron, S. R., Dornbusch, S. M., Hess, R. D., Hornik, R. C., Philips, D. C., Walker, D. F., & Weiner, S. S. (1980). *Toward Reform of Program Evaluation*. San Fancisco: Jossey Bass.

Cullen, E. (1997). Can a prison be a therapeutic community? The Grendon template. In E. Cullen, L. Jones & R. Woodward (Eds), *Therapeutic Communities for Offenders*, pp. 75–99. Chichester: John Wiley.

Dahle, K.-P. (1995). *Therapiemotivation hinter Gittern*. Regensburg: Roderer.

Dolan, B. (1997). A community based TC: The Henderson hospital. In E. Cullen, L. Jones & R. Woodward (Eds), *Therapeutic Communities for Offenders*, pp. 47–74. Chichester: John Wiley.

Dolan, B., & Coid, J. (1993). *Psychopathic and Antisocial Personality Disorders*. London: Gaskell.

Dolde, G. (1996). Zur Bewährung der Sozialtherapie im Justizvollzug von Baden-Württemberg: Tendenzen aus einer neueren Rückfalluntersuchung. *Zeitschrift für Strafvollzug und Straffälligenhilfe*, **45**, 290–297.

Donenberg, G. R., Lyons, J. S., & Howard, K. I. (1999). Clinical trials versus mental health services research: Contributions and connections. *Journal of Clinical Psychology*, **55**, 1135–1146.

Dowden, C., & Andrews, D. A. (1999). What works for female offenders: a meta-analytic review. *Crime and Delinquency*, **45**, 438–452.

Dünkel, F., & Geng, B. (1994). Rückfall und Bewährung von Karrieretätern nach Entlassung aus dem sozialtherapeutischen Behandlungsvollzug und aus dem Regelvollzug. In M. Steller, K.-P. Dahle & M. Basqué (Eds), *Straftäterbehandlung*, pp. 34–59. Pfaffenweiler: Centaurus.

Egg, R. (1990). Sozialtherapeutische Behandlung und Rückfälligkeit im länger-fristigen Vergleich. *Monatsschrift für Kriminologie und Strafrechtsreform*, **73**, 358–368.

Farrington, D. P., Ohlin, L. E., & Wilson, J. Q. (1986). *Understanding and Controlling Crime: Toward a New Research Strategy*. New York: Springer Verlag.

Farrington, D. P., Sampson, R. J., & Wikström, P.-O. (Eds) (1993). *Integrating Individual and Ecological Aspects of Crime*. Stockholm: Allmanna Forlaget.

Feldman, P. (1989). Applying psychology to the reduction of juvenile offending and offences: Methods and results. *Issues in Criminological and Legal Psychology*, **14**, 3–32.

Foxhall, K. (2000). Research for the real world. *APA Monitor on Psychology*, **31**(7), 1–9.

Garrett, P. (1985). Effects of residential treatment of adjucated delinquents: A meta-analysis. *Journal of Research in Crime and Delinquency*, **22**, 287–308.

Genders, E., & Player, E. (1995). *Grendon: A Study of a Therapeutic Prison*. Oxford: Clarendon Press.

Gendreau, P. (1995). The principles of effective intervention with offenders. In A. J. Harland (Ed.), *Choosing Correctional Options that Work: Defining the Demand and Evaluating the Supply*. Thousand Oaks, CA: Sage.

Gendreau, P., & Goggin, C. (1996). Principles of effective programming. *Forum on Corrections Research*, **8**(3), 38–41.

Gendreau, P., Goggin, C., & Smith, P. (1999). The forgotton issue in effective correctional treatment: Program implementation. *International Journal of Offender Therapy and Comparative Criminology*, **43**, 180–187.

Gendreau, P., Little, T., & Goggin, C. (1995). A meta-analysis of the predictors of adult offender recidivism: What works? *Criminology*, **34**, 575–607.

Gensheimer, L. K., Mayer, J. P., Gottschalk, R., & Davidson II, W. S. (1986). Diverting youth from the juvenile justice system: A meta-analysis of intervention efficacy. In S. J. Apter & A. Goldstein (Eds), *Youth Violence: Programs and Prospects*, pp. 39–57. Elmsford, NY: Pergamon Press.

Gottschalk, R., Davidson II, W. S., Gensheimer, L. K., & Mayer, J. P. (1987). Community-based interventions. In H. C. Quay (Ed.), *Handbook of Juvenile Delinquency*, pp. 266–289. New York: John Wiley.

Hall, G. C. N. (1995). Sexual offender recidivism revisited: A meta-analysis of recent treatment studies. *Journal of Consulting and Clinical Psychology*, **63**, 802–809.

Haney, C., & Zimbardo, P. (1998). The past and future of U.S. prison policy. Twenty-five years after the Stanford Prison Experiment. *American Psychologist*, **53**, 709–727.

Hanson, R. K., & Bussière, M. T. (1996). Predicting relapse: A meta-analysis of sexual offender recidivism studies. *Journal of Consulting and Clinical Psychology*, **66**, 348–362.

Hanson, R. K., & Harris, A. J. R. (2000). *The Sex Offender Need Assessment Rating (SONAR): A Method for Measuring Change in Risk Levels*, User report. Ottawa: Solicitor General Canada.

Hanson, R. K., & Wallace-Capretta, S. (2000). *Predicting Recidivism among Male Batterers*, User report. Ottawa: Solicitor General Canada.

Hare, R. D. (1991). *The Hare Psychopathy Checklist—Revised*. Toronto: Multi-Health.

Hart, S. D. (1998). Psychopathy and risk for violence. In D. J. Cooke, A. E. Forth & R. D. Hare (Eds), *Psychopathy: Theory, Research and Implications for Society*, pp. 355–373. Dordrecht: Kluwer.

Hawkins, J. D., Herrenkohl, T., Farrington, D. P., Brewer, D., Catalano, R. F., & Harachi, T. W. (1998). A review of predictors of youth violence. In R. Loeber & D. P. Farrington (Eds), *Serious and Violent Juvenile Offenders*, pp. 106–146. Thousand Oaks: Sage.

Hemphill, J. F., Hare, R. D., & Wong, S. (1998). Psychopathy and recidivism: A review. *Legal and Criminological Psychology* 3, 139–170.

Hoge, R. D., & Andrews, D. A. (1996). *Assessing the Youthful Offender: Issues and Techniques*. New York: Plenum.

Hollin, C. R. (1995). The meaning and implications of 'programme integrity'. In J. McGuire (Ed.), *What Works: Reducing Reoffending*, pp. 195–208. Chichester: John Wiley.

Hollin, C. R. (1999). Treatment programs for offenders: Meta-analysis, "what works", and beyond. *International Journal of Law and Psychiatry*, **22**, 361–372.

Howard, K. I., Martinovich, Z., & Black, M. (1997). Outpatient outcomes. *Psychiatric Annals*, **27**, 108–112.

Howard, K. I., Orlinsky, D. E., & Lueger, R. J. (1994). Clinically relevant outcome research in individual psychotherapy: new models guide the researcher and clinician. *British Journal of Psychiatry*, **165**, 4–8.

Izzo, R. L., & Ross, R. R. (1990). Meta-analysis of rehabilitation programs for juvenile delinquents. A brief report. *Criminal Justice and Behavior*, **17**, 134–142.

Krause, M. S., Howard, K. J., & Lutz, W. (1998). Exploring individual change. *Journal of Consulting and Clinical Psychology*, **66**, 838–845.

Laws, D. R. (1999). Relapse prevention: the state of the art. *Journal of Interpersonal Violence*, **14**, 285–302.

Le Blanc, M. (1998). Screening of serious and violent juvenile offenders. In R. Loeber & D. P. Farrington (Eds), *Serious and Violent Juvenile Offenders*, pp. 167–193. Thousand Oaks, CA: Sage.

Lilienfeld, S. O. (1994). Conceptual problems in the assessment of psychopathy. *Clinical Psychology Review*, **14**, 17–38.

Lipsey, M. W. (1992a). Juvenile delinquency treatment: A meta-analytic inquiry into variability of effects. In T. D. Cook, H. Cooper, D. S. Cordray, H. Hartmann, L. V. Hedges, R. L. Light, T. A. Louis & F. Mosteller (Eds), *Meta-analysis for Explanation*, pp. 83–127. New York: Russell Sage Foundation.

Lipsey, M. W. (1992b). The effect of treatment on juvenile delinquents: results from meta-analysis. In F. Lösel, D. Bender & T. Bliesener (Eds), *Psychology and Law: International Perspectives*, pp. 131–143. Berlin: de Gruyter.

Lipsey, M. W.(1995). What do we learn from 400 research studies on the effectiveness of treatment with juvenile delinquents. In J. McGuire (Ed.), *What works: Reducing Reoffending*, pp. 63–78. Chichester: John Wiley.

Lipsey, M. W., & Derzon, J. H. (1998). Predictors of violent or serious delinquency in adolescence and early adulthood: A synthesis of longitudinal research. In R. Loeber & D. P. Farrington (Eds), *Serious and Violent Juvenile Offenders*, pp. 86–105. Thousand Oaks, CA: Sage.

Lipsey, M. W., & Wilson, D. B. (1998). Effective intervention for serious juvenile offenders. In R. Loeber & D. P. Farrington (Eds), *Serious and Violent Juvenile Offenders*, pp. 313–345. Thousand Oaks, CA: Sage.

Lipton, D., Martinson, R., & Wilks, J. (1975). *The Effectiveness of Correctional Treatment*. New York: Praeger.

Lloyd, C., Mair, G., & Hough, M. (1994). *Explaining Reconviction Rates: A Critical Analysis*. London: Home Office.

Loeber, R., Farrington, D. P., Stouthamer-Loeber, M., & Van Kammen, W. B. (1998). *Antisocial Behavior and Mental Health Problems*. Mahwah, NJ: Lawrence Erlbaum.

Logan, C. H., Gaes, G. G., Harer, M., Innes, C. A., Karacki, L., & Saylor, W. G. (1991). *Can Meta-analysis Save Correctional Rehabilitation?* Washington, DC: Federal Bureau of Prisons.

Lösel, F. (1993). The effectiveness of treatment in institutional and community settings. *Criminal Behaviour and Mental Health*, **3**, 416–437.

Lösel, F. (1995a). Increasing consensus in the evaluation of offender rehabilitation? Lessons from research syntheses. *Psychology, Crime and Law*, **2**, 19–39.

Lösel, F. (1995b). Evaluating psychosocial interventions in prison and other penal contexts. In European Committee on Crime Problems (Ed.), *Psychosocial Interventions In the Criminal Justice System*, pp. 79–114. Strasbourg: Council of Europe.

Lösel, F. (1995c). The efficacy of correctional treatment: A review and synthesis of meta-evaluations. In J. McGuire (Ed.), *What Works: Reducing Reoffending*, pp. 79–111. Chichester: Wiley.

Lösel, F. (1996). Changing patterns in the use of prisons: An evidence-based perspective. *European Journal on Criminal Policy and Research*, **4**(3), 108–127.

Lösel, F. (1998). Treatment and management of psychopaths. In D. J. Cooke, A. E. Forth & R. D. Hare (Eds), *Psychopathy: Theory, Research and Implications for Society*, pp. 303–354. Dordrecht: Kluwer.

Lösel, F. (2000a). The efficacy of sexual offender treatment: A review of German and international evaluations. In P. J. van Koppen & N. Roos (Eds), *Rationality, Information and Progress in Psychology and Law*, pp. 145–170. Maastricht: Metajuridica Publications.

Lösel, F. (2000b). Existe un tratamiento eficaz para la psicopatía? Qué sabemos y que deberíamos saber. In A. Raine & J. Sanmartin (Eds), *Violencia y Psicopatía*, pp. 236–272. Barcelona: Ariel.

Lösel, F., & Bender, D. (in press). Protective factors and resilience. In D. P. Farrington & J. Coid (Eds), *Early Prevention of Adult Antisocial Behavior*. Cambridge: Cambridge University Press.

Lösel, F., & Bliesener, T. (1989). Psychology in prison: Role assessment and testing of an organizational model. In H. Wegener, F. Lösel & J. Haisch (Eds), *Criminal Behavior and the Justice System: Psychological Perspectives*. New York: Springer Verlag.

Lösel, F., & Bliesener, T. (1994). Some high-risk adolescents do not develop conduct problems: A study of protective factors. *International Journal of Behavioral Development*, **17**, 753–777.

Lösel, F., & Egg, R. (1997). Social-therapeutic institutions in Germany: Description and evaluation. In E. Cullen, L. Jones & R. Woodward (Eds), *Therapeutic Communities in Prisons*, pp. 181–203. Chichester: John Wiley.

Lösel, F., & Koferl, P. (1989). Evaluation research on correctional treatment in West Germany: A meta-analysis. In H. Wegener, F. Lösel & J. Haisch (Eds), *Criminal Behavior and the Justice System: Psychological Perspectives*, pp. 334–355). New York: Springer Verlag.

Lösel, F., Koferl, P., & Weber, F. (1987). *Meta-Evaluation der Sozialtherapie*. Stuttgart: Enke.

Lösel, F., & Nowack, W. (1987). Evaluationsforschung. In J. Schultz-Gambard (Ed.), *Angewandte Sozialpsychologie*, pp. 57–87. München: Psychologie Verlags Union.

Lösel, F., & Pomplun, O. (1998). *Jugendhilfe statt Untersuchungshaft. Eine Evaluationsstudie zur Heimunterbringung*. Pfaffenweiler: Centaurus.

Lösel, F., & Wittmann, W. W. (1989) The relationship of treatment integrity and intensity to outcome criteria. *New Directions for Program Evaluation*, **42**, 97–108.

Lynam, D. R., Caspi, A., Moffitt, T. E., Wikström, P.-O., Loeber, R., & Novak, S. (in press). The interaction between impulsivity and neighborhood context on offending: The effects of impulsivity are stronger in poorer neighborhoods. *Journal of Abnormal Psychology*, in press.

McCord, J. (1978). A thirty-year follow-up of treatment effects. *American Psychologist*, **33**, 284–289.

McCord, J., & Ensminger, M. E. (1997). Multiple risks and comorbidity in an African American population. *Criminal Behaviour and Mental Health*, **7**, 339–352.

McGuire, J. (Ed) (1995). *What Works: Reducing Reoffending—Guidelines for Research and Practice*. Chichester: John Wiley.

McMurran, M., & Hodge, J. (Eds) (1994). *The Assessment of Criminal Behaviors of Clients in Secure Settings*. London: Jessica Kingsley.

Monahan, J. (1981). *Predicting Violent Behavior: An Assessment of Clinical Techniques*. Beverly Hills, CA: Sage.

Moos, R. (1975). *Evaluating Correctional and Community Settings*. New York: John Wiley.

Mulvey, E. (2000). *The Use of Measurement Instruments in Assessing Early Intervention Strategies, Paper presented at the NATO Advanced Research Workshop "Multiproblem Violent Youth: A Foundation For Comparative Research on Needs, Interventions and Outcomes"*. Krakow, Poland, 30 August–2 September 2000.

Orlinsky, D. E. (1994). Research-based knowledge as the emergent foundation for clinical practice in psychotherapy. In P. F. Talley et al. (Eds), *Psychotherapy Research and Practice: Bridging the Gap*, pp. 99–123. New York: Basic Books.

Orlinsky, D. E., Grawe, K., & Parks, B. K. (1994). Process and outcome in psychotherapy. In A. E. Bergin & S. L. Garfield (Eds), *Handbook of Psychotherapy and Behavior Change*, 4th ed., pp. 270–376. New York: John Wiley.

Ortmann, R. (2000). *Längsschnittstudie zur Evaluation der Wirkung der Sozialtherapie sowie Ansätze zur Effizienzsteigerung*. Freiburg im Breisgau: Max-Planck-Institut für ausländisches und internationales Strafrecht.

Palmer, T. (1992). *The Re-emergence of Correctional Intervention*. Newbury Park, CA: Sage.

Pawson, R., & Tilley, N. (1994). What works in evaluation research. *British Journal of Criminology*, **34**, 291–306.

Pearson, F. S., Lipton, D. S., & Cleland, C. M. (1996). *Some Preliminary Findings from the CDATE Project, Paper presented at Annual Meeting of the American Society of Criminology*, Chicago, IL, November 1996.

Petrosino, A. (1997). *What Works Revisited Again: A Meta-analysis of Randomized Experiments in Delinquency Prevention*, Doctoral Dissertation, Rutgers University.

Pfäfflin, F. (1999). Ambulante Behandlung von Sexualstraftätern. In R. Egg (Ed.), *Sexueller Mißbrauch von Kindern*, pp. 137–156. Wiesbaden: Kriminologische Zentralstelle.

Polizzi, D. M., MacKenzie, D. L., & Hickman, L. J. (1999). What works in adult sex offender treatment? A review of prison- and non-prison-based treatment programs. *International Journal of Offender Therapy and Comparative Criminology*, **43**, 357–374.

Prentice, D. A., & Miller, D. T. (1992). When small effects are impressive. *Psychological Bulletin*, **112**, 160–164.

Prentky, R., & Burgess, A. W. (1992). Rehabilition of child molesters: A cost-benefit analysis. In A. W. Burgess (Ed.), *Child Trauma I: Issues and Research*, pp. 417–442. New York: Garland.

Quinsey, V. L., Harris, G. T., Rice, M. E., & Cormier, C. A. (1998). *Violent Offenders: Appraising and Managing Risk.* Washington, DC: American Psychological Association.

Rawlings, B. (1999). Therapeutic communities in prisons: A research review. *Therapeutic Communities: The International Journal for Therapeutic and Supportive Organizations*, **20**, 177–193.

Redondo, S., Garrido, V., & Sánchez-Meca, J. (1997). What works in correctional rehabilitation in Europe: A meta-analytical review. In S. Redondo, V. Garrido, J. Pérez, & R. Barbaret (Eds), *Advances in Psychology and Law*, pp. 498–523. Berlin: de Gruyter.

Redondo, S., Sánchez-Meca, J., & Garrido, V. (1999). The influence of treatment programmes on the recidivism of juvenile and adult offenders: An European meta-analytic review. *Psychology, Crime and Law*, **5**, 251–278.

Roberts, A. R., & Camasso, M. J. (1991). The effect of juvenile offender treatment programs on recidivism: A meta-analysis of 46 studies. *Notre Dame Journal of Law, Ethics and Public Policy*, **5**, 421–444.

Roberts, C. (1995). Effective practice and service delivery. In J. McGuire (Ed.), *What Works: Reducing Reoffending*, pp. 221–236. Chichester: Wiley.

Ross, R. R., & Ross, B. (Eds) (1995). *Thinking Straight.* Ottawa: Cognitive Centre.

Rutter, M. (1997). Comorbidity: Concepts, claims and choices. *Criminal Behaviour and Mental Health*, **7**, 265–285.

Rutter, M., Giller, H., & Hagell, A. (1998). *Antisocial Behavior by Young People.* Cambridge: Cambridge University Press.

Rutter, M., Maughan, B., Mortimore, P., & Ouston, J. (1979). *Fifteen Thousand Hours: Secondary Schools and Their Effects on Children.* Cambridge, MA: Harvard University Press.

Sampson, R. J., & Laub, J. H. (1993). *Crime in the Making: Pathways and Turning Points through Life.* Cambridge, MA: Harvard University Press.

Sampson, R. J., Raudenbush, S. W., & Earls, F. (1997). Neighborhoods and violent crime: A multilevel study of collective efficacy. *Science*, **277**, 918–924.

Serin, R. (1995). Treatment responsivity in criminal psychopaths. *Forum on Corrections Research*, **7**(3), 23–26.

Sherman, L., Gottfredson, D., MacKenzie, D., Eck, J., Reuter, P., & Bushway, S. (1997). *Preventing Crime: What Works, What Doesn't, What's Promising*, Report to the United States Congress: University of Maryland.

Spencer, A. P. (1999). *Working with Sex Offenders in Prisons and through Release to the Community.* London: Jessica Kingsley.

Thornberry, T. P. (1998). Membership in youth gangs and involvement in serious and violent offending. In R. Loeber & D. P. Farrington (Eds), *Serious and Violent Juvenile Offenders*, pp. 147–166. Thousand Oaks, CA: Sage.

Tonry, M. (1996). Controlling prison population size. *European Journal on Criminal Policy and Research*, **4**(3), 26–45.

Weisburd, D., Petrosino, A., & Mason, G. (1993). Design sensitivity in criminal justice experiments: Reassessing the relationship between sample size and statistical power. In M. Tonry & N. Morris (Eds), *Crime and Justice*, Vol. 17. Chicago: University of Chicago Press.

Weisz, J. R., Donenberg, G. R., Weiss, B., & Han, S. S. (1995). Bridging the gap between laboratory and clinic in child and adolescent psychotherapy. *Journal of Consulting and Clinical Psychology*, **63**, 688–701.

Welsh, B. C., & Farrington, D. P. (2000). Correctional intervention programs and cost-benefit analysis. *Criminal Justice and Behavior*, **27**, 115–133.

Werner, E. E., & Smith, R. S. (1992). *Overcoming the Odds*. Ithaca: Cornell University Press.

Wexler, H. (1997). Therapeutic communities in American prisons. In E. Cullen, L. Jones & R. Woodward (Eds), *Therapeutic Communities for Offenders*, pp. 161–179. Chichester: John Wiley.

White, P., Bradley, C., Ferriter, M., & Hatzipetrou, L. (1998). *Managements for People with Disorders of Sexual Preference and for Convicted Sexual Offenders*. The Cochrane Library.

Whitehead, J. T., & Lab, S. P. (1989). A meta-analysis of juvenile correctional treatment. *Journal of Research in Crime and Delinquency*, **26**, 276–295.

Wikström, P.-O., & Loeber, R. (in press). Do disadvantaged neighborhoods cause well-adjusted children to become adolescent delinquents? *Criminology*, in press.

Wittmann, W. W. (1985). *Evaluationsforschung*. Berlin: Springer Verlag.

Woody, G. E., McLellan, A. T., Luborsky, L., & O'Brien, C. P. (1985). Sociopathy and psychotherapy outcome. *Archives of General Psychiatry*, **42**, 1081–1086.

PART II: IMPLEMENTING SPECIFIC PROGRAMS

PROLOGUE

The first four chapters in this section pertain to specific programs for juvenile offenders. Chapter 5 reflects the work of Scott Henggeler, the premier researcher in the area of intensive, community-based programs for juvenile delinquents. This chapter by Daniel Edwards, Sonja Schoenwald, Scott Henggeler and Keller Strother presents a detailed discussion of the structures that have been developed to support the dissemination of Multisystemic Therapy (MST). They detail the site assessment process, which involves examining a range of contextual factors critical to the start-up, sustainability and fidelity of MST. As well, the chapter reviews the multilevel systems that enhance treatment implementation, including their innovative measures of therapist and supervisor adherence to the model. In Chapter 6, Arnold Goldstein and Barry Glick share their ideas about evaluating community and residential Aggression Replacement Training programs based on two decades of hands-on experience within the juvenile justice system. Their suggestions for program management and recommendations about how to deal with implementation challenges are particularly valuable.

Chapter 7 by Dean Fixsen, Karen Blase, Gary Timbers and Montrose Wolf review their data on the key implementation factors derived from 15 years of attempted replications of the Teaching-Family Model. Over 30 years of research, evaluation and program experience with this model has made a major contribution to understanding of how programs for delinquents develop and evolve. The model's delineation of the integrated clinical, administrative, evaluation and supervision systems necessary to ensure quality assurance and treatment integrity is a singular achievement in the field of human services. In Chapter 8 by Gary Bernfeld, one Canadian adaptation of the Teaching-Family Model's approach to home-based services is described. Particularly interesting is the presentation of the multilevel challenges involved in implementing an integrated treatment within a fragmented service delivery system.

Chapters 9 and 10 review the work of model programs for adult offenders. First, Peter Raynor and Maurice Vanstone describe the STOP Reasoning and

Rehabilitation program in Mid-Glamorgan in Wales. They focus on the lessons learned from STOP and the multilevel processes necessary to facilitate successful implementation. Ralph Serin and Denise Preston, in Chapter 10, focus on their experience with a Canadian program for adult violent offenders. They present in great detail issues related to program implementation which impact on treatment integrity.

Overall, these chapters provide us with a unique perspective on the *process* of how effective correctional programs operate, by looking into the "black box" of treatment. They explore the concepts, knowledge and "practice wisdom" which impact on treatment integrity and implementation. We believe that our growing understanding of these concerns will enable us to be more successful in the services that we deliver. Moreover, this should also "bridge the gap" between research and practice.

Chapter 5

A MULTILEVEL PERSPECTIVE ON THE IMPLEMENTATION OF MULTISYSTEMIC THERAPY (MST): ATTEMPTING DISSEMINATION WITH FIDELITY

DANIEL L. EDWARDS,* SONJA K. SCHOENWALD,[†] SCOTT W. HENGGELER[†] AND KELLER B. STROTHER*

* MST Institute, Mt Pleasant, South Carolina, USA
[†] Family Services Research Center, Department of Psychiatry and Behavioral Sciences, Medical University of South Carolina, USA

I. MULTISYSTEMIC THERAPY: AN OVERVIEW AND BRIEF HISTORY

A. Overview of the model

Multisystemic Therapy (MST) is an intensive, family- and community-based treatment that targets the multiple determinants of serious behavioral and emotional problems in children and adolescents and seeks to prevent out-of-home placement (Henggeler, Mihalic, Rone, Thomas, & Timmons-Mitchell, 1998). Originated by Henggeler and colleagues (Henggeler & Borduin, 1990;

Offender Rehabilitation in Practice. Edited by G. A. Bernfeld, D. P. Farrington and A. W. Leschied.
© 2001 John Wiley & Sons, Ltd.

Henggeler, Schoenwald, Borduin, Rowland, & Cunningham, 1998), MST was first developed in the 1970s to be a comprehensive, evidence-based treatment model in an era when most researchers and policy makers had concluded that nothing works with this challenging population. The first clinical trials supported the efficacy of MST with inner-city youth in Memphis, Tennessee (Henggeler et al., 1986) and with families of abused and neglected children (Brunk, Henggeler, & Whelan, 1987). Since that time, six additional clinical trials have been published and MST has been widely recognized as an effective, evidence-based treatment for chronic antisocial behavior and other serious clinical problems (Kazdin & Weisz, 1998).

The success of MST has led to the implementation of MST programs at over 40 sites in the United States and Canada, and implementation has recently begun in Norway. This effort to provide training and consultation in MST to provider organizations in other states and countries has been conducted primarily by MST Services, which has the exclusive licensing agreement with the Medical University of South Carolina to disseminate MST technology and intellectual property. The mission of MST Services has been to foster conditions at community sites that promote therapist, supervisor and organizational adherence to MST protocols—adherence linked with favorable long-term outcomes for referred youths and families. This chapter describes the approach currently being taken to transport MST to community-based sites in ways that maximize program fidelity.

Based on social ecological (Bronfenbrenner, 1979) and pragmatic family systems (Haley, 1976; Minuchin, 1974) models of behavior, the central thrusts of MST are consistent with available evidence (e.g. causal modeling studies; Elliott, 1994) on the multiple determinants of antisocial behavior in youth (see Table 5.1). Determinants include family factors such as low parental monitoring, high conflict, low warmth, inconsistent or harsh disciplinary practices and parental problems; peer factors such as negative peer associations; school factors such as problems with academic and social performance, and poor family–school relations; and community factors such as transience, disorganization and criminal subculture. From the social-ecological perspective, the child and her or his family are "nested" within the network of these multiple interactive systems that influence the quality of the child's development. Certain interactions within these systems directly involve the child (e.g. parenting practices, the teacher's day-to-day instruction and classroom management, etc.), and other interactions do not involve the child but indirectly influence her or his development (e.g. relations at the parent's workplace).

In MST, interventions target the reciprocal interactions within and between systems, such as those between parents, between parents and children, between families and schools, or between the child and her/his

Table 5.1 Risk and resiliency factors

Context	Risk factors	Resiliency factors

Individual	Low verbal skills
	Favorable attitudes toward
	   antisocial behavior
	Psychiatric symptomatology
	Cognitive bias to attribute
	   hostile intentions to others
		Intelligence
		Being first born
		Easy temperament
		Conventional attitudes
		Problem solving skills

Family	Lack of monitoring
	Ineffective discipline
	Low warmth
	High conflict
	Parental difficulties (e.g. drug
	   abuse, psychiatric conditions,
	   criminality)
		Attachment to parents
		Supportive family environment
		Marital harmony

Peer	Association with deviant peers Poor relationship skills Low association with prosocial peers	Bonding with prosocial peers

School	Low achievement
	Dropout
	Low commitment to education
	Aspects of the schools, such as
	   weak structure and chaotic
	   environment
		Commitment to schooling

Neighborhood and community	High mobility
	Low community support
	   (neighbors, church, etc.)
	Criminal subculture
		Ongoing involvement in
		   church activities
		Strong indigenous support
		   network

peer network. Nine treatment principles (see Table 5.2) guide the nature of contact between therapists and families and the development and implementation of treatment interventions. Together, these principles are used to operationalize MST and support the overriding purpose of treatment, which is to empower parents with the skills and resources necessary to address the inevitable difficulties that arise in rearing adolescents, and to empower youth to cope with family, peer, school and neighborhood problems.

Treatment in MST programs has typically been delivered using a home-based, intensive, and time-limited (i.e. 3–5 months) model of service delivery. Treatment sessions are active, collaborative, highly focused and held as often as daily early in treatment. Sessions may be conducted in the home or in other settings in the natural ecology—at the child's school, at a

Table 5.2   MST treatment principles

1.   The primary purpose of assessment is to understand the "fit" between the identified problems and their broader systemic context.
2.   Therapeutic contacts emphasize the positive and use systemic strengths as levers for change.
3.   Interventions are designed to promote responsible behavior and decrease irresponsible behavior among family members.
4.   Interventions are present-focused and action-oriented, targeting specific and well-defined problems.
5.   Interventions target sequences of behavior within and between multiple systems that maintain the identified problems.
6.   Interventions are developmentally appropriate and fit the developmental needs of the youth.
7.   Interventions are designed to require daily or weekly efforts by family members.
8.   Intervention effectiveness is evaluated continuously from multiple perspectives with providers assuming accountability for overcoming barriers to successful outcomes.
9.   Interventions are designed to promote treatment generalization and long-term maintenance of therapeutic change by empowering caregivers to address family members' needs across multiple systemic contexts.

recreational center or at any other setting where family members feel comfortable. To facilitate intensive work with families, therapists carry low caseloads (4–6 families per therapist), and families have access to their therapist (or a member of his/her team) 24 hours a day, 7 days per week. Although each therapist carries a designated caseload, therapists work closely in small teams of two to four therapists, receiving supervision together and providing coverage for one another's families.

B. Clinical trials supporting the efficacy of MST

MST is a well-validated treatment model (Kazdin & Weisz, 1998), with eight randomized clinical trials completed and several additional randomized studies underway. Early outcome research supported the short-term efficacy of MST in treating inner-city adolescents (Henggeler et al., 1986), maltreating families (Brunk et al., 1987), and a small sample of juvenile sex offenders (Borduin, Henggeler, Blaske & Stein, 1990). Later studies conducted in both university (Borduin et al., 1995) and community mental health (Henggeler, Melton, Brondino, Scherer, & Hanley, 1997; Henggeler, Melton, Smith, Schoenwald, & Hanley, 1993; Henggeler, Melton, & Smith, 1992) settings supported the longer term efficacy of MST in treating serious antisocial behavior in youth. Likewise, recent randomized trials have supported the effectiveness of MST with substance abusing and dependent juvenile offenders (Henggeler, Pickrel, & Brondino, 1999) and youths presenting mental health emergencies (Henggeler, Rowland et al., 1999). Overall, in comparison with control groups, treated youth in studies of MST have shown: significantly improved family relations and family functioning; reduced drug use in juvenile offenders; 25–70 per cent decreases in long-term rates of rearrest among violent and chronic juvenile offenders; and 47–64 per cent reductions in days in out-of-home placements. These latter findings have led reviewers to conclude that MST is a highly cost-effective treatment model (Aos, Phipps, Barnoski & Lieb, 1999), achieving over $60,000 in average net gain per youth served by MST in terms of reduced placement costs, criminal justice savings and crime victim benefits. As a point of comparison, such savings compare favorably to the cost-ineffectiveness of boot camps which achieve an average net *loss* of $7,511 per youth. Finally, MST has been extremely effective at engaging families in treatment, with recent clinical trials (Henggeler, Pickrel & Brondino, 1999; Henggeler, Rowland et al., 1999) evidencing treatment completion rates of 98 and 97 per cent, respectively.

Currently, numerous studies are further examining the effectiveness of MST, evaluating its generalizability with other client populations, and investigating the use of MST in different models of service delivery. For example, the effectiveness of MST within the context of juvenile drug courts and as an alternative to out-of-home placements for physically abused children is being evaluated in Charleston. Studies of neighborhood-based (Randall, Swenson, & Henggeler, 1999) and school-based (Cunningham & Henggeler, 2001) MST programs are underway. In addition, MST-based continua of care (i.e. MST outpatient, MST home-based, MST-friendly foster care and short-term residential treatment) are funded for evaluation in randomized trials at two sites. In addition, randomized trials of MST are being conducted by investigators not affiliated with the Family Services Research Center (FSRC) or MST Services in Delaware (Miller, 1998), Canada (Leschied, Principal Investigator), Galveston, TX (Thomas, Principal Investigator), at Vanderbilt University (Weiss, Principal Investigator) and Wayne State University with a pediatric sample (Ellis, Principal Investigator).

In recent years, studies have demonstrated the importance of treatment fidelity in achieving significant positive outcomes. Henggeler et al. (1997) disseminated MST to two communities geographically removed from the developers of MST and weekly consultation with an MST expert did not occur. Youth and family outcomes obtained in this study varied greatly and were not as positive overall as had been obtained in previous clinical trials. Measures of therapist adherence were collected throughout the study, and subsequent analyses indicated a significant positive correlation between adherence to the MST model and youth outcomes at follow-up. Specifically, high scores on the MST therapist adherence measure predicted lower rates of rearrest and incarceration 1.7 years post-treatment. This finding has been replicated in a recent study with substance abusing and dependent juvenile offenders (Henggeler et al., 1999). Together, these findings highlight the importance of program fidelity and of examining the processes associated with fidelity.

C. Treatment dissemination

Given the success of MST at achieving decreased out-of-home placements for troubled youth, decreasing recidivism and demonstrating cost savings (Schoenwald, Ward, Henggeler, Pickrel & Patel, 1996; Aos, Phipps, Barnoski & Lieb, 1999), MST has begun to capture the attention and interest of legislators, policy makers and leaders in the fields of juvenile justice, mental health and child welfare. Over the past 5 years, MST has been disseminated by MST Services to more than 20 states in the United States; Ontario, Canada; and Norway. Through the dissemination process, efforts have focused on how to optimize program fidelity at sites that are geographically distant from Charleston, SC, which is the home of MST Services and the Medical University of South Carolina.

To date, the dissemination of MST has occurred largely in response to the interest of child-serving agencies (i.e. Juvenile Justice, Mental Health, Social Services) and service providers in establishing MST programs. During the past 2 years, initiatives sponsored by the Office of Juvenile Justice and Delinquency Prevention (i.e. the Blueprints program; a grant awarded to the Consortium for Children, Families and the Law) have generated additional demand for MST on the part of local and state agencies. Thus, dissemination has generally been "stakeholder" driven, rather than systematically pursued by the developers of MST. Our experiences trying to meet community demand for MST programs illuminated service system and organizational factors that influence the implementation of MST. These factors are similar to those identified in the transfer of technology literature (see Schoenwald & Henggeler, in press). Thus, whereas evidence from clinical trials supporting the association between treatment adherence and outcomes informed the development of a training, supervision and consultation process aimed at supporting clinician adherence to MST, our efforts to "transport" (Hoagwood, Hibbs Brent & Jensen, 1995) MST to diverse community settings prompted the development of a systematic "site assessment" of contextual factors relevant to program start-up, sustainability and fidelity to the model (see Appendix A: Site assessment checklist).

This site assessment process is designed to: assess the philosophical compatibility of MST with community agency and consumer groups; identify referral and funding incentives and disincentives that could impact long-term sustainability of the program; establish the interagency collaboration necessary for the MST program and client families to take the lead in clinical decision making; and to align the structure, procedures and culture of the organization hosting the MST program to support therapist adherence to MST and provider accountability for family engagement and outcomes. As described subsequently, the range of issues that are addressed in the site assessment process can be conceptualized along dimensions similar to those proposed by Bernfeld, Blase, and Fixsen (1990) in the description of the "multilevel perspective".

II. IMPLEMENTATION WITH INTEGRITY: A MULTILEVEL PERSPECTIVE

In their examination of human services organizations and service delivery systems, Bernfeld et al. (1990) proposed that competing variables in multilevel systems often account for program failure and, therefore, that these implementation variables must be identified and manipulated as a prerequisite to program success. The implementation variables operate at multiple levels (i.e. society, organization, program and client) and interact in a reciprocal and dynamic fashion. In the view of Bernfeld and colleagues, the optimal qualities of systems (i.e. macro) and behavioral (i.e. micro) models may be combined to form a "behavioral systems perspective" (Bernfeld et al., 1990, p. 192) that permits broader and deeper analysis of implementation variables and permits self-corrective steps to be taken on the basis of feedback occuring within the system. In the following sections, efforts made to implement MST with fidelity at remote sites are examined with respect to the multiple levels of influence.

A. Societal factors

At the societal level are economic, political and social issues that shape the views of key stakeholders in the community regarding the treatment of serious antisocial behavior in adolescents. For example, if the political mandate of a state's juvenile justice system is more consistent with a punishment than a rehabilitative stance, officials from that agency may prohibit any youth who has committed an index offense from participation in MST. In such a scenario, the referral base will most likely be insufficient for sustaining an MST program for serious offenders. The referral base problem represents a service system manifestation of a broader political context.

The MST site assessment process is designed to prompt key community stakeholders to identify major political, economic and social drivers of interest in MST and to articulate how these and other (i.e. organizational, clinical) factors could impact the implementation of an MST program. Key stakeholders typically include representatives from juvenile justice, mental health, education, family court and social welfare agencies and other entities (i.e. third-party payors) who may fund services. Consistent with research on the adoption of innovations (Rogers, 1995), several "local champions" are often needed to cultivate a community context supportive of MST.

The first objective of the site assessment process, then, is to assist those individuals who wish to introduce an MST program into their community in collaborating with other key stakeholders to identify community needs and desired outcomes. MST programs are more likely to be successful in communities where key stakeholders are committed to:

- decreasing rates of out-of-home placements;
- finding alternatives to incarceration and residential treatment;
- rehabilitating adolescent offenders (versus punishing them);
- achieving cost savings;
- preserving family integrity.

When the compatibility of the stakeholders' goals and MST goals is established, the second objective of the site sssessment is to help stakeholders identify extra-organizational and organizational factors that can influence a provider agency's ability to achieve those goals. For example, the site assessment process helps stakeholders identify a sufficient referral base and concomitant funding for the MST program within the community. Although many successful MST programs are funded through either some form of case rate mechanism or receive complete program-level funding, identifying funding for MST program start-up and continued operations can be challenging for many reasons. In most states, for example, traditional guidelines for reimbursement for mental health services focus on the provision of a predetermined quantity of services (i.e. reimbursement based on number of hours of face-to-face contact) rather than on the attainment of treatment goals as in MST. Service delivery mechanisms that focus on face-to-face contact with the referred youth cause problems for MST programs which emphasize:

(a) direct contact between therapist, caregivers and other family members;
(b) considerable telephone contact with other key participants in the youth's ecology (e.g. teachers or principals);
(c) clinical supervision and consultation for 3 hours per week on average; and
(d) constantly decreasing contact between therapist and family once the

family has begun to learn the skills and strategies necessary to effectively monitor and manage the referred youth.

Additional funding problems occur when communities have financial disincentives for public agencies to use community-based services versus institution-based services (Henggeler, Mihalic, et al., 1998). For example, referral sources might be required to pay for a community-based treatment like MST but not for incarceration, or a provider organization might receive significantly higher reimbursement rates for providing more restrictive services. Similarly, changes in funding (e.g. funds diverted toward building a county juvenile detention center) or in public attitudes (e.g. increased desire to have gang-related youth incarcerated) might lead to a significant decrease in referrals to an MST program and a resultant loss of funding.

When such disincentives are identified during the site assessment, they must be proactively addressed. Generally, the strategy has been to demonstrate to key stakeholders how each disincentive leads to program failure. Appropriate reimbursement mechanisms and incentives must be developed to help restructure the environment to promote higher utilization of community-based services like MST. This restructuring is challenging and generally requires assisting the stakeholders to focus on outcomes for the youth and families served, rather than on the provision of quantities of traditional service delivery packages (e.g. residential beds, clinic hours).

A third objective of the site assessment process is creating relationships among providers that allow MST therapists to take the lead in the clinical decision-making process for clients. MST programs emphasize accountability for youth and family outcomes, but a program cannot be accountable if it does not have clinical decision-making authority. On occasion, the introduction of an MST program into a community is seen as a threat to the viability of other programs that serve the target population, including home-based as well as outpatient, day-treatment and inpatient programs. Alternatively, MST might be viewed suspiciously as the latest mental health "fad" to come down the pike. Nonetheless, MST program leadership and therapists must be able to collaborate with other providers and child-serving agencies in determining the appropriate treatment for the youth and his/her family. The prospective MST provider and the key stakeholders in the community are responsible for engaging other providers and agencies and building relationships that will facilitate the delivery of clinical services. When such a collaborative atmosphere is established, the MST provider organization, assisted by consultation with MST Services, is responsible for maintaining those relationships through respectful dealings with other professionals and high-quality interventions with the families served.

The expansion of the Youth Villages Intercept program in Tennessee (see Henggeler, Mihalic et al., 1998, pp. 61–62) provides an excellent case study in the development of positive relationships between the MST provider and critical players in state and local service systems. There, the MST program (Intercept) began with a well-executed needs analysis (i.e. interviews with the heads of child-serving agencies as well as juvenile court judges) and matured into a statewide program serving hundreds of referred youth and their families in six regions of the state each year. One key to growth was the organization's willingness to assume financial responsibility for keeping children and youth in their homes under a capitated funding arrangement with the state.

B. Organizational factors

Consistent with the maxim that "every [administrative] decision is a treatment decision" (Bernfeld et al, 1990, p. 199), recent findings in children's mental health services research indicate a significant relationship between client outcomes and the culture or climate of the provider organization (Glisson & Himmelgarn, 1996); that is, outcomes are shaped by the context within which therapists work. Thus, MST provider organizations are strongly encouraged to implement policies and procedures to support clinician fidelity to MST.

Thus far, the dissemination of MST has relied heavily upon individuals within the provider organization to generate interest in and commitment to the MST ideals—both internally and externally—through their personal energy, education and negotiation skills, and leadership. In the dissemination of MST by Youth Villages, for example, administrators, supervisors, and MST counselors found it necessary to devote significant time and energy to explaining the program to those outside professionals whose beliefs about treatment, punishment and family preservation differed markedly from the MST model. The importance of organizational climate has led to the investment of significant resources in fostering administrative understanding of MST during the site assessment process and continuing through all aspects of program implementation.

Internally, administrators proactively and concretely support MST therapists through policies (e.g. flextime, comptime [compensation time], insurance for transporting clients) and resources (cell phones and pagers). In addition, because MST therapists frequently work with multiproblem families who are involved with several different social service agencies, efforts are made to reduce documentation as much as possible so that state and agency paperwork dovetail with the process of MST. A related issue is establishing salaries that are competitive and attractive when compared with salaries received by clinicians providing traditional office-based outpatient therapy. Indeed, because the nature of MST demands greater accessibility of therapists (i.e. often working evenings and weekends) and a much higher degree of supervision and accountability than is customary in mental health settings, significantly higher salaries are warranted. The formal site assessment process (Strother, Schoenwald, & Swenson, 1998), therefore, examines and clarifies each of these organizational issues before moving ahead to develop MST programs.

C. Program factors

The implementation of evidence-based treatment models depends upon the ability of key individuals within the provider organization (e.g. administrators, supervisors and therapists) to "translate knowledge and theory into practice with integrity" (see Chapter 1 of this book by Alan Leschied, Gary Bernfeld and David Farrington). To assist with that translation, the site assessment process includes the development of a document that establishes individualized MST goals and guidelines for each MST provider. This document specifies the resolution of numerous administrative and clinical details, including the definition of the target population, participant inclusion and exclusion criteria, program goals, referral criteria and procedures for opening, closing and reporting on clinical cases. Moreover, within these details is a subset of program elements that experience has shown are necessary conditions for program success. These criteria, presented in Henggeler, Mihalic et al. (1998), include the following requirements:

- therapists must be full-time employees assigned to the MST program;
- MST teams must consist of between two and four therapists per team (plus the supervisor);
- caseloads may not exceed six families per therapist, with the normal caseload being four to six families;
- MST clinical supervisors must be assigned to the MST program at least 50 per cent of the time per team (with a strong preference for full-time supervisors);
- teams must participate in group supervision at least once per week, and group telephone consultation with an MST expert once per week.

In addition to these administrative structures, MST Services also provides assistance and consultation with regard to personnel decisions pertaining to the MST supervisor and clinicians. To a significant extent, the success of an MST program hinges upon the individual characteristics (e.g. motivation, sense of accountability, willingness to accept productive criticism from others) and abilities (e.g. organizational, clinical and interpersonal skills) of the individual therapists and supervisors. The supervisor's ability to build cohesion among team members while promoting adherence to the model is an important aspect of a program's success.

To facilitate team and supervisor competencies and to promote program fidelity, the dissemination process has incorporated a strong emphasis on continuous therapist and supervisor training and professional development. The training protocol for therapists and supervisors involves four distinct components: an initial orientation and overview of the treatment model (5 days), quarterly booster trainings (1.5 days), weekly on-site MST supervision (average 2 hours; Henggeler & Schoenwald, 1998) and telephone consultation with an MST expert (average 1 hour; Schoenwald, 1998). In addition to the rigorous training, therapists' adherence to the MST treatment model is monitored continuously via monthly surveys of a standardized Therapist Adherence Measure (Henggeler & Borduin, 1992) administered to families. The adherence measures are scored using an Internet-based scoring system (www.mstinstitute.org) which provides immediate feedback to supervisors and therapists.

As the on-site representatives of MST, supervisors are expected to acquire expertise in the MST model sooner and in greater depth than other team members. The development of supervisor competencies is typically facilitated through additional consultations (i.e. outside the regularly scheduled 1 hour team consultation) with an MST expert who provides developmentally appropriate feedback to the supervisors and helps to monitor team growth. In stepwise fashion, MST consultants help supervisors to: identify opportunties to teach and provide necessary clinical oversight; develop objectives for supervision which are case- and therapist- specific and consistent with the MST treatment model; and develop a plan to give therapists feedback in ways that optimize clinical outcomes.

Although MST was originally designed for and validated with chronic and violent juvenile offenders and their families, many communities have expressed interest in applying MST to other populations of youth presenting serious clinical problems; for example, abused and neglected children and their families, substance-abusing youth and youth with serious emotional disturbances (SED). Inclusion of additional populations of youths presenting serious clinical problems necessitates additional training for MST clinical staff. In Galveston, Texas, for example, MST was introduced as part of a foundation and state initiative to treat a large, mostly Hispanic American youth gang population. This adaptation of MST, although relatively minor, nonetheless required that therapists receive additional training and support in order to successfully work with such youths and their families. For example, therapists rode along with police officers on patrol to learn the neighborhoods and to build collaborative relationships with local law enforcement. Seminars on local youth gangs and gang rivalries were also provided to help MST staff understand gang culture and gain necessary expertise.

D. Client factors

MST is known for its success in achieving positive clinical outcomes with referred youth and their families in controlled clinical trials. That MST has been effective with a broad range of youth without regard to gender, age, household income, family composition or race has also contributed to interest in the model. But the question remains: Why is MST successful? Several characteristics of the model have been proposed to explain its success (Henggeler, Schoenwald, & Pickrel, 1995).

First, MST addresses the multiple known determinants of serious anti-social behavior in adolescents (i.e. individual, family, school, peer and community factors associated with antisocial behavior) in a comprehensive yet individualized manner (Henggeler, Schoenwald et al., 1998). MST therapists are taught that "the client is the ecology", and that all aspects of the youth's social ecology must be examined to understand the specific risk and protective factors for each youth and his or her family. Interventions are then individualized to strategically address the key determinants of the identified problems.

Second, the identified problems are treated in the natural ecology of the youth and family. Treatment is provided in home, school and neighborhood settings. Providing treatment where problems occur helps to remove barriers to service access, engage families, obtain more valid assessment and outcome data, and enhance treatment generalization. Thus, the high ecological validity of MST significantly promotes sustained outcomes.

Third, the success of MST has been attributed to a quality assurance protocol that brings a level of rigor to community settings that has been previously reserved for clinical trials conducted in university settings (Weisz, Donenberg, Han & Weiss, 1995). Initially, this protocol included MST training (see p. 108) being implemented under the watchful eye of an MST developer or expert. With the rapid growth of MST beyond clinical trials and out into many communities, the need for a cadre of full-time dedicated doctoral-level professionals to provide consultation and training developed very quickly. These consultants (aka. MST "experts") are primarily responsible for ensuring the effective implementation of MST at the client level. As such, consultants' primary objectives include monitoring and supporting clinician and supervisor adherence to the MST treatment principles and use of appropriate and effective evidence-based treatment modalities. To become MST experts, doctoral or experienced master's level clinicians participate in a rigorous training process that has been recently specified in a training manual (Schoenwald, 1998).

III. MULTICOMPONENT EVALUATION OF MST PROGRAMS: MONITORING IMPLEMENTATION AND OUTCOMES

Recent findings regarding service system initiatives (e.g. Bickman, 1996; Bickman, Summerfelt, Firth, & Douglas, 1997) and service effectiveness (Burns, Hoagwood, & Maultsby, 1998; Jensen, Hoagwood, & Petti, 1996) have focused attention on the specific clinical interventions being delivered in children's mental health settings (Schoenwald, Henggeler, Brondino, & Rowland, 1999). Consistent with this attention and in response to community demands for MST programs, a training and quality assurance package has been developed which facilitates dissemination efforts. The package is designed to optimize therapist adherence to the MST model and provider accountability for meaningful, measurable outcomes. Quality assurance mechanisms include a pre-training site assessment, technical assistance for program start-up, an introductory 5-day orientation training for all MST staff, on-site task-oriented supervision, quarterly booster training, use of adherence measures and weekly case consultation with an MST expert. In addition, manuals describing procedures for supervision (Henggeler & Schoenwald, 1998) consultation (Schoenwald, 1998) and organizational procedures (Strother, Swenson, & Schoenwald, 1998) are made available to providers engaged in the training process.

A. Mechanisms to promote quality assurance

1. The site assessment and technical assistance during program start-up

The extent to which organizational and service system factors influence the implementation of MST is an empirical question, albeit one the Family Services Research Center is investigating with, see p. 113, funding from the National Institutes of Mental Health (Schoenwald, Principal Investigator) and the Office of Juvenile Justice and Delinquency Prevention (Henggeler, Principal Investigator). Anecdotal evidence from the efforts of MST Services to disseminate MST across the United States and Canada suggests, however, that contextual factors do impact program implementation and success. Thus, the MST training and quality assurance package begins with the site assessment process that allows the potential provider organization and representatives from referring and reimbursement agencies and consumer groups to discuss the extent to which the establishment of an MST program is both desirable and viable. The site assessment process also includes technical assistance in developing procedures for outcomes and adherence monitoring.

2. Training

The 5-day orientation training is provided on-site using essentially the same protocol that has been used in successful clinical trials of MST with violent and chronic juvenile offenders. The format includes both didactic and ex-periential components, and the topics of instruction include research on the major psychological and sociological models regarding serious clinical problems in youth and a range of evidence-based assessment and interven-tion strategies used in MST (e.g. behavior therapy, cognitive behavior therapy, pragmatic family therapies). Quarterly booster training sessions are conducted on-site as therapists gain field experience with MST. The purpose of these $1\frac{1}{2}$ day boosters is to provide additional training in areas identified by therapists and clinical supervisors and to facilitate in-depth examination, enactment and problem-solving of particularly difficult challenges that arise in working with referred youth and their families.

3. Weekly on-site supervision

MST supervision sessions are the primary forum in which supervisors obtain evidence of clinicians' development of the conceptual and behavioral skills required to implement MST effectively. As such, supervision serves three interrelated purposes:

(1) development of case-specific recommendations to speed progress toward outcomes for each client family;
(2) monitoring of therapist adherence to MST treatment principles in all cases; and
(3) advancement of clinicians' trajectories with respect to each aspect of the ongoing developmental process through which clinicians learn to im-plement MST consistently and effectively.

Thus, just as MST therapists are encouraged to "do whatever it takes" to achieve treatment goals with families, supervisors must be prepared to expend considerable effort in promoting clinicians' adherence to the MST protocol.

4. Quality assurance monitoring

Currently, therapist adherence to treatment principles is measured by a 26-item, Likert-format, MST Therapist Adherence Measure (Henggeler &

Borduin, 1992). Therapist adherence as measured by this scale has been significantly associated with youth outcomes at the 1.7 year follow-up in a study with violent and chronic juvenile offenders (Henggeler et al., 1997), and these findings have been replicated, in part, in a study with substance abusing or dependent juvenile offenders (Henggeler, Pickrel, et al., 1999). In light of the link between therapist adherence to MST treatment principles and youth outcomes, the current standard quality assurance protocol for MST teams includes therapist adherence monitoring on a monthly basis with each family, with the primary caregiver providing ratings via telephone interviews. Internet-based data collection and response mechanisms allow for real-time scoring, and supervisors can use survey results to provide immediate feedback to therapists.

Likewise, supervisor adherence is measured via a recently developed 43-item, Likert-format, MST Supervisor Adherence Measure (Schoenwald, Henggeler, & Edwards, 1998). This instrument assesses adherence to the model of MST supervision as specified in the MST Supervisory Manual (Henggeler & Schoenwald, 1998) as reported by therapists on the MST team. Supervisor adherence is evaluated bimonthly, and therapists can respond using the Internet (www.mstinstitute.org), which promotes confidentiality and provides timely feedback for MST consultants who work with the supervisors. When incorporated with other sources of feedback (e.g. client outcomes, consultant observations, continued funding and sufficient referrals), such continuous evaluation provides the basis for consultant feedback to multiple levels of the system and increases the likelihood that corrective actions will be taken early in the course of program implementation.

5. Weekly consultation with an MST expert

As described on p. 109, MST consultants or "experts" are the individuals primarily responsible for ensuring the effective implementation of MST at the client level. The primary objective of weekly consultation is to monitor and support clinician and supervisor adherence to the MST treatment principles, and to facilitate use of appropriate and effective evidence-based treatment modalities (Schoenwald, 1998). Patterns of questions or clinical concerns that arise during the course of weekly consultation also provide the basis for the quarterly booster trainings which are provided by the MST consultant on site.

B. Evaluation studies of dissemination efforts

It remains to be seen whether the aforementioned quality assurance mechanisms can facilitate the level of treatment fidelity required to achieve the types of positive outcomes observed in the MST clinical trials. A project funded by the Office of Juvenile Justice and Delinquency Prevention (OJJDP) will allow an examination of the relationship between supervisory practice, therapist adherence and youth outcomes in community settings (Henggeler et al., under review). This study involves the ongoing measurement of therapist and supervisor adherence using protocols described on pp. 111–112. Information about the child's living situation, school status, emotional indicators, rearrest, and out-of-home placements is obtained from the caregiver via telephone at treatment termination, 6 months and 12 months post-treatment. State agencies provide corroborating information about arrests, reports of child abuse or neglect, and out-of-home placements including psychiatric hospitalization and incarceration up to 1 year post-treatment. This focus on "real world" longitudinal outcomes, using a multi-method, multi-respondent format, is rare in mental health settings but is most likely an essential component of successful dissemination. Rigorous evaluation focusing on real-world outcomes has been a hallmark of the development and dissemination of MST (Henggeler, Mihalic et al., 1998) and will continue with the collaboration of sites interested in providing state of the art services.

Finally, a project recently funded by the National Institute of Mental Health (Schoenwald, Principal Investigator) includes organizational and extra-organizational factors in an examination of the transportability of MST to real-world practice settings. The study evaluates a social-ecological model of treatment transportability in which linkages between treatment outcomes, therapist adherence, supervisory practices, organizational variables and extra-organizational factors (e.g. referral and reimbursement mechanisms, interagency relations) are delineated. Hopefully, the results of these investigations will inform future efforts to make effective treatment models available in community service systems.

IV. SUMMARY AND KEY IMPLICATIONS

MST has proven to be a clinically effective and cost effective alternative to out-of-home placement of youths presenting serious clinical problems. Such outcomes, obtained via delivery of intensive family-based treatment, have clear implications for mental health and juvenile justice policy. First, a sizable portion of resources currently devoted to expensive, ineffective and often deleterious (e.g. boot camps) out-of-home placements should be shifted toward intensive, empirically supported community interventions. Second, community interventions should: be intensive, comprehensive and individualized; provide time-limited treatment with access to aftercare; deliver

ecologically valid and evidence-based interventions; and incorporate protocols that promote a high degree of quality assurance. Third, policy mandates
should include guidelines or strategies to promote dissemination of successful treatments that include attention to the multiple levels of impact on the
local community.

References

Aos, S., Phipps, P, Barnoski, R., & Lieb, R. (1999). *The Comparative Costs and Benefits of Programs to Reduce Crime: A Review of National Research Findings with Implications for Washington State, Version 3.0* Olympia, WA: Washington State Institute for Public Policy.

Bernfeld, G. A., Blase, K. A., & Fixsen, D. L. (1990). Towards a unified perspective on human service delivery systems: Application of the teaching-family model. In R. J. McMahon & R. Dev. Peters (Eds), *Behavior Disorders of Adolescence*. New York: Plenum.

Bickman, L. (1996). A managed continuum of care: More is not always better. *American Psychologist*, **51**(7), 689–701.

Bickman, L., Summerfelt, W. T., Firth, J., & Douglas, S. (1997). The Stark County Evaluation Project: Baseline results of a randomized experiment. In D. Northrup & C. Nixon (Eds), *Evaluating Mental Health Services: How Do Programs for Children "Work" in the Real World?* Newbury Park, CA: Sage.

Borduin, C. M., Henggeler, S. W., Blaske, D. M., & Stein, R. J. (1990). Multisystemic treatment of adolescent sexual offenders. *International Journal of Offender Therapy and Comparative Criminology*, **35**, 105–114.

Borduin, C. M., Mann, B. J., Cone, L. T., Henggeler, S. W., Fucci, B. R., Blaske, D. M., & Williams, R. A. (1995). Multisystemic treatment of serious juvenile offenders: Long-term prevention of criminality and violence. *Journal of Consulting and Clinical Psychology*, **63**, 569–578.

Bronfenbrenner, U. (1979). *The Ecology of Human Development: Experiments by Nature and Design*. Cambridge, MA: Harvard University Press.

Brunk, M., Henggeler, S. W., & Whelan, J. P. (1987). A comparison of multisystemic therapy and parent training in the brief treatment of child abuse and neglect. *Journal of Consulting and Clinical Psychology*, **55**, 311–318.

Burns, B. J., Hoagwood, K. H., & Maultsby, L. T. (1998). Improving outcomes for children and adolescents with serious emotional and behavioral disorders: Current and future directions. In M. H. Epstein, K. Kutash & A. J. Duchnowski (Eds), *Outcomes for Children and Youth with Emotional and Behavioral Disorders and Their Families: Programs and Evaluation Best Practices*, pp. 685–707. Austin, TX: Pro-ED.

Cunningham, P. B. & Henggeler, S. W. (2001). Implementation of an empirically-based drug and violence prevention and intervention program in public school settings. *Journal of Clinical Child Psychology*, **30**, 221–232.

Elliott, D. S. (1994). Serious violent offenders: Onset, developmental course, and termination—The American Society of Criminology 1993 Presidential address. *Criminology*, **32**, 1–21.

Glisson, C., & Hemmelgarn, A. (1996). The effects of organizational climate and interorganizational coordination on the quality and outcomes of children's service systems. *Child Abuse and Neglect*, **22**, 401–421.

Haley, J. (1976). *Problem Solving Therapy*. San Francisco: Jossey-Bass.

Henggeler, S. W. (1999). Multisystemic therapy: An overview of clinical procedures, outcomes, and policy implications. *Child Psychology and Psychiatry Review*, **4**, 2–10.

Henggeler, S. W., & Borduin, C. M. (1990). *Family Therapy and Beyond: A Multisystemic Approach to Treating the Behavior Problems of Children and Adolescents*. Pacific Grove, CA: Brooks/Cole.

Henggeler, S. W., & Borduin, C. M. (1992). *Multisystemic Therapy Adherence Scales*, Unpublished. Department of Psychiatry and Behavioral Sciences, Medical University of South Carolina.

Henggeler, S. W., Schoenwald, S. K., Liao, J. G., Letourneau, E. J., & Edwards, D. L. (under review). *Transporting Efficacious Treatments to Field Settings: The Link between Supervisory Practices and Therapist Fidelity in MST Programs*.

Henggeler, S. W., Melton, G. B., Brondino, M. J., Scherer, D. G., & Hanley, J. H. (1997). Multisystemic therapy with violent and chronic juvenile offenders and their families: The role of treatment fidelity in successful dissemination. *Journal of Consulting and Clinical Psychology*, **65**, 821–823.

Henggeler, S. W., Melton, G. B., & Smith, L. A. (1992). Family preservation using multisystemic therapy: An effective alternative to incarcerating serious juvenile offenders. *Journal of Consulting and Clinical Psychology*, **60**, 953–961.

Henggeler, S. W., Melton, G. B., Smith, L. A., Schoenwald, S. K., & Hanley, J. (1993). Family preservation using multisystemic therapy: Long-term follow-up to a clinical trial with serious juvenile offenders. *Journal of Child and Family Studies*, **2**, 283–293.

Henggeler, S. W., Mihalic, S. F., Rone, L., Thomas, C., & Timmons-Mitchell, J. (1998). Multisystemic therapy. In D. S. Elliott (Series Ed.), *Blueprints for Violence Prevention*. Boulder, CO: University of Colorado, Center for the Study and Prevention of Violence, Institute for Behavioral Sciences.

Henggeler, S. W., Pickrel, S. G., & Brondino, M. J. (1999). Multisystemic treatment of substance abusing and dependent delinquents: Outcomes, treatment fidelity, and transportability. *Mental Health Services Research*, **1**, 171–184.

Henggeler, S. W., Rodick, J. D., Borduin, C. M., Hanson, C. L., Watson, S. M., & Urey, J. R. (1986). Multisystemic treatment of juvenile offenders: Effects on adolescent behavior and family interactions. *Developmental Psychology*, **22**, 132–141.

Henggeler, S. W., Rowland, M. D., Randall, J., Ward, D. M., Pickrel, S. G., Cunningham, P. B., Miller, S. L., Edwards, J. E., Zealberg, J., Hand, L., & Santos, A. B. (1999). Home-based multisystemic therapy as an alternative to the hospitalization of youths in psychiatric crisis: Clinical outcomes. *Journal of the American Academy of Child and Adolescent Psychiatry*, **38**, 1331–1339.

Henggeler, S. W., & Schoenwald, S. K. (1998). *Multisystemic Therapy Supervisory Manual*. Charleston, SC: MST Institute.

Henggeler, S. W., Schoenwald, S. K., Borduin, C. M., Rowland, M. D., & Cunningham, P. B. (1998). *Multisystemic Treatment for Antisocial Behavior in Children and Adolescents*. New York: Guilford Press.

Henggeler, S. W., Schoenwald, S. K., & Pickrel, S. G. (1995). Multisystemic therapy: Bridging the gap between university- and community-based treatment. *Journal of Consulting and Clinical Psychology*, **63**, 709–717.

Hoagwood, K., Hibbs, E., Brent, D., & Jensen, P. (1995). Introduction to the special section: Efficacy and effectiveness in studies of child and adolescent psychotherapy. *Journal of Consulting and Clinical Psychology*, **63**, 683–687.

Jensen, P. S., Hoagwood, K., & Petti, T. (1996). Outcomes of mental health care for children and adolescents: II. Literature review and application of a comprehensive model. *Journal of the American Academy of Child and Adolescent Psychiatry*, **35**, 1064–1077.

Kazdin, A. E. & Weisz, J. R. (1998). Identifying and developing empirically-supported child and adolescent treatments. *Journal of Consulting and Clinical Psychology*, **66**, 19–36.

Miller, M. L. (1998). *The Multisystemic Therapy Pilot Program: Final Evaluation*. Wilmington, DE: Evaluation, Research, and Planning.

Minuchin, S. (1974). *Families and Family Therapy*. Cambridge, MA: Harvard University Press.

Randall, J., Swenson, C. C. & Henggeler, S. W. (1999). Neighborhood solutions for neighborhood problems: An empirically-based violence prevention collaboration. *Health, Education, and Behavior*, **26**, 806–820.

Rogers, E. M. (1995). *Diffusion of Innovations*, 4th ed. New York: Free Press.

Schoenwald, S. K. (1998). *Multisystemic Therapy Consultation Guidelines*. Charleston, SC: MST Institute.

Schoenwald, S. K. & Henggeler, S. W. (in press). Mental health services research and family-based treatment: Bridging the gap. In H. Liddle, G. Diamond, R. Levant, J. Bray & D. Santisteban (Eds), *Family Psychology Intervention Science*. Washington, DC: American Psychological Association.

Schoenwald, S. K., Henggeler, S. W., Brondino, M. J, & Rowland, M. D. (2000). Multisystemic therapy: Monitoring treatment fidelity. *Family Process*, **39**, 83–103.

Schoenwald, S. K., Ward, D. M., Henggeler, S. W., Pickrel, S. G., & Patel, H. (1996). MST treatment of substance abusing or dependent adolescent offenders: Costs of reducing incarceration, inpatient, and residential placement. *Journal of Child and Family Studies*, **5**, 431–444.

Schoenwald, S. K., Henggeler, S. W., & Edwards, D. L. (1998). *MST Supervisor Adherence Measure*, Unpublished. Charleston, SC: MST Institute.

Strother, K. B., Schoenwald, S. K., & Swenson, M. E. (1998). *Multisystemic Therapy Organizational Manual*. Charleston, SC: MST Institute.

Washington State Institute for Public Policy (1998). *Watching the Bottom Line: Cost-effective Interventions for Reducing Crime in Washington*. Olympia, WA: Evergreen State College.

Weisz, J. R., Donenberg, G. R., Han, S. S., & Weiss, B. (1995). Bridging the gap between laboratory and clinic in child and adolescent psychotherapy. *Journal of Consulting and Clinical Psychology*, **63**, 688–701.

Acknowledgements

The writing of this manuscript was supported by grants #97-JN-FX-0016 and #98-JN-FX- 0015 from the Office of Juvenile Justice and Delinquency Prevention (OJJDP).

APPENDIX A: SITE ASSESSMENT CHECKLIST

MST SERVICES

Site assessment checklist

Provider: _____   Prepared by: _____

Site: _____   Training dates: _____

Overview of the community service system:

☐ Identify organizations and agencies affected by the MST program (i.e. schools, social services, juvenile justice, etc.) that need to be "on board" to ensure the successful implementation of the MST program.

☐ Develop an invitation list for the Monday of the 5-Day orientation training. This list will include representatives from all agencies that need to be "on board", including their management, front line staff and critical "opinion leaders".

☐ What evidence exists that these organizations and agencies are "on board"? Please include copies of any memoranda of agreement regarding the support of the MST program in terms of collaboration, referrals or reimbursement.

☐ Confirm that the provider organization will be able to take the "lead" on cases with the buy-in of other organizations and agencies (i.e. MST therapists will be able to "take the lead" for clinical decision making on each case). The organization sponsoring the MST program has responsibility for initiating collaborative relationships with these organizations and agencies. Each MST therapist sustains these relationships through ongoing, case-specific collaboration.

☐ Describe the funding sources for MST program (e.g. program funding, fee for service, case rate, capitated rate, performance contract).

☐ Identify any potential financial disincentives for referral sources to use MST program (i.e. referral source must pay for MST but not for placing the youth in an out-of-home setting).

☐ If applicable for program evaluation, include copies of memoranda of agreement regarding commitment from appropriate archival agencies to provide outcome data at the time of case closure and during follow-up phase. A separate memorandum is needed for each agency that has the authority to remove children from their home (Juvenile Justice, Social Services/Child Welfare and Mental Health).

Overview of sponsoring and/or provider organization or agency:

☐ Describe the factors contributing to the interest in MST (e.g. significant public sector policies or initiatives, federal or state level funding for training, third-party payer and/or managed care's impact on the service environment, etc.).

☐ Include the provider organization's statements of mission and service philosophy (attaching a recent annual report or program brochure may be an easy way to accomplish this objective).

☐ Identify an individual or individuals who will be responsible for weekly telephone calls to families for purpose of tracking adherence of therapists.

☐ If applicable for program evaluation, confirm that procedures for obtaining informed consent to participate in structured program evaluation are in place, or will be developed, and that therapists will be trained to obtain this consent as part of the standard intake process.

☐ If applicable for program evaluation, confirm that all staff members with responsibility for data entry, including therapists, supervisors and administrative staff, will have access to the Internet for data entry on the MST Institute website.

MST program "Goals and Guidelines":

☐ Define the target population for the MST program (ages, defining "labels", problem profiles, etc.).

☐ Document the details of the referral process including:
referral sources;
anticipated availability of referrals;
referral criteria (inclusionary and exclusionary); and
referral procedures (step-by-step details, names, phone numbers, etc.).

☐ Establish written, measurable goals for the MST program.

☐ Discuss how program-level outcomes will be measured.

Confirm that the following "required" program practices can be implemented:

☐ MST therapists will be full-time master-level or highly competent, clinically skilled bachelor-level professionals assigned to the MST program solely.

☐ MST clinical supervisors will be either PhD level or experienced master-level professionals.

☐ Confirm that the MST clinical supervisor will have credible authority over the MST clinicians. Describe the clinical and administrative lines of authority.

☐ MST therapists will operate in teams of no fewer than two and no more than four therapists (plus the supervisor) and use a home-based model of service delivery.

☐ MST clinical supervisors will be assigned to the MST program a minimum of 25 per cent of the time (50% time, or full-time carrying a partial case load, is preferable) per MST team to conduct weekly team clinical supervision, facilitate the weekly MST telephone consultation and be available for individual clinical supervision for crisis cases. Supervisors carrying a partial caseload should be assigned to the program on a full-time basis.

☐ MST caseloads will not exceed six families per therapist with a normal range being four to six families per therapist. A normal caseload consists of three or four "active" cases.

☐ The expected duration of treatment is 3–5 months.

☐ In order to achieve outcomes through consistent adherence to the MST model, MST therapists must track progress and outcomes on each case weekly by completing case summaries and by participating in group supervision and MST consultation. Please confirm that all therapists will participate in these activities.

☐ Confirm that MST teams will have access to a good-quality speaker-phone, a fax machine, a computer with Internet access for administering adherence measures.

☐ MST therapists will be accessible at times that are convenient to their clients and in times of crisis, very quickly. Issues to be addressed in this area include:

the full-time and dedicated nature of the MST therapist role;
the use of flex/comptime;
policies allowing for the use of personal vehicles to transport clients; and
the use of pagers and/or cellular phones.

☐ The MST program will have a 24 hour/day, 7 day/week on-call system to provide coverage when MST therapists are on vacation or taking personal time. This system must be staffed by professionals who know the details of each MST case and understand MST.

☐ Discuss outcome focused personnel evaluation policies including the strengths of contract formats that make incentive bonuses for therapists possible.

☐ Confirm that there is an organizational understanding that account-ability for client outcomes begins with the therapists but clearly lies within the entire organization, including the team, supervisor and administration.

Clinical practices:

☐ Confirm that supervision practices can conform to the following format: weekly MST group consultation, weekly group clinical supervision and individual supervision only as needed due to case crises.

☐ Confirm that discharge criteria will be outcome-based rather than being focused on treatment duration or other criteria.

☐ Discuss how aftercare referrals will be made. Will such referrals be carefully managed and limited to those that target specific, well-defined problems? MST assumes that most cases should need minimal "formal" aftercare services.

Training:

☐ Discuss the administration's expectations for the training program and outline specific objectives for the training program. (Outside of developing an effective team of MST therapists, organizational expectations or desired outcomes of the training program need to be clearly articulated and built into the implementation plans or they will not be meet.)

Chapter 6

AGGRESSION REPLACEMENT TRAINING: APPLICATION AND EVALUATION MANAGEMENT

Arnold P. Goldstein* and Barry Glick[†]

* Center for Research on Aggression, Syracuse University, New York, USA
[†] G&C Consultants, Scotia, New York, USA

This chapter describes the procedures and curriculum which constitute Aggression Replacement Training (ART); their diverse application in agency, school and residential settings; and an extended series of evaluations of their behavior change efficacy. Throughout these examinations, particular emphasis is placed upon describing program management and implementation challenges and solutions.

ART PROCEDURES AND CURRICULUM

Counselors, teachers, juvenile corrections staff and others who deal with aggressive juvenile delinquents understand that these juveniles often make use of high levels of acting-out-behaviors combined with substandard and deficient alternative prosocial behaviors. Many of these juveniles are skilled in fighting, bullying, intimidating, harassing and manipulating others.

Offender Rehabilitation in Practice. Edited by G. A. Bernfeld, D. P. Farrington and A. W. Leschied.
© 2001 John Wiley & Sons, Ltd.

However, they are frequently inadequate in more socially desirable behaviors, such as negotiating differences; identifying their own and others feelings; dealing appropriately with accusations; and responding effectively to failure, teasing, rejection or anger. ART is our response to such antisocial behavior excesses and prosocial behavior deficits. It is a multimodal, psychoeducational intervention that consists of skillstreaming, anger-control training and moral reasoning training. These three components, when integrated and coordinated as we have designed, constitute a cognitive-behavioral intervention program targeted to the participating youths thinking, affect and overt behavior.

Skillstreaming

Skillstreaming, a 50-skill intervention curriculum of prosocial behaviors, is systematically taught to chronically aggressive adolescents (Goldstein, Sprafkin, Gershaw & Klein, 1980) and younger children (McGinnis & Goldstein, 1984; 1990). The skillstreaming curriculum is implemented with small groups of juveniles (preferably six to eight). The following teaching procedures are employed:

- Modeling—The groups see several examples of experts using the behaviors and the skills in which they are weak or lacking.
- Role playing—Individuals are given several guided opportunities to practice and rehearse competent-interpersonal behaviors.
- Performance feedback—Instructors praise and provide feedback on how well the juveniles' role playing of the skill matched the expert model's portrayal of it. Reinstruction is given when necessary.
- Generalization training—Juveniles are encouraged to practice what they have seen modeled and tried in their role play via a series of activities, such as regularly completing skill homework assignments, that are designed to increase the chances that the skills learned in the training setting will be available for them to use when needed in their real-life environment—the institution, the home, the school, the community or other real-world settings.

The prosocial skills that participating youngsters learn from these procedures are listed in Table 6.1.

Anger control training

Anger control training, first developed by Feindler, Marriott and Iwata (1984), is partially based on the earlier anger control and stress inoculation

Table 6.1 Skillstreaming skills for adolescents

Group	Description	Skill
I	Beginning social skills	1. Listening 2. Starting a conversation 3. Having a conversation 4. Asking a question 5. Saying thank you 6. Introducing yourself 7. Introducing other people 8. Giving a compliment
II	Advanced social skills	9. Asking for help 10. Joining in 11. Giving instructions 12. Following instructions 13. Apologizing 14. Convincing others
III	Skills for dealing with feelings	15. Knowing your feelings 16. Expressing your feelings 17. Understanding the feelings for others 18. Dealing with someone else's anger 19. Expressing affection 20. Dealing with fear 21. Rewarding yourself
IV	Skill alternatives to aggression	22. Asking permission 23. Sharing something 24. Helping others 25. Negotiating 26. Using self-control 27. Standing up for your rights 28. Responding to teasing 29. Avoiding trouble with others 30. Keeping out of fights
V	Skills for dealing with stress	31. Making a complaint 32. Answering a complaint 33. Sportsmanship after the game 34. Dealing with embarrassment 35. Dealing with being left out 36. Standing up for a friend 37. Responding to persuasion 38. Responding to failure 39. Dealing with confusing messages 40. Dealing with an accusation 41. Getting ready for a difficult conversation 42. Dealing with group pressure

continued

Table 6.1 (*cont.*)

Group	Description	Skill
VI	Planning skills	43. Deciding on something to do 44. Deciding what caused a problem 45. Setting a goal 46. Deciding on your abilities 47. Gathering information 48. Arranging problems by importance 49. Making a decision 50. Concentrating on a task

research of Novaco (1975) and Meichenbaum (1977). Its goal is to teach juveniles to control their own anger. In anger control training, the participating juveniles must bring to each session one or more descriptions of recent anger-arousing experiences. Usually these experiences are written in their "hassle log". During 10 sessions, the juveniles are trained to respond to their hassles with a chain of behaviors that include:

- identifying triggers (external events and internal self-statements that provoke an anger response);
- identifying cues (individual kinesthetic or physical experiences, such as tightened muscles, flushed faces and clenched fists that let the individual know that the emotion he or she is experiencing is anger);
- using reducers (techniques that are designed to lower the individual's level of anger, such as deep breathing, counting backward, imaging a peaceful scene or imagining the long-term consequences of one's behavior);
- using reminders (self-statements, such as "stay calm", "chill out" and "cool down", or non-hostile explanations of others' behaviors);
- Using self-evaluation (reflecting on how well the hassle was responded to by identifying triggers and cues, using reminders, and using reducers and then praising or rewarding oneself for effective performance).

The juvenile trainees, who participate in both skillstreaming and anger control training, are thus knowledgeable about what to do (from skillstreaming) and what not to do (from anger control training) in circumstances that instigate aggression. But because aggressive behavior is so consistently, immediately and richly rewarded in many of the real-world settings in which juveniles live, work, go to school and interact, they may still consciously choose to behave aggressively. Thus, we believed that it was important to add a values-oriented component to this intervention approach. The final component of ART, therefore, is moral reasoning training.

Moral reasoning training

Moral reasoning training is a set of procedures designed to enhance the juvenile's sense of fairness, justice and concern with the needs and rights of others. In a pioneering series of investigations, Kohlberg (1969, 1973) demonstrated that exposing juveniles to a series of moral dilemmas (through discussion groups that include juveniles reasoning at differing levels of morality) arouses cognitive conflict. When resolved, this cognitive conflict will frequently advance a juvenile's moral reasoning to that of his or her peers in the group who reason at a higher level. Such advancement of moral reasoning is a reliable finding, but, as with many other single-component interventions, efforts to use it alone as a means of enhancing actual, overt moral behavior have resulted in mixed success (Arbuthnot & Gordon, 1983; Zimmerman, 1983).

We thus reasoned that Kohlberg's moral reasoning training (and in recent implementations of ART, the closely related approach, social problem solving developed by Gibbs, 1999), has marked potential for providing constructive direction toward sociability. It can aid in moving them away from antisocial behavior when juveniles have in their behavioral repertoires the actual skills for acting prosocially or for successfully inhibiting antisocial or more aggressive behaviors. Because a combination of all three components—skillstreaming, anger control training and moral reasoning training—is stronger than any component alone, we used all three to constitute ART.

We and others have offered the ART curriculum in a variety of time frames, but a 10-week sequence has emerged as a "core" curriculum in several of its research evaluations (see Table 6.2).

APPLICATION INNOVATIONS

Since its inception in 1987, ART programs have been put in place in a substantial number of agencies, schools and residential settings in the United States and beyond. A number of such programs have creatively implemented its procedure and curriculum, and in the present section we wish to share a sense of a number of these applied innovations.

Table 6.2 ART core curriculum

Week	Skillstreaming	Moral reasoning	Anger control
1.	*Expressing a complaint* 1. Define what the problem is, and who's responsible for it 2. Decide how the problem might be solved 3. Tell the person what the problem is and how it might be solved 4. Ask for a response 5. Show that you understand his or her feelings 6. Come to an agreement on the steps to be taken by each of you	1. The used car 2. The dope pusher 3. Riots in public places	*Introduction* 1. Rationale: presentation and discussion 2. Rules: presentation and discussion 3. Training procedures: presentation and discussion 4. Contract for anger control training, initial history taking 5. Antecedent provocations–behavioral response–consequences (A–B–C)
2.	*Responding to the feelings of others (empathy)* 1. Observe the other person's words and actions 2. Decide what the other person might be feeling, and how strong the feelings are 3. Decide whether it would be helpful to let the other person know you understand his or her feelings 4. Tell the other person, in a warm and sincere manner, how you think he or she is feeling	1. The passenger ship 2. The case of Charles Manson 3. LSD	*Assessment* 1. Hassle log: purpose and mechanics 2. Anger self-assessment: physiological cues 3. Anger reducers: reducer 1: deep breathing training; reducer 2: refocusing, backward counting; reducer 3: peacful imagery

3. *Preparing for a stressful conversation*
1. Imagine yourself in the stressful situation
 	
2. Think about how you will feel and why you will feel that way
3. Imagine that other person in the stressful situation. Think about how that person will feel and why
4. Imagine yourself telling the other person what you want to say
5. Imagine what he or she will say
6. Repeat the above steps using as many approaches as you can think of
7. Choose the best approach
	1. Shoplifting
	
	2. Booby trap
	
	3. Plagiarism
		Triggers
		1. Identification of provoking stimuli:
		   a. direct triggers (from others);
		   b. indirect triggers (from self)
		2. Role play: triggers + cues + anger reducer
		3. Review of hassle logs

4. *Responding to anger* 1. Listen openly to what the other person has to say 2. Show that you understand what the other is feeling 3. Ask the other person to explain anything you don't understand 4. Show that you understand why the other person feels angry 5. If it is appropriate, express your thoughts and feelings about the situation	1. Toy revolver 2. Robin Hood case 3. Drugs	*Reminders (Anger reducer 4)* 1. Introduction to self-instruction training 2. Modeling use of reminders under pressure 3. Role play: triggers + cues + reminders + anger reducer 4. Homework assignments and review of hassle log

continued

Table 6.2 (*cont.*)

Week	Skillstreaming	Moral reasoning	Anger control

5.	*Keeping out of fights*
	1. Stop and think about why you want to fight
	2. Decide what you want to happen in the long run
	3. Think about other ways to handle the situation besides fighting
	4. Decide the best way to handle the situation and do it
		1. Private country road
		
		2. New York versus Gerald Young
		
		3. Saving a life
			Self-evaluation
			1. Review of reminder homework assignment
			2. Self-evaluation of post-conflict reminders:
			  a. self-reinforcement techniques;
			  b. self-coaching techniques
			3. Review of hassle log post-conflict reminders

6.	*Helping others* 1. Decide if the other person might need and want your help 2. Think of the ways you could be helpful 3. Ask the other person if he or she needs and wants your help 4. Help the other person	1. The kidney transplant 2. Perjury 3. Misrepresentation	*Thinking ahead (anger reducer 5)* 1. Estimating future negative consequences for current acting out 2. Short-term versus long-term consequences 3. Worst to least consequences 4. Role play: "If ... then" thinking ahead 5. Role play: triggers + cues + reminders + anger reducers + self-evaluation + skillstreaming skill
7.	*Dealing with accusation* 1. Think about what the other person has accused you of 2. Think about why the person might have accused you 3. Think about ways to answer the person's accusations 4. Choose the best way and do it	1. Lt Berg 2. Perjury 3. Doctor's responsibility	*The angry behavior cycle* 1. Review of hassle logs 2. Identification of own anger-provoking behavior 3. Modification of own anger-provoking behavior 4. Role play: triggers + cues + reminders + anger reducers + self-evaluation + skillstreaming skill

8. *Dealing with group pressure*
1. Think about what other people want to do and why
2. Decide what you want to do

3. Decide how to tell the other people what you want to do
4. Tell the group what you have decided

1. Noisy child

2. The stolen car

3. Discrimination

Full sequence rehearsal
1. Review of hassle logs
2. Role play: triggers + cues + reminders + anger reducers + self-evaluation + skillstreaming skill

9. *Expressing affection*
1. Decide if you have good feelings about the other person
2. Decide wheter the other person would like to know about your feelings
3. Decide how you might best express your feelings
4. Choose the right time and place to express your feelings.
5. Express affection in a warm and caring manner

1. Defense of other persons
2. Lying in order to help someone
3. Rockefeller's suggestion

Full sequence rehearsal
1. Review of hassle logs
2. Role play: triggers + cues + reminders + anger reducers + skillstreaming skill

10. *Responding to failure*
1. Decide if you have failed.
2. Think about both the personal reasons and the circumstances that have caused you to fail
3. Decide how you might do things differently if you tried again
4. Decide if you want to try again
5. If it is appropriate, try again, using your revised approach

1. The desert
2. The threat

3. Drunken driving

Full sequence rehearsal
1. Review of hassle logs
2. Role play: triggers + cues + reminders + anger reducers + self-evaluation + skillstreaming skill

An alternative school: Positive Alternative Learning (PAL) program (St Louis)

An especially noteworthy feature of the PAL program is its major outreach to the interpersonal systems of its target youths. After a student learns a new behavior, a new perception, a new way of coping or responding in an ART series, he or she goes out to interact with key people who respond to these new ways of being. If these real-world figures respond with indifference or even hostility to the youngster's efforts, the new behaviors and perceptions rapidly disappear. If, on the other hand, they respond with interest, praise or approval, the behavioral changes have a much better chance to endure. At PAL the real-world figures are the school's staff, PAL peers and the young-sters' parents. The program makes an energetic and sustained effort to reach out to such figures, makes clear in concrete terms precisely how they can contribute positively to the behavior-change process and monitors whether such a contribution is in fact being made. With regard to parents of PAL students, for example, PAL holds weekly parent empowerment meetings. At the beginning of each youth's stay at PAL, his or her parents are required as a condition of the youth's acceptance into the program to attend parent meetings for 8 weeks. Each parent meeting contains major elements of ART programming. If a parent fails to attend, a PAL staff member goes to the home the next morning and conducts an on-site skill lesson. If the parent continues to miss meetings, the youth is suspended from the program. Since the program's inception, only a few students have been dropped for parental non-attendance.

A community agency (Brooklyn, NY)

The Brownsville Neighborhood Youth Action Center offers a strong and consistent expectation for success. Beginning with their first trainee contact, program staff verbally and behaviorally deliver the message that "you can succeed, stay out of jail, get your equivalency diploma, find and keep a job, and get along better with your family." Staff commitment to trainee success has been shown in the research literature, as well as in this particular program, to motivate, encourage and set a standard that many youths emulate. In brief, the message of this agency's ART program is "expect the best of your trainees; it helps them to achieve it."

A school district (Erie, PA)

The school district's most significant achievement is its ability to stimulate and sustain staff involvement in ART delivery at numerous program sites over a long period of time. How do they do it? In brief, trainers are motivated by active participation in program development and amendment and by a process of consensus building and ongoing opportunity for trainer feedback. While program strategy (ART and others) and organizing philosophy are set largely at the district supervisory level, commitment to participatory management is communicated to, and carried out by, trainer staff at the program's tactical level. Program staff contribute substantially and on a continuing basis to decisions about their own program's content, intensity, staffing, structure and more. Clearly, the sense of joint ownership is a major factor in developing and maintaining high levels of districtwide staff motivation.

A limited security delinquency facility (Taberg, NY)

The centerpiece of the overall Taberg program is ART, and it is competently administered by the center's staff. Yet trainees' learning and performance of ART's prosocial lessons are greatly influenced by (and also influence in return) the attitudes of the significant people to whom the youths relate day after day—in this particular instance, the Taberg staff. The operating manual notes in this regard:

> It is imperative that Taberg staff be impeccable role models. Residents need staff whom they can emulate; who convey a genuine concern and caring, with unconditional positive regard and empathic understanding. As positive role models we must be ever cognizant of our own interpersonal interactions with both residents and colleagues and exhibit an ability to appropriately handle conflict, decision making, problem solving and planning. In order to demonstrate a genuine concern for youth, staff must be warm and friendly, yet firm in holding residents accountable to expectations for their growth and development. We will need a staff capable to achieve a delicate balance between establishing close, personal relationships with youth and yet perform roles as adult authority figures. Staff always have to demonstrate and model respectful behavior, toward residents and colleagues. As staff engage in the serious profession of being change agents their interactions and interventions with one another are as crucial to the habilitative process as our interventions and interactions with residents. To be successful in our mission, staff must work cooperatively and supportively with one another as members of a treatment team. Inherent to this team spirit are characteristics which all staff need to possess:
>
> 1. Involvement: An ability to develop and demonstrate a commitment to the group with which one works as well as a commitment to the Taberg program.

2. Initiative: Willingness to accept responsibility; contribute more than may be required even when it may seem risky or beyond one's role or function.
3. Understanding of self: The ability to possess a knowledge of one's own feelings, values, beliefs, abilities, limitations and needs.
4. Understanding others: A willingness to explore and listen to what others (co-workers) feel, believe, think and need.
5. Openness: An ability to say what is on one's mind—is able and willing to confront peers constructively to enhance job performance; is clear about where he/she stands.
6. Listening ability: Is willing and able to listen carefully to what others say and mean; listens for necessary information and instructions; asks questions to assist in better understanding of what he/she has heard.
7. Uses feedback: Is able and willing to accept constructive criticism from others in a positive manner; avoids being defensive and personalizing feedback; learns from ... experiences and is able to make changes which will improve job performance.
8. Ability to communicate: Shares and receives information/data with co-workers.
9. Participates in decision making: Is willing to take the time and energy to share in the decision-making process.
10. Perseverance: Does not abandon youth or staff with whom he/she is working (is able to work under stress, without giving up).
11. Self-development: Takes the initiative to continually expand ... knowledge and experience in order to reach the highest level of his/her professional development.

A residential school district (Children's Village, NY)

Staff training for competency in ART group leadership at Children's Village is operationalized as an apprenticeship program in which novice trainers participate in a series of orienting workshops followed by practice group experiences ("trainees" are staff playing the roles of residents). These experiences are followed by the supervised running of actual ART groups, and finally by the unsupervised running of groups.

The challenge of intervention work—whether ART or another effort—is generalization. Does the training extend beyond the training room to other settings, and does it endure over time? At Children's Village, a major effort is made to extend the outcomes of the ART meetings to both the campus residence settings and to the residents' families. Using both formal and informal means of communication, the school, cottage, staff and family regularly communicate and collaborate in the skill acquisition and skill performance efforts. Such generalization is not easily accomplished, but the effort at Children's Village to do so is broad and energetic, and stands as a model to be emulated.

A residential family treatment center (Aneby, Sweden)

The program in Aneby possesses two operational qualities that promote the generalization of learned skills. One is careful training of all staff in the ART rationale and procedures. Though only a portion of the staff become group trainers for skillstreaming, anger control training or moral reasoning training sessions, all staff have daily interactions with residents and their families. Consistent with our notion that all staff serve as transfer coaches, supervisory, social work, teaching, psychology, office maintenance and housekeeping personnel are all trained and expected to reward competent skill use when they see it and to coach such competency when skills should be used but are not.

Like many treatment organizations, this agency holds regular staff supervisory meetings. These are, however, far more than typical case conferences. In addition to discussion of client-related concerns, considerable time and energy are devoted to examining staff behavior (and, in a sense, counseling staff). In other words, this agency is keenly aware that in an organization espousing the remedial value of modeling, staff behavior toward clients and one another is a potent force. Often clients learn not so much from what staff say, but from what they do. These staff meetings are one more significant ingredient in the successful learning and generalization of ART programs at Aneby.

A statewide system (Washington State)

In 1997, the State of Washington passed the Community Juvenile Accountability Act (CJAA) which provides community-based programs that emphasize youth accountability and the development of the skills for youth to function in a manner consistent with public safety. CJAA programs must include: a risk assessment; reduce risk factors associated with juvenile offending, and employ interventions of demonstrated effectiveness. The legislation charged the Washington State Institute for Public Policy to identify and evaluate the array of existing programs. As a result of that effort, ART was identified as one of five programs for possible CJAA implementation in Washington State. In the Fall of 1998, each juvenile court within each Washington State County decided which program it would implement with CJAA funds. ART was selected by 23 county jurisdictions, and, in this still in-progress application of its procedures, ART has yielded initial comparative outcomes indicating it to be the most cost effective of the nine alternative intervention approaches simultaneously being used and examined.

EVALUATIONS OF EFFECTIVENESS

Annsville Youth Center

Our first evaluation of ART was conducted at a New York State Division for Youth facility in central New York State (Goldstein & Glick, 1987). A total of 60 youths at Annsville were included, most of them incarcerated at this limited-security institution for such crimes as burglary, unarmed robbery, criminal mischief and various drug offenses. Of these, 24 youngsters received the 10- week ART program described earlier (see Table 6.2). As already mentioned, this program required them to attend three sessions per week, one each of skillstreaming, anger control training and moral reasoning training. An additional 24 youths were assigned to a no-ART, brief instruction control group. This group controlled for the possibility that any apparent ART-derived gains in skill performance were due not to ART *per se*, but to the youngsters' enhanced motivation to display skills they already possessed but simply were not using. A third group, the no-treatment control group, consisted of 12 youths not participating in either ART or the brief instruction control group.

   The overall goal of this evaluation was to examine the effectiveness of ART for the purpose of:

1.   Skill acquisition: Do the youngsters learn the 10 skillstreaming skills in the ART curriculum?
2.   Minimal skill transfer: Can the youngsters perform the skills in response to new situations similar in format to those in which they were trained?
3.   Extended skill transfer: Can the youngsters perform the skills in response to new situations dissimilar in format and more "real-lifelike" than those in which they were trained?
4.   Anger control enhancement: Do the youngsters actually demonstrate fewer altercations or other acting-out behaviors as reflected in weekly behavior incident reports, completed for all participating youths by the center's staff?
5.   Impulse reduction: Are the youngsters rated as less impulsive and more reflective and self-controlled in their interpersonal behaviors?

Analyses of study data revealed, first, that youths undergoing ART compared with youths in both control groups, significantly acquired and transferred (minimal and extended) 4 of the 10 skillstreaming skills: making a complaint, getting ready for a difficult conversation, dealing with someone else's anger and dealing with group pressure. Similarly significant ART versus control group comparisons emerged on both the number and intensity of in-facility acting-out behaviors (as measured by the behavior incident reports) as well as on staff-rated impulsiveness.

Following completion of the project's posttesting, in Week 11 new ART groups were formed for the 36 youths in the two control groups. As before, these sessions were held three times per week for 10 weeks and duplicated the first-phase ART sessions in all other major respects (curriculum, group size, materials, etc.). Our goal in this second phase was an own control test of the efficacy of ART, with particular attention to discerning possible reductions in acting-out behaviors by comparing, for these youths, their behavior incident reports during Weeks 11 through 20 (when in ART) with their behavior incident reports from the period when they had served as control group members (Weeks 1 through 10). Both of the statistical comparisons (number and severity) conducted to test these replication effects yielded positive results.

Real-world figures such as family and peers frequently express indifference or even hostility toward trainees' use of newly learned prosocial skills. As a result, incarcerated delinquents experience considerable difficulty in effecting the transfer of skills from the more protective and benign training environment to the community environment. Family and peers frequently serve as reinforcers of antisocial behaviors, ignoring or even punishing constructive alternative actions. Our hope was that ART would serve as a sufficiently powerful intervention to effect at least moderate carryover of in-facility ART gains.

In order to test for such possible transfer effects, we constructed a global rating measurement of community functioning. During the 1-year period following initiation of ART at Annsville, 54 youths were released from this facility. A total of 17 had received ART; 37 had not. We contacted the Division for Youth team members (analogous to parole officers) around New York State to whom the 54 released youths regularly reported and, without informing the workers as to whether the youths had or had not received ART, asked the workers to complete global rating measurements for each of the Annsville youths. In four of the six areas—namely, home and family, peer, legal and overall—ART youths were rated significantly higher with regard to in-community functioning than were youths who had not received ART. In the areas of school and work, no significant differences emerged.

MacCormick Youth Center

Our second evaluation of the efficacy of ART was conducted at MacCormick Youth Center, a New York State Division for Youth maximum-security facility for male juvenile delinquents between the ages of 13 and 21 (Goldstein & Glick, 1987). In essence, this second evaluation project sought to replicate the exact procedures and findings of the Annsville project and to include youths incarcerated for substantially more serious felonies. A total of 51 youths were in residence at MacCormick at the time of the evaluation. Crimes committed by these youths included murder, manslaughter, rape, sodomy, attempted murder, assault and armed robbery. In all its procedural and experimental particulars, the MacCormick evaluation project replicated the effort at Annsville. It employed the same preparatory activities, materials, curriculum, testing, staff training, residential training, supervision and data analysis procedures.

On 5 of the 10 skillstreaming skills, significant acquisition and/or transfer results emerged. These findings essentially replicate the Annsville skillstreaming results. In contrast to the Annsville results, however, the MacCormick data also yielded a significant result on the sociomoral reflection measure (Gibbs, Basinger & Fuller, 1992). At MacCormick, but not at Annsville, youths participating in moral reasoning training sessions grew significantly in moral reasoning stages over the 10-week intervention period.

Regarding overt, in-facility behavior, youths receiving ART, compared with those who did not, increased significantly over their base rate levels in their use of constructive, prosocial behaviors (e.g. offering or accepting criticism appropriately, employing self-control when provoked) and decreased significantly in their rated levels of impulsiveness. In contrast to the Annsville findings, MacCormick youths who received ART did not differ from controls in either the number or intensity of acting-out behaviors. Annsville, internally, is not a locked facility. Its 60 youths live in one dormitory, in contrast to the locked, single-room arrangement at MacCormick. MacCormick's staff is twice the size of Annsville's, and the facility operates under a considerably tighter system of sanctions and controls than does Annsville. Because of these operational differences, the opportunity for acting-out behaviors is lower across all conditions at MacCormick as compared with Annsville. A "floor effect" therefore seemed to be operating at MacCormick that made a decrease in acting-out at MacCormick less likely to be a direct result of ART participation than at Annsville. At Annsville, such behaviors were contextually more possible at base rate, and they could (and did) decrease over the intervention period. At MacCormick, all youths started with low base rates and, likely for these same contextual reasons (e.g. sanctions, controls, rich staffing, etc.), they remained low. Subjects' use of prosocial behaviors, to which no floor or ceiling influences were relevant, did increase differentially as a function of the ART intervention.

A community-based evaluation

The findings of our first two investigations revealed ART to be a multimodal, habilitation intervention of considerable potency with incarcerated juvenile delinquents: It enhanced prosocial skill competency and overt prosocial behavior and reduced levels of impulsiveness. And, in one of the two samples studied, decreases (where possible) in the frequency and intensity of acting-out behaviors and enhancement of participants' levels of moral reasoning were verified.

Furthermore, some evidence provided independently revealed ART to lead to valuable changes in community functioning. In light of the general movement away from residential-based and toward community-based programming for delinquent youths, this possibility for community change led to our third evaluation of the efficacy of ART. This evaluation sought to discern the value of ART when provided to 65 youths on a postrelease basis, while youths were living in the community (Goldstein, Glick, Irwin, Pask-McCartney & Rubama, 1989). We were aware of the potent contribution to effective community functioning that parents and others make in the lives of delinquent youths. This belief led to our attempt to discern the effects of offering ART not only to the youths, but also to their parents and other family members.

This community-based project was essentially a three-way comparison of ART provided directly to youths plus ART provided to the youths' parents or other family members (Condition 1), versus ART for youths only (Condition 2), versus a no-ART control group (Condition 3). For the most part, participating youths were assigned to project conditions on a random basis, with departures from randomization becoming necessary on occasion as a function of the five-city, multisite, time-extended nature of the project. Largely as a result of how long the New York State Division for Youth had aftercare responsibility for youths discharged from their facilities, the ART program that was offered to project participants was designed to last 3 months, with sessions meeting twice per week, for a total of approximately 24 sessions. Each session, $1\frac{1}{2}$ to 2 hours long, was spent in:

(a) brief discussion of current life events and difficulties;
(b) skillstreaming training of a skill relevant to the life events/difficulties discussed; and
(c) anger control training or moral reasoning training on an alternating basis.

Once weekly, an ART session was held for the parents and other family members of a sample of participating youths. Those parents selected to

Table 6.3   Frequency of rearrest by condition in the community-based evaluation

Condition	Total N	Rearrested N	Per cent rearrested
Youth ART plus parent/sibling ART	13	2	15
Youth ART only	20	6	30
No-ART control	32	14	43

participate, but who did not appear, were provided ART in modified form via a weekly home visit or telephone call.

Since the different ART groups comprising the project's two treatment conditions chose which of the 50 skillstreaming skills they wished to learn, different groups learned different (if overlapping) skills. We did not, therefore, examine in our statistical analyses participant change on individual skills. Instead, analyses focused on total skill change for the youths participating in ART (Conditions 1 and 2) versus each other and non-ART control group youths (Condition 3). Results indicated that, although results for the two ART conditions did not differ significantly, participants in each of these conditions increased significantly in their overall interpersonal skill competence when compared to Condition 3 (no-ART) youths. A similarly significant outcome emerged (both ART groups versus no-ART group) for decrease in self-reported anger levels in response to mild (e.g. minor nuisance, unfair treatment) but not severe (e.g. betrayal of trust, control/coercion, physical abuse) anger-provoking situations.

A particularly important evaluation criterion in delinquency intervention work is recidivism. The majority of previously incarcerated youths who recidivate do so within the first 6 months following their release (Maltz, 1984). Thus, the recidivism criterion employed in this project, rearrest, was tracked during the first 3 months, in which youths received ART, and during the 3 subsequent no-ART months. Condition 3 youths, of course, received no ART during the entire tracking period. Analyses examining the frequency of rearrest by condition showed a significant effect for ART participation. Both Condition 1 and Condition 2 youths were rearrested significantly less than were youths not receiving ART. A substantial decrease in rearrest occurred when the youths' families (i.e. parents and siblings) participated simultaneously in their own ART groups. Table 6.3 represents the actual frequency and percentages of rearrests by condition.

From this study it appears that teaching family members interpersonal skills and anger control techniques reciprocal to those the delinquent youths are learning may well provide the youths with a more responsive and prosocially reinforcing real-world environment—an environment in which prosocial instead of antisocial behaviors are supported, encouraged and reinforced.

The gang intervention project

Our research group's fourth ART evaluation (Goldstein, Glick, Carthan & Blancero, 1994), in which trainees were all gang members, also grew from a systems-oriented spirit. If our community-based effort captured that part of the delinquent youths' interpersonal world made up of family members and turned it, at least in part, toward a prosocially reinforcing direction, could the same be done with delinquent gang youths and their peer groups (i.e. other gang members)? Could we use ART not only to teach youths to behave more prosocially but also to increase the likelihood that their prosocial efforts in real life would be met by acceptance, support and even praise from fellow gang members?

This project was conducted in two Brooklyn, New York, community based agencies: the Brownsville Community Neighborhood Action Center and Youth DARES of Coney Island. Each agency conducted three 4-month sequences of ART. Within each sequence, trainees were all members of the same gang. We constituted a control group for each sequence whose members were also from the same gang but from a gang different than the one to which the ART trainees belonged. Thus, across both agencies, 12 different gangs participated in the program—six receiving ART, six as no-ART controls. All the youths, ART and controls, received the same educational, vocational and recreational services offered by the two participating agencies.

Repeated measures analysis of variables crossing project conditions (ART versus control) with time of measurement (pre- versus poststudy) revealed a significant interaction effect favoring ART participants for each of the seven skillstreaming categories—beginning social skills, advanced social skills, skills for dealing with feelings, skill alternatives to aggression, skills for dealing with stress, and planning skills—as well as on a total skills score.

None of the ANOVA comparisons between ART scores and control group scores for the study's measure of anger control yielded significant differences. Of the five community domains, only work adjustment yielded a significant difference. This result accords well with (and no doubt largely reflects) the real-world employment pattern for project participants. For example, in the months immediately following their ART sequence, the majority of the participating Lo-Lives left their gang and took jobs in retail businesses. At an analogous point in time, following their own ART participation, a substantial minority of the participating Baby Wolfpack members obtained employment in the construction trades.

Arrest data were available for the youths participating in our first two ART gang intervention sequences and their respective control groups. Five of the 38 ART participants (13%) and 14 of the 27 control group members (52%) were rearrested during the 8-month tracking period ($\chi^2 = 6.08$,

$p < 0.01$). Our primary rationale for working with intact gangs in this project was the opportunity afforded by such a strategy to capture a major portion of the youth's environment and turn it in a prosocial direction. The question was, once trainees learned specific prosocial behaviors, would the transfer and maintenance of these skills be facilitated or discouraged by the people with whom the youths regularly interacted in the real-world environment? Our favorable outcome verified by rearrest rates implies the possibility that a more harmonious and prosocially promotive post-ART peer environment was created. While it is important for future research to examine this possibility more directly, it is of considerable interest to note that similar rearrest outcomes were obtained in our earlier attempt to create a prosocially reinforcing post-ART environment for delinquent youths by employing this intervention with them and their families. For these youths (ART for self and family), rearrest rates on follow-up were 15 per cent for no-ART control group youths, the comparable figure was 43 per cent. Both of these outcomes from the community-based project closely parallel the outcomes found here (13 and 52%, respectively) for the presence or absence of support from a rather different type of "family"—fellow gang members.

The efficacy evaluations we have described suggest that ART is an effective intervention. It appears to promote the acquisition and performance of skills, improve anger control, decrease the frequency of acting-out behaviors and increase the frequency of prosocial behaviors. Beyond facility walls, its effects persist—less fully perhaps than when the juvenile is in a controlled environment, but the effects persist nonetheless. In general, the potency of the results appears to be sufficiently adequate that its continued implementation and evaluation with chronically aggressive juveniles is clearly warranted. This encouraging conclusion is supported by additional investigations evaluating the efficacy of ART with delinquent and aggressive juveniles that were conducted by other investigators in widely dispersed research sites: Texas (Coleman, Pfeiffer & Oakland, 1991), Pennsylvania (Amendola, pers. comm.), Michigan (White, pers. comm.) Washington State (Curulla, 1990), Ohio (Leeman, Gibbs & Fuller, 1991), Brisbane, Australia (Jones, 1990), and Lima, Peru (Masias & Anicama, 1995).

PROGRAM MANAGEMENT

Management of a four-study, multisite delinquency intervention evaluation program lasting 7 years and involving dozens of facility and agency staff as well as hundreds of delinquent juvenile trainees required diverse planning, training, supervision, data collection, data analysis, budget management and resource coordination efforts. What have these efforts taught us?

Program planning

These investigations were supported by research grants from the New York State Division of Criminal Justice Services, a state agency concerned with the creation, evaluation and dissemination of effective interventions for juvenile delinquents. Three of the four studies described (Annsville, MacCormick and the community) were conducted at New York Sate Division for Youth locations with juvenile delinquents in that agency's charge. The final (gang) program investigation was conducted at two, private non-profit, community-based agencies: The Brownsville Neighborhood Youth Action Center and Youth DARES, both located in Brooklyn, New York.

Our experiences with these programs provide valuable information for both those who seek to replicate this project as well as those who are managing other programs. Starting from the beginning of project planning, project managers must seek to plan not only good science (design, measurement, analysis), but also to conduct skilled consultations and negotiations among the many interested parties. Open, honest and frequent communication among several agencies and facilities maximized our opportunity to reflect their thinking in program planning and meet their needs as they defined them in such plans.

Just as in skillstreaming itself, in which trainee motivation is enhanced when the skill curriculum is negotiated with the trainee, staff motivation to participate in program procedures and implement them is enhanced when major aspects of the program are negotiated. Such a planning strategy need not negate research requirements such as standardization of intervention procedures nor disturb randomness of assignment to a particular condition. However, it does provide all interested parties with a genuine sense of participation in program planning and a shared ownership of program outcomes.

A crucial planning consideration, relevant to both the participatory process as just described and the ultimate design of the research to be conducted, is the notion of rigor–relevance balance. Good intervention evaluation research, in both our view and that of the several agency and staff collaborators with whom we worked, is both experimentally rigorous and highly relevant to the real lives of its recipients. Lindsley (1964) spoke of three orientations to experimentation on intervention effectiveness. The "rigorless magician" orientation is reflected in the "shoot from the hip", "impressions-count-for-everything" stance held by the individual who eschews objective measurement of effect and relies totally on his or her "clinical judgment". At the opposite extreme is the "rigor mortician", so fixated on objective measurement that he or she sacrifices the richness, the uniqueness and the individuality of the phenomena being studied in the effort to obtain standardized measurement information. At an intermediate position, and to be recommended, is the "rigorous clinician". Here, a fruitful balance of the rigor of experimental design and measurement, and relevance to the real world of those being studied, is striven for. Perhaps aided by the fact that our participatory planning team consisted of both principal investigator researchers and agency-staff clinicians, our program-evaluation goal clearly became that of the rigorous clinician.

Training, monitoring and supervision

Program integrity, defined as the degree to which program implementation is faithful to, consistent with or corresponds to the program plan, is primarily a function of three related management activities—training, monitoring and supervision. In each of the studies described, we initiated these functions by distributing to the staff at the participating agencies copies of the training process manual, *Aggression Replacement Training* (Goldstein and Glick, 1987). This manual describes all ART procedures and their implementation in a highly comprehensive, stepwise, concrete manner. We urged the staff to read and reread this manual prior to the next step in the training process, the trainer's workshop. Here, all staff of the participating agencies underwent an intensive, participatory, experiential series of lessons in the actual conduct of ART groups. These workshops also gave the project manager the opportunity, based on overt displays of ART-relevant competence and incompetence, to select from among the workshop participants those staff members who would actually serve as project trainers. The workshops also enabled the project managers to determine which of the three components of the ART staff members were most able and willing to lead.

Once each project's ART sessions with participating juveniles actually began, we initiated an ongoing process of regular monitoring and supervision. This process took several forms, depending partly on the physical distance of the facility or agency from where the project managers were located, but also on the competence levels of particular trainers. We accomplished such monitoring and supervision by regular visits to the training sites where we observed ART sessions in progress and met with the group facilitators afterwards to offer feedback. We supplemented this on-site supervision by requiring trainers to keep weekly session notes, which they mailed to the managers for feedback. We held twice weekly (and often lengthy) telephone conversations. Most of the latter were regularly scheduled, but some occurred on an as-needed basis as issues or crises arose.

Perhaps the most valuable feature of this multipronged training, monitoring and supervision process was the opportunities it provided not only to point out and correct intervention delivery "errors" (trainer behaviors departing from ART manual procedures), but also the chances it offered to "catch trainers being good". Trainers, as the participating juveniles them-selves, are often especially deserving of recognition and praise for skilled enactment of training procedures. Unfortunately, trainers often do not receive this recognition, although it helps to maintain and improve performance.

Each of the two evaluations of ART in residential settings lasted a year. Each of the community and gang ART evaluations lasted 2 years. How do research managers keep staff trainers interested, involved and true to inter-vention procedures as planned during such extended periods? The ART programs offered to participating juveniles within these respective programs were 20–32 sessions long, conducted on a twice- a-week basis. How do trainers keep juveniles with short attention spans, most of whom have found antisocial behavior to be consistently rewarding, interested and motivated to attend, participate in and use the lessons of an intervention designed to teach prosocial alternative behaviors?

Our first answer to these often daunting questions is "it ain't easy!" It was our clear sense in the management of this and other research programs that satisfactory program initiation was conducted much more easily than was satisfactory program maintenance. At launch time, all are often excited and eager to "travel" several miles down the road. However, when implementa-tion feels routine, novelty has long since departed and problems—both anticipated and unexpected—have arisen, the state of continuing to be eagerly involved and rigorous in our application of intervention procedures can and does become problematic.

Maintaining motivation

We used two classes of motivators—extrinsic and intrinsic. Extrinsic moti-vators are tangibles provided in advance of or following competent perform-ance. For staff trainers—in the community and gang studies, but not the institutional studies in which it was not permitted—project grant monies were used to pay for participation. Juveniles were "paid" also, in all four studies, but they were not paid with money. Although we had wanted to offer them money for participation, the funding agency disallowed this request. Instead, we provided them with food; we also provided movie privileges when deserved, and we gave each juvenile a specially designed "Angerbuster" T-shirt, as well as other material reinforcers.

Intrinsic motivators—reinforcers inherent in the intervention itself, or in-tangibles associated with it—began early in each program's implementation. In the two residential studies, before the program began, we placed a series of posters throughout each facility proclaiming in one or another way to both juveniles and staff that ART was coming and that it would provide the juveniles a special opportunity if they participated. For staff, as noted earlier, program participation also was preceded by motivation-enhancing involvement in program planning and decision making. This provided them with a sense of program ownership. As the program developed, for many staff the primary intrinsic motivators became their enhanced sense of professional competence and their enhanced belief that they were significantly intervening for the better in the lives of some very troubled juveniles.

For the juveniles themselves, intrinsic motivation followed primarily from their growing sense that the skills they were learning were, in fact, relevant and functional in their everyday lives in the facility, on the street, at school and at home. We promoted such skill relevance and function, especially after the initial 10 weeks of the program were completed, by regular use of "negotiating the curriculum". Rather than, for example, beginning each skillstreaming session with a staff member modeling a skill, which they had selected, staff members were asked to engage the juveniles in a brief discussion of their current life events and concerns, and from that discussion the skill to be taught was mutually selected. Thus, a juvenile recently fired from his job in a fast food outlet for telling his boss to "shove it" may profitably choose to learn, and be taught the skill "standing up for your rights". The shy juvenile, wanting to reach out to an opposite sex peer but afraid to do so, will become more motivated to remain in the group and learn its lessons if he or she is taught "starting a conversation" and uses it effectively with that peer.

Finally, as both folklore and several hundred studies of the consequences of positive reinforcement make clear, for both the staff trainers and juvenile delinquent trainees, "catching them being good" was our most consistently effective motivation maintainer. For staff, such praise following competent implementation of ART procedures and, for juveniles, such approval following competent skill use (or role playing, homework completion or dilemma discussion) regularly appeared to promote the desire for them to continue their involvement in program activities.

As project managers, we had overall management responsibility for both agency staff and participating juveniles. But agency staff also had management obligations, in their case "hands on", "front line", or "direct care" obligations, including the motivation of trainee attendance and participation. In one of our program's investigations, it was instructive to observe that the two agencies which participated employed contrasting motivational tactics. One, following the lead we sought to operationalize in our own management style, was managed mostly by using the "carrots" of the "carrots and stick" approach—i.e. praise, material reinforcers, communication of both positive expectations for change and staff availability (and eagerness) to assist in such change. The second agency relied much more heavily on the "stick" for its motivational effort, primarily by reiteration of the judge's threat of more time in or a return to detention for failure to attend ART sessions. This latter agency had many times more attendance and management problems over the course of its project participation than did the former.

Coordination of functions and resources

As noted at the outset, a number of organizations and agencies were "interested parties" over the life of this research and evaluation program—a university; a state-agency funding source; two private agencies and a state agency providing implementation sites; media representatives; and a number of state and local political figures. Their interests, with rare exceptions, intersected and were not a source of management difficulty. Yet, they were repeatedly sources requiring management activity. Grant proposals, quarterly project reports, meeting and implementation schedules, budgets, evaluation measures and other reports, forms, memos and accountings each had to be prepared in an accurate and timely manner. Meetings had to be regularly (and sometimes irregularly) prepared for, scheduled and conducted, with an eye to both team building and the project's ultimate evaluation goals. The several interested parties—their sheer number and dispersed locations—also meant many planned and unplanned telephone conversations. In some of these conversations the content mattered a great deal. For some, the act of calling was primarily to solidify the relationship-maintaining goal.

Adding to the picture of diverse and numerous management requirements was the fact that the mass media developed considerable interest in ART, especially as we implemented it with juvenile gangs. Newspaper and television reporters, both local and national, became a presence, first to appreciate, and then to contend with, over the course of the evaluation sequence. They, too, have their own legitimate needs and demands, but on more than a few occasions their presence functioned as an intrusive detriment to appropriate intervention implementation. Tactful, but firm, management intervention proved necessary here (e.g. knowing when and how to say "no", enforcing schedules, protecting confidentiality and so forth).

Data collection and analysis

In operational terms, evaluating the efficacy of ART was a multistage process. While reflecting the primary goal of standardization across conditions and studies, we also had to be responsive to the realities of the participating agencies and institutions. Even given realities—such as staff schedules, other juvenile programs in operation, security needs and confidentiality needs—data collection proceeded in a generally "as planned" manner in all four program studies.

The specific management requirements constituting this aspect of the program included the following:

- the developing and selecting of appropriate evaluation measures;
- duplicating and disseminating measures to study sites;
- instructing site staff in measurement administration;
- preparing a measurement schedule;
- administering tests to participating juveniles and staff as scheduled and in a standardized manner;
- scoring and recording of the measures thus administered;
- conducting appropriate data analyses.

Although we had our share of missing answers, participants who did not show up, last-minute scheduling changes and similar events, the procedures and contents of the measurement effort remained intact.

Management principles

We recommend that administrators or research managers consider following a more general, strategic set of valuable management principles as they design and implement their own ART programs.

1. Give respect to get respect. The biblical teaching urging you to do unto others as you would have them do unto you is an especially valuable management principle for successful program implementation. Ideally, the project manager will—with consistency and initiative—seek to overtly demonstrate respect for each participating staff member's job knowledge and skill performance. The program-implementing staff members, in turn, should be urged to display similarly respectful attitudes and behaviors, when appropriate, toward participating juveniles' opinions, choices and overt behaviors. When staff members perceive themselves and their work to be respected, on-line performance of project responsibilities may be enhanced, feedback may more freely be given and received and staff self-esteem may be favorably affected. Similarly beneficial consequences can also emerge as participating trainees experienced respect from staff and one another.
2. Employ and encourage open and honest communication. Underpinning the effort to promote mutual respect is open and honest communication between and among management, staff and juveniles. Not only staff but especially participating juveniles, know when half-truths are being told

or information is being withheld. Such departures from open and "straight up" communication can seriously sabotage important aspects of program procedure. We urge, on both ethical and pragmatic grounds, that "telling it like it is" be adopted as a management principle. Even when the message is more work for the person to whom we are speaking, or disappointing, open and honest communication must be sought. The adage: "We can agree to disagree" can provide a basis for open dialogue and honest interchange.

3. Define roles and responsibilities clearly. Early and open communication is especially necessary, in regard to who is to do what, when and how, as well as who "reports" to whom, about what and when. Such clear definition of roles and responsibilities is the backbone of successful program management. It must be made explicit to study participants as early as the initial invitation. If offered early and explicitly, discussed openly and concretized fully so that cross-cutting lines of authority and obligation are minimized, subsequent role/responsibility confusion or conflict is less likely to occur.

4. Share project planning, process and product. In a number of ways, a research program will benefit greatly when decision making about its substance and implementation, as well as the fruits it yields, are not owned exclusively by its management but, instead, are genuinely shared. In addition to "up front" matters such as program planning and process, the sense of ownership and participatory sharing also should fully characterize project products. The "products" of the present program were most importantly the intangible sense of accomplishment as juveniles changed, became less aggressive and more prosocially skilled, dropped out of gangs, stayed out of juvenile detention, got jobs or went back to school. These were big victories, with credit to all participants openly offered. Such a spirit of shared ownership should and did characterize tangible products of the program. This included invitation to professional meetings, workshops or other agencies to describe the program and its results; joint authorship of descriptive articles, chapters and monographs; and financial remuneration for one's project time and effort. Clearly, the shared ownership of project planning, process and product meant a better project in all three regards.

The management strategies we have described and the management tactics we have sought to implement form an ethically responsible and pragmatically functional means for planning and conducting a long-term research program, as well as for disseminating its outcomes. Used conscientiously, such strategies and tactics can yield utilitarian research outcomes fully reflecting the rigor–relevance balance sought by rigorous clinicians.

References

Arbuthnot, J., & Gordon, D. A. (1983). Moral reasoning development in correctional intervention. *Journal of Correctional Education*, **34**(2), 133–138.

Coleman, M., Pfeiffer, S., & Oakland, T. (1991). *Aggression Replacement Training with Behavior Disordered Adolescents*, Unpublished, University of Texas.

Curulla, V. L. (1990). *Aggression Replacement Training in the Community for Adult Learning Disabled Offenders*. Unpublished, University of Washington.

Feindler, E. L., Marriott, S. A., & Iwata, M. (1984). Group anger control training for junior high school delinquents. *Cognitive Therapy and Research*, **8**(4), 299–311.

Gibbs, J. (1999). Moral reasoning training. In A. P. Goldstein (Ed.), *The Prepare Curriculum*. Champaign, IL: Research Press.

Gibbs, J., Basinger, K. S., & Fuller, D. (1992). *Moral Maturity: Measuring the Development of Sociomoral Reflection*. Hillsdale, NJ: Erlbaum.

Goldstein, A. P., & Glick, B. (1987). *Aggression Replacement Training*. Champaign, IL: Research Press.

Goldstein, A. P., Glick, B., Carthan, M., & Blancero, D. (1994). *The Prosocial Gang: Implementing Aggression Replacement Training*. Thousand Oaks, CA: Sage.

Goldstein, A. P., Glick, B., Irwin, M. J., Pask-McCartney, C., & Rubama, I. (1989). *Reducing Delinquency: Intervention in the Community*. New York: Pergamon Press.

Goldstein, A. P., Sprafkin, R., Gershaw, J., & Klein, P. (1980). *Skillstreaming the Adolescent*. Champaign, IL: Research Press.

Jones, Y. (1990). *Aggression Replacement Training in a High School Setting*, Unpublished, Center for Learning and Adjustment Difficulties, Brisbane, Australia.

Kohlberg, L. (1969). Stage and sequence: The cognitive-developmental approach to socialization. In D. A. Goslin (Ed.), *Handbook of Socialization Theory and Research*. Chicago: Rand McNally.

Kohlberg, L. (Ed.) (1973). *Collected Papers on Moral Development and Moral Education*. Cambridge, MA: Harvard University, Center for Moral Education.

Leeman, L. W., Gibbs, J., & Fuller, D. (1991). *Evaluation of Multi-component Treatment Program for Juvenile Delinquents*, Unpublished, Ohio State University.

Maltz, D. (1984). *Recidivism*. New York: Academic Press.

Masias, C., & Anicama, J. (1995). *Experiencias en la Applicación de Programa Preventivo y de Sustitución de la Violencia: El Programa ART en Drogas, Violencia y Ecología*. Lima: Cedro.

Meichenbaum, D. (1977). *Cognitive Behavior Modification: An Integrative Approach*. New York: Plenum.

McGinnis, E., & Goldstein, A. P. (1984). *Skillstreaming the Elementary School Child*. Champaign, IL: Research Press.

McGinnis, E., & Goldstein, A. P. (1990). *Skillstreaming in Early Childhood*. Champaign, IL: Research Press.

Novaco, R. W. (1975). *Anger Control: The Development and Evaluation of an Experimental Treatment*. Lexington, MA: Lexington Books.

Zimmerman, D. (1983). Moral education. In *Prevention and Control of Aggression*, Center for Research on Aggression. New York: Pergamon Press.

Chapter 7

IN SEARCH OF PROGRAM IMPLEMENTATION: 792 REPLICATIONS OF THE TEACHING-FAMILY MODEL

DEAN L. FIXSEN,* KAREN A. BLASE,[†] GARY D. TIMBERS[‡] AND MONTROSE M. WOLF[§]

* FYI Consulting, Calgary, Alberta, Canada
[†] Calgary Women's Emergency Shelter, Calgary, Alberta, Canada
[‡] BIABH Study Center, Morganton, North Carolina, USA
[§] Department of Human Development & Family Life, University of Kansas, Lawrence, Kansas, USA

This chapter discusses a solution-oriented and incremental approach to solving major social problems. If we are to solve important social problems, such as child abuse, delinquency and illiteracy, researchers need to generate effective programs that can be replicated and social service providers need to implement those programs with fidelity. The Teaching-Family Model, based on over 30 years of research, evaluation and program experience, has been replicated across North America. We present an analysis of 792 attempted replications over a period of 15 years. The analysis reveals certain aspects of the treatment program that were found to be sufficient conditions for treatment program implementation and survival. These "site

Offender Rehabilitation in Practice. Edited by G. A. Bernfeld, D. P. Farrington and A. W. Leschied.
© 2001 John Wiley & Sons, Ltd.

services" are described and the implications for effective practices in services for children are presented.

Children, families and vulnerable adults face a multitude of problems in our society. The statistics are clear and the newspapers each day carry personal reminders of the tragedies that abound in families, schools and neighborhoods across North America. For a number of these difficult problems, the popular conception is that "nothing works". Juvenile delinquency, teenage pregnancy, school dropouts, illiteracy, poverty, low birth weight babies, child abuse and neglect, domestic violence, and so on seem to occur at alarming rates in spite of our efforts as a society.

Part of the problem lies with the kinds of research that have been supported for the past several decades across North America. During his term as president of the American Psychological Association, Frank Farley (1994) identified this issue and suggested a change in the research agenda:

> I want SOLUTIONS to the problems confronting us. We already KNOW THE STATISTICS. Psychology has the greatest potential of any creation of the human mind in the past several centuries to SOLVE some of these dreadful problems and we must focus on those SOLUTIONS. We need more solution-oriented research, more research directed at solving these massive human problems. Significant parts of our research establishment have for decades been enslaved in a publish or perish paradigm they can't seem to break out of, and it often encourages quick studies on easy and minor problems. According to citation analyses, the overwhelming majority of published studies have no demonstrable effect on anyone, anywhere, anytime, and the vast submerged corpus of unpublished research presumably has even less impact! These are often clever studies, bringing to bear monumental research methods and skills upon minor topics apparently to no end. No end, at least, where the critical problems confronting the human race are concerned.
>
> (p. 3, capitalization in the original)

Another part of the problem lies with the providers of human services. Many research and evaluation studies have pointed to effective intervention processes but these are often ignored or are "conceptually adopted" without significant change in actual services. Lipsey (1992) examined over 400 studies of treatment for delinquent behavior and found that:

> "When the researcher was more closely involved in the design, implementation, and monitoring of treatment, the effects were larger. While this could reflect some experimenter bias artifact, it is also plausible that it represents the effects of greater treatment integrity, i.e., consistent delivery of the treatment as intended to all clients.
>
> (p. 10)

Shadish (1984) studied adoption rates of social science solutions and found that:

When an attempt is made to implement those solutions, powerful social networks are activated whose interests have been ignored and who are, therefore, often hostile to implementing the solution.

(p. 727)

There is no doubt that applied research is difficult to do and that organizational changes to accommodate new intervention strategies and techniques are fraught with barriers and administrative headaches. These also is no doubt that our society needs to find ways to work toward solutions to these problems so that we can begin to see incremental improvements over time for all children in North America. The human suffering and the costs to society are too great to ignore.

IMPLEMENTATION

Other than most chemical interventions and some surgical interventions, any treatment endeavor in the human services is labor intensive. It is the skillful interaction of a practitioner with a child, parent or other adult that produces benefits. The more difficult the problem, the more skillful and complete the performance of the practitioner must be in order to achieve a beneficial outcome. The practitioner–child or practitioner–adult interaction is where and how treatment is actualized in the human services.

What do practitioners implement? Consider for a moment Table 7.1 concerning treatment procedures or whole treatment programs. Poor outcomes are relatively easy to achieve while good outcomes only occur under specific conditions. Thus, if we are to solve important social problems researchers need to generate effective programs that can be replicated and practitioners need to implement those programs with fidelity. Under those conditions we can produce good outcomes. Anything else results in the status quo: poor outcomes for children and families and social problems that remain intractable from one generation to the next.

Table 7.1   The sources of good outcomes for children and families

Program characteristics	Poorly implemented	Well implemented
Replicable effectiveness	Poor outcome	Good outcome
Non-replicable effectiveness	Poor outcome	Poor outcome

The Teaching-Family Model

Any discussion of implementation begs the questions of implementation of what, by whom, when, under what conditions, how? If implementation is "a means to some end" (*Webster's New World Dictionary*, 1972), what are the "means" and what is the "end"? There must be a plan in order to have implementation. Usually, in human services we are referring to some procedure or set of procedures intended to provide benefits to people. That is "what" we are trying to implement. For many of us working with difficult children and families, the plan is the Teaching-Family Model (see also Chapter 8 by Gary Bernfeld in this book).

The Teaching-Family Model was initiated in 1967 with the opening of Achievement Place, a group home for delinquent children. In the 1960s, 1970s and 1980s the National Institute of Mental Health (NIMH) Center for the Study of Crime and Delinquency provided funding for research on treatment and for evaluation of the Teaching-Family training and replication efforts across the United States. The product of this effort is a treatment model that has demonstrated generality as it has been adapted to community-based and campus-based treatment agencies; to treatment foster care, home-based treatment and classroom service delivery settings; and to children and adults with a variety of problems such as severe mental health problems, mental handicaps, autism, abuse and neglect, educational delays, substance abuse and so on (Phillips, 1968; Phillips, Phillips, Fixsen & Wolf, 1974; Braukmann, Fixsen, Phillips & Wolf, 1975; Black, Downs, Brown & Bastien, 1984; Blase, Fixsen & Phillips, 1984; McClannahan, Krantz, McGee & MacDuff, 1984; Fixsen & Blase, 1993; Blase, 1994; Wolf, Kirigin, Fixsen, Blase & Braukmann 1995).

Goals of the Teaching-Family Model

The goals of the Teaching-Family Model were specified in *The Teaching-Family Handbook* (Phillips et al., 1974) and have been adopted by the Teaching-Family Association (1994). The goals are to be:

- Humane: Characterized by compassion, consideration, respect, acceptance, positive regard, cultural sensitivity and adherence to the *Standards of Ethical Conduct of the Teaching-Family Association* (1993).
- Effective: Progress toward resolving referral issues and achieving treatment goals, with high expectations for improvement and low tolerance for deviance. Research and evaluation demonstrate the current helpfulness of practices and provide for the systematic evolution of the Teaching-Family Model.
- Individualized: Each aspect of the program is tailored to the unique history, strengths and needs of each child and family. The treatment

goals are based on the special needs of the child and family as assessed by family members and referral agents, in conjunction with the observations and descriptions of behavior by the practitioner.

- Satisfactory to stakeholders: The program applications are satisfactory to children, parents, allied professionals, referral sources and funding agents with respect to the cooperation, communication, effectiveness and concern of the practitioner.
- Cost efficient: The program is affordable, practical and do-able with respect to costs related to treatment and support systems.
- Replicable: The program is teachable, practical and do-able with respect to treatment implementation and support systems.
- Integrated: The program seeks to simultaneously achieve all of the above goals. No one goal can be emphasized to the detriment of any other goal.

Teaching-parents in group homes

To accomplish these goals, each Teaching-Family group home treatment program is directed by a married couple known as teaching-parents. They, along with one or two assistants, are the practitioners who comprise the sole staff of a group home for up to 7 youths. The couple lives in the home 24 hours a day, 7 days a week. The availability of a live-in couple facilitates consistent treatment, localizes accountability, models family-style living and facilitates cost-effective treatment. Teaching-parents have wide-ranging responsibilities. They design and carry out treatment procedures to correct problem behaviors and to teach appropriate alternative behavior. They supervise the activities of the youths in school, in the community, in their natural homes and in the group home. They establish and maintain positive relationships with the parents of the youths, the juvenile court, the social service department, the schools, the mental health department, community civic groups and so on. They are responsible for working with a board of directors or other administrative entity to develop budgets and policies to operate the home (Phillips et al., 1974).

The Teaching-Family Model was established on the strength of research on the behavior of delinquent children residing in group homes (see Braukmann & Fixsen, 1975; Fixsen & Blase, 1993; and Wolf et al., 1995 for summaries of the research on treatment practices). Research is important, but it is only a first step. To be helpful, the research findings must be useful in context (e.g. group home, classroom, foster home, therapist's office). Interventions have to be feasible and effective in the actual environments where people live, learn, work and play. Thus, the single-variable approach to research in the laboratory is replaced by a multi-component approach to research in human service settings (Reppucci & Saunders, 1974).

For example, "Our original idea for improving school behavior was to teach the school teachers how to use the token economy in school. We quickly discovered, however, that the teachers were not very enthusiastic about having our youths in their classrooms let alone the extra work involved in learning and implementing a token economy for them" (Wolf et al., 1995, p. 16). This led to the creation of a "daily report card" that was simple for the teachers to use and still led to large improvements in the youths' social and academic behaviors in the classroom (Bailey, Wolf & Phillips, 1970). Experiences like this led us down the road toward mission-oriented research and program development (Fixsen, Phillips & Wolf, 1978).

Thus, the treatment setting must be seen as a "natural laboratory" where research is conducted to find practical solutions to everyday problems. In these natural laboratories, research and practice exert a mutual influence and each stimulates progress in the other. In this way, more studies can be done that have applications and not just implications for clinical practice (Azrin, 1977).

The research and evaluation data on the effectiveness of the procedures and processes that define the Teaching-Family Model can be accessed in the literature (see the references at the end of this chapter) and are not the subject of this chapter. In this chapter we will focus our attention on the empirical bases for the processes we have found to be useful and practical over the past 30 years for assessing and assuring implementation at several levels of treatment and program operations.

15 YEARS OF IMPLEMENTATION DATA

Achievement Place, the prototype group home for the Teaching-Family Model, opened in 1967. The data presented below cover the period from 1967 through 31 December 1982, a 15-year period. During the 15-year period covered by the data, the Teaching-Family Model was conceived, developed and replicated in group homes across the United States. As shown in Figure 7.1, during this time a total of 792 couples (the teaching-parents who operate Teaching-Family group homes) participated in training and started work in 303 Teaching-Family group homes. The data represent a total of 1,077 "Teaching-Parent years" of experience in providing treatment to delinquent, abused, neglected, emotionally handicapped mentally handi-capped, and autistic children nationally.

Figure 7.1 shows that the growth of Teaching-Family Model group homes was fairly linear from 1972 through 1982 with about 30 new homes added each year. The number of teaching-parents increased in a more geometric fashion as more couples were being recruited and trained for existing group homes (replacement couples) as well as new ones (new home couples). The

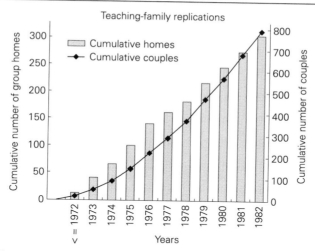

Figure 7.1   The cumulative number of teaching-parent couples (bar graph) and the cumulative number of Teaching-Family group homes operating (line graph) for the years 1967 through 1982.

303 Teaching-Family group homes were located in 32 different states and in one Canadian province.

As noted above, human services are labor intensive. Thus, each practitioner is a replication of a treatment program and these data represent 792 attempted replications of the Teaching-Family Model. This huge range of data provides an excellent opportunity to look at program implementation empirically to see what makes a difference.

Initial replication attempts

First, however, we should note that the development, replication and implementation of the Teaching-Family Model did not occur in the nice linear fashion implied by Figure 7.1. It almost ended in 1971 when we attempted our first replication of the Achievement Place group home program (see Blase et al., 1984 and Wolf et al., 1995 for a more complete description of the early replication experiences).

A nearby community had called and asked us to help them establish a group home "like Achievement Place". It took us almost 2 years to obtain the funding, locate and renovate the house, secure the necessary zoning and licensing, find a couple brave enough to be the teaching-parents, and prepare the couple by having them participate in the best academic masters degree program that we could offer at the University of Kansas.

As soon as the new group home opened and youths started living with our new teaching-parents, it was clear that things were not going well. The youths were fighting among themselves, defiant, running away, skipping school and generally creating mayhem. Clearly, this was not a replication of the beautiful program that had been created at Achievement Place! We started driving back and forth between the two homes comparing the new couple and what they did with Lonnie and Elaine Phillips, the teaching-parents who were doing so well at Achievement Place. We spent hours each day observing and making video tapes and audio tapes trying to figure out what the differences were. As soon as we thought we had found something, we tried to get the new couple to implement it to see if things improved.

After a few months of this, the board of directors called us to a meeting and fired us! Fortunately, we had already started two more attempted replications by this time and these other two homes continued to provide us with a replication laboratory while we learned our lessons the hard way. Otherwise, the whole enterprise might have ended with that first dramatic failure to replicate.

Lessons from a failure to replicate

Out of this difficult and embarrassing experience, some hard lessons were learned. First, the hours of observation and videotapes helped us to discover the 'teaching interaction' and reminded us of the importance of relationships. Lonnie and Elaine Phillips easily established warm and caring relationships with the youths and others and were natural teachers of a huge range of social behaviors at Achievement Place. They were so natural that we never saw how they did it until we had the second couple as a comparison. Since then, the teaching interaction has been refined and evaluated (Phillips et al., 1974: Ford, 1974; Bedlington et al., 1978; Ford, Evans, & Dworkin, 1982) and has become the cornerstone of the entire Teaching-Family Model.

Second, the masters degree training turned out to be ineffective and impractical with respect to teaching specific treatment skills. It was too much to ask trainees to translate theory and general statements of principles into actual effective practices, and 18 months of attending classes was not timely or practical for widespread dissemination in any case. Thus, a 1-week preservice workshop was created (Braukmann, Fixsen, Kirigin et al., 1975) that provided introductory information and lots of behavior rehearsals specifically designed to teach the skills needed to work with delinquent children in a group home.

Third, after that first disaster, we wanted to get our feedback in smaller doses and in a more timely manner while we still had a chance to do something about it. To this end, we established an evaluation system

(Phillips, Phillips, Fixsen, and Wolf, 1974) to regularly solicit the opinions of consumers such as parents, teachers, social service workers, court workers and board members via mail out questionnaires and telephone interviews. In addition, a youth interview was developed to get the opinions of the children who lived in the group home regarding the behavior of the teaching-parents and the care and treatment being provided. Finally, a professional in-home evaluation was included to directly observe and rate the skills being acquired by the youths, the skills of the teaching-parents in using the treatment components and the development of other components of the Teaching-Family Model such as family-style living.

Fourth, criteria were established to certify teaching-parents and recognize their full implementation of the Teaching-Family Model (Phillips et al., 1974; Braukmann et al., 1975). An initial evaluation was scheduled about 6 months after completion of the preservice workshop then an annual evaluation was scheduled at 12 months after the preservice workshop and annually thereafter. Any couple who met criterion on each evaluation component on an annual evaluation were certified as professional teaching-parents. This meant that the couple had to achieve a score of "satisfied" (6.0) or better on a 7-point scale that ranged from "completely satisfied" (7.0) to "completely dissatisfied" (1.0) on the consumer evaluation, youth evaluation and professional in-home evaluation components.

Putting our lessons to good use

We quickly put our newly discovered information to use in 1972 and by the end of that year the fourth set of teaching-parents, Gary and Barbara Timbers, became the first couple to successfully replicate the Achievement Place/Teaching-Family Model group home program. In addition, the first replication couple decided they still wanted to be teaching-parents and went through the revised training before becoming teaching-parents in another group home. They did very well as teaching-parents, were certified and enjoyed a long tenure in that home. Clearly, the new training course was more functional.

With this bit of encouragement we cautiously proceeded with more attempted replications of the Teaching-Family Model. We held "dissemination conferences" where we invited 30–40 decision makers at a time (e.g. juvenile judges, welfare directors, researchers, political leaders) to Kansas where we described the Teaching-Family Model and had them visit Achievement Place or one of the replication homes nearby. We also sent out information on the model to anyone who asked. And, we continued to publish research, to present at professional meetings and to participate in professional and public discussions of delinquency, mental health and community-based programming issues.

As Figure 7.1 shows, there was no shortage of interested individuals and groups who wanted to replicate the Teaching-Family Model.

An analysis of proximity

By 1975 our organization in Kansas had attempted 60 replications of the Teaching-Family Model group home treatment program in Kansas and in 17 other states. As we did training and evaluations for new homes we also began losing group homes as couples left and were not replaced by teaching-parents or the boards decided to close their homes.

The loss of homes was cause for considerable concern. Each group home represented a significant investment in terms of the start up resources to purchase and furnish a home, the effort required to clear all the zoning hurdles and obtain a license to operate, the time needed to establish referral and funding sources, the education of teachers, board members, neighbors and other consumers; the cost of recruiting and training and evaluating teaching-parent couples and so on. Thus, the loss of a group home was a worrisome and costly problem.

Figure 7.2 shows an analysis of the first 60 replication group homes for the Kansas organization. As we analyzed the results for these homes, we found that 52 per cent of the in-state homes continued to operate for 5 years or more while only 17 per cent of the out-of-state homes operated that long.

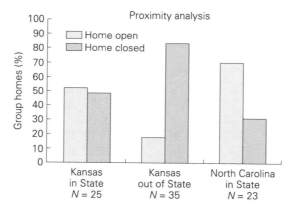

Figure 7.2 The impact of proximity of the group home and the support staff on the survival rates of Teaching-Family group homes sponsored by the Kansas staff and by the staff in North Carolina.

We began looking at our own behavior and found that we knew a lot more about the Kansas homes. We were there more often to give advice and support and help solve problems, the teaching-parents came to see us more often, we called them more often and so on. Proximity seemed to be very important to these communication and support functions.

At about this same time we began to see the spectacular results coming from our colleagues in North Carolina as well. In 1973 three graduate students from the University of Kansas (Gary Timbers, Karen Blase, Dennis Maloney) had moved to Morganton to start a new organization of group homes to serve children in the western half of North Carolina. All three had participated in the Kansas training and research efforts in support of Teaching-Family homes.

When we analyzed the data from the Teaching-Family group homes in North Carolina we found an even more positive result. As shown in Figure 7.2, over 70 per cent of their homes (all in-state) operated for 5 years or more.

Proximity allowed more frequent contact, more support and more immediate assistance with program implementation problems, all of which seemed to be related in important ways to the survival rates of the Teaching-Family group homes.

The Teaching-Family Association

In 1975 we began a series of meetings involving the organizations that were training and supporting teaching-parents in the United States. Given the diversity in locations, populations served, operating requirements of different states and so on we decided to try and define the essential elements of the Teaching-Family Model and develop an organization to set national standards for teaching-parent certification and standards governing the organizations providing training and support for teaching-parents. In 1978 the first meeting of the Teaching-Family Association was held with teaching-parents and support staff convening to share their procedures and their research.

Between 1975 and 1978 the participants in these meetings defined the key aspects of *organizations* of Teaching-Family Model homes (we call them Teaching-Family sites). The staff at Teaching-Family sites provide staff selection, preservice and inservice training, ongoing staff consultation, staff evaluations, program evaluation and facilitative administration to group homes within reasonable proximity (usually 2–3 hours driving time) to the training and support staff.

The keys to implementation

The Teaching-Family Association (1980) published a directory listing all the Teaching-Family group homes that were affiliated with a Teaching-Family

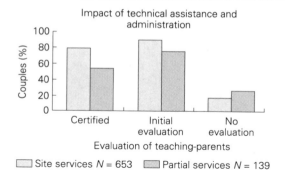

Figure 7.3   The impact of site support services (i.e. selection, training, consultation, evaluation, administration) on implementation of the Teaching-Family Model.

site and, therefore, had been receiving the full complement of services (i.e. selection, training, consultation, evaluation, administration) mandated by the Teaching-Family Association through the end of 1979.

This permitted an interesting comparison. Using the Teaching-Family Association directory as the guide, we found that 653 couples had received the preservice training, in-home consultation, regular evaluation and facilitative administrative supports mandated by the Teaching-Family Association. The remaining 139 couples had received preservice training and evaluation services, but not the full complement of site services.

Figure 7.3 shows the results of this analysis. Those teaching-parent couples who received full site services were certified (annually) more often (79 versus 53%) and received the initial evaluation (after 6 months) more often (89 versus 75%). These data point to more complete implementation of the Teaching-Family Model by those couples who received full site services that included consultation and administrative support in addition to preservice training and evaluation.

The percentages in Figure 7.3 are based on eligibility for evaluation. That is, in the site services group there were 394 couples who had been in the home 365 days or longer and were eligible for the certification evaluation, 546 couples who had been in the home for 183 days or longer and were eligible for the initial evaluation and 107 couples who had been in the home for less than 183 days and were not eligible for an evaluation yet. Comparable numbers for the partial services group are 64, 104 and 35 couples.

We also looked at the survival rates of the group homes and found another dramatic difference. Figure 7.4 shows that only 17 per cent of the 219 group homes that received site services closed within 5 years while 85 per cent of the 84 group homes that received only partial services (training and evaluation) closed within 5 years. These results are very clear. Those teaching-parent couples who received the full complement of site services

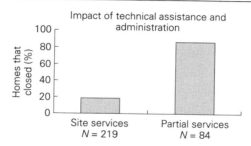

Figure 7.4 The impact of site support services (i.e. selection, training, consultation, evaluation, administration) on survival rates for Teaching-Family group homes.

(i.e. selection, training, consultation, evaluation, administration) achieved certification criteria 1.5 times more often and the group homes closed at a rate that was one-fifth that for homes receiving partial services (i.e. staff training and evaluation). Thus, site services were related to greater implementation of the Teaching-Family Model resulting in higher quality services and better survival rates.

CONCLUSION

The first 15 years of research and development of the Teaching-Family Model demonstrated that it is possible to generate effective programs that can be replicated and implemented carefully. Achievement Place provided a prototype for developing the treatment program and the attempted replications provided a natural laboratory for developing the support systems necessary to assure routine implementation by practitioners. Research and practice have exerted a mutual, beneficial influence at each stage.

The data from the first 792 teaching-parent couples and the first 303 Teaching-Family group homes have several implications for practices in programs for delinquent children and for other human services as well:

1. Having well-researched procedures working well in a prototype program is a good place to start, but it is not sufficient to assure replicability and implementation. Replication of the prototype is a critical step in the development of the prototype program itself. As Sidman (1960) pointed out, replication is the key to science and the key to real knowledge. This was certainly true in the evolution of the Teaching-Family Model. Our early replication attempts provided the laboratory for us to learn what was really critical to the success we had seen at Achievement Place, the prototype group home. Comparing, contrasting, evaluating as

best we could, implementing new knowledge as quickly as we could and puzzling over what we were missing set the stage for further description and elaboration of the treatment model itself.

2. Program development and widespread implementation is mostly an inductive process where we start with a problem, look for a solution and take data of some kind to serve as a guide as we oscillate our way toward our goal. This idea might be best illustrated by the cartoon that says, "Ready, fire, aim." As more replications of the treatment model were opened, we were presented with a variety of problems and barriers that had to be overcome to allow others to use the treatment model (e.g. government regulations, community concerns, funding, etc). Practical issues internal to the operations of the treatment unit regarding time management, costs, staff turnover, recruitment, personnel issues, etc. also began to surface and had to be dealt with in a programmatic way. We also discovered there are many aspects to operating a treatment environment, with treatment planning and treatment procedures being just two of many (see Table 8.1 in this book). To be successful, a treatment approach must be able to comfortably fit within existing operating structures or must be able to specify new ones and be able to create them to fit the treatment program. As program developers, we had to look beyond our immediate interests in treatment and see the broader context in which we operated. Treatment can only exist and flourish in a supportive environment where the various parts are working in concert. In addition, the treatment model itself must compete for survival and for effectiveness on a scale that exposes the whole enterprise to the vagaries of larger systems of politics, finance and community influences (see also Bernfeld, Blase & Fixsen, 1990, for a further discussion of these factors).

3. All the time and attention given to changing the behavior of children begins to pale compared to the time and effort required to initiate and sustain program settings and adult staff behavior across replications in order to assure implementation. For example, Teaching-Family site services that were critical to the quality of care provided to children and families and to the longer term survival of the services themselves included (see also Table 8.3 in this book):

    a. staff selection;
    b. staff training;
    c. staff supervision and treatment consultation;
    d. staff evaluation;
    e. facilitative administration and program management.

4. Human services are labor intensive. In a very real sense, the practitioner *is* the treatment program. We have found that we can teach many of the

important skills needed to be a good practitioner of the Teaching-Family Model. Still, there are many skills and approaches to life that we need to select for during the hiring process. These include caring and commitment, common sense, intelligence, willingness to learn, philosophical fit and background knowledge.

5.   The work with children and families is too important to leave to mom and pop couples who have raised their own children or to whatever skills BA or MA level staff may have. Program-specific training must be provided to assure implementation of procedures and coordination of efforts. Thus, as soon as a practitioner is employed in a Teaching-Family treatment setting, a 1-year training program commences. First, we provide a 6-day, skill-oriented preservice workshop to teach the basic skills involved in providing Teaching-Family treatment. Then we provide "shadow training" where a consultant (described below) shares responsibility for decision making and implementing treatment for a few weeks. The consultant and the practitioner work on *in vivo* skill development and applications and work on clinical judgement and implementation of values and philosophy in the context of daily interactions with children, families and staff. We need to make sure the child and family get the treatment they need at the same time that the new practitioner is learning the basics.

6.   A consultant/supervisor is needed to facilitate implementation by focusing on the professional development of the practitioner (especially treatment planning, treatment implementation and clinical judgement). The consultant provides coaching for skill development as well as personal and emotional support to each practitioner. It is the nature of work with children and families that a practitioner will come face to face with his or her own issues in one family or another. The consultant can help practitioners over these personal hurdles while maintaining quality treatment for children and families. Consultants have a very important role in the Teaching-Family Model. Consultants integrate treatment, training, consultation, evaluation and administrative systems and promote a systematic flow of information among all these program components. They help to conduct interviews to select practitioners, they are trainers and evaluators, they are the supervisors of practitioners within the organizational scheme of things, they tutor and support new practitioners, they help deal with difficult child and family issues and they contribute in many ways to the development of new treatment technology and operating systems. Almost without exception, consultants started out as practitioners and then obtained the extra training to become consultants.

7.   Regular evaluations of staff performance is another key to implementation of replicable procedures. For example, to be certified as a practitioner

in the Teaching-Family Model a practitioner must participate in and successfully complete a series of events over the course of 1 year. This includes:

a. complete the preservice workshop;
b. receive regular consultation and supervision;
c. complete the initial performance evaluation at 6 months;
d. continue to receive regular consultation and supervision;
e. complete the annual performance evaluation;
f. meet all criteria and ethical standards on the annual evaluation.

Certification must be renewed each year by completing the annual performance evaluation and meeting all criteria and ethical standards. A practitioner performance evaluation at 6 months, 12 months and annually thereafter has four main parts:

a. Youth consumer evaluation: Children are interviewed by an evaluator and asked to provide ratings and comments about the practitioner's cooperation, communication, effectiveness, fairness, concern, helpfulness and availability.
b. Staff practices evaluation: Children are interviewed by an evaluator and asked about any potential abusive practices used by staff. This interview helps to prevent and detect practices that might infringe on the youths' rights and safety.
c. General consumer evaluation: A brief questionnaire is mailed out to parents; all mental health, court and social service employees that have involvement with each child; all the youths' teachers and principals; and other stakeholder agencies asking them to provide ratings and comments about the practitioner's cooperation, communication, effectiveness and advocacy.
d. Professional in-home evaluation: Two qualified evaluators review the treatment plan and treatment efforts made to date, then directly observe the treatment being provided over a 2–4 hour visit. The evaluators systematically review motivation system records and youth files and directly observe and rate treatment planning, teaching skills, relationships with youths, use of the motivation systems, use of self-government systems, family-style living, intervention progress, clinical judgement and record keeping.

8. Successful treatment programs require an organization that has clear goals, clear philosophy, clear lines of communication, well-practised feedback loops and integrity at the point of implementation. With everything working in harmony, good treatment practices have a chance to be implemented with excellence. We have found that the performance of practitioners embodies the performance of the entire program model.

The performance of practitioners reflects how well the selection process worked, how good the preservice training was, how well the consultation process has functioned and the degree to which administrative practices actually facilitate the treatment processes. No one evaluation will provide enough information on these broader issues, but looking across 5 or 10 or 20 evaluations starts to point out where consistent problems are occurring and where program efforts need to be focused. Thus, the performance evaluations for practitioners are the prompts for administrators and other staff to make continuous, incremental improvements to the treatment model itself and to the overall operations of the agency.

This may seem like a lot of work and administrators always wonder where the funds will come from to recruit and support practitioners in these ways. But, the data are clear. If we want well-implemented treatment programs that benefit children and families in a sustained manner, these are the supports we must offer. Otherwise, we will continue using public resources that only maintain the status quo: poor outcomes for children and families and social problems that remain intractable from one generation to the next.

References

Azrin, N. H. (1977). A strategy for applied research: Learning based but outcome oriented. *American Psychologist*, **February**, 140–149.

Bailey, J. S., Wolf, M. M., & Phillips, E. L. (1970). Home-based reinforcement and the modification of pre-delinquents' classroom behavior. *Journal of Applied Behavior Analysis*, **3**, 223–233.

Bedlington, M. M., Solnick, J. V., Schumaker, J. B., Braukmann, C. J., Kirigin, K. A., & Wolf, M. M. (1978). *Evaluating Group Homes: The Relationship between Parenting Behaviors and Delinquency*, Paper presented at the American Psychological Association Convention, Toronto, Ontario.

Bernfeld, G. A., Blase, K. A., & Fixsen, D. L. (1990). Towards a unified perspective on human service delivery systems: Application of the Teaching-Family Model. In R. J. McMahon & R. DeV. Peters (Eds), *Behavior Disorders of Adolescence*, pp. 191–205. New York: Plenum.

Black, D., Downs, J., Brown, L., & Bastien, J. (1984). *Social Skills in the School*. Boys Town, NE: Father Flanagan's Boys' Home.

Blase, K. A. (1994). *School-based Teaching Interactions and Motivation Systems*. Calgary, Alberta: FYI Consulting.

Blase, K., Fixsen, D., & Phillips, E. (1984). Residential treatment for troubled children: Developing service delivery systems. In S. C. Paine, G. T. Bellamy & B. Wilcox (Eds), *Human Services that Work: From Innovation to Standard Practice*, pp. 149–165. Baltimore, MD: Paul H. Brookes Publishing.

Braukmann, C. J., & Fixsen, D. L. (1975). Behavior modification with delinquents. In M. Hersen, R. M. Eisler & P. M. Miller (Eds), *Progress in Behavior Modification*, Vol. 1, pp. 191–231. New York: Academic.

Braukmann, C. J., Fixsen, D. L., Kirigin, K. A., Phillips, E. A., Phillips, E. L., & Wolf, M. M. (1975). Achievement Place: The training and certification of teaching-parents. In W. S. Wood (Ed.), *Issues in Evaluating Behavior Modification*, pp. 131–152. Champaign, IL: Research Press.

Braukmann, C. J., Fixsen, D. L., Phillips, E. L., & Wolf, M. M. (1975). Behavioral approaches to treatment in the crime and delinquency field. *Criminology*, **13**, 299–331.

Farley, F. (1994, February). President's corner. *The Monitor*. Washington, DC: American Psychological Association.

Fixsen, D. L., & Blase, K. A. (1993). Creating new realities: Program development and dissemination. *Journal of Applied Behavior Analysis*, **26**, 597–615.

Fixsen, D. L., Phillips, E. L., & Wolf, M. M. (1978). Mission-oriented behavior research: The Teaching-Family Model. In A. C. Catania & T. A. Brigham (Eds), *Handbook of Applied Behavior Analysis: Social and Instructional Processes*, pp. 603–628. New York: Irvington Publishers.

Ford, D. (1974). *Parent–Child Interaction in a Token Economy*, Masters degree thesis, University of Kansas.

Ford, D., Evans, J. H., & Dworkin, L. K. (1982). Teaching interaction procedures: Effects upon the learning of social skills by an emotionally disturbed child. *Education and Treatment of Children*, **5**, 1–11.

Lipsey, M. W. (1992). *The Effects of Treatment on Juvenile Delinquents: Results from Meta-analysis*, Paper presented at the NIMH meeting for potential applicants to prevent youth violence. Bethesda, MD: National Institute of Mental Health.

McClannahan, L. E., Krantz, P. J., McGee, G. G., & MacDuff, G. S. (1984). Teaching-Family Model for autistic children. In W. P. Christian, G. T. Hannah & T. J. Glahn (Eds), *Programming Effective Human Services*, pp. 383–406. New York: Plenum.

Phillips, E. L. (1968). Achievement Place: Token reinforcement procedures in a home-style rehabilitation setting for pre-delinquent boys. *Journal of Applied Behavior Analysis*, **1**, 213–223.

Phillips, E. L., Phillips, E. A., Fixsen, D. L., & Wolf, M. M. (1974). *The Teaching-Family Handbook*, 2nd ed. Lawrence, KS: University Press of Kansas.

Reppucci, N. D., & Saunders, J. T. (1974). Social psychology of behavior modification: Problems of implementation in natural settings. *American Psychologist*, **September**, 649–660.

Shadish, W. R., Jr (1984). Lessons from the implementation of deinstitutionalization. *American Psychologist*, **39**, 725–738.

Sidman, M. (1960). *Tactics of Scientific Research*. New York: Basic Books.

Teaching-Family Association (1980). *Directory of the Teaching-Family Association*. Boys Town, NE: Father Flanagan's Boys' Home.

Teaching-Family Association (1993). *Standards of Ethical Conduct of the Teaching-Family Association*. Asheville, NC: Teaching-Family Association.

Teaching-Family Association Newsletter (1994). *Elements of the Teaching-Family Model*. Asheville, NC: Teaching-Family Association.

Wolf, M. M., Kirigin, K. A., Fixsen, D. L., Blase, K. A., & Braukmann, C. J. (1995). The Teaching-Family Model: A case study in data-based program development and refinement (and dragon wrestling). *Journal of Organizational Behavior Management*, **15**, 11–68.

Chapter 8

THE STRUGGLE FOR TREATMENT INTEGRITY IN A "DIS-INTEGRATED" SERVICE DELIVERY SYSTEM

Gary A. Bernfeld

Behavioural Sciences Technology Program, St Lawrence College, Kingston, Ontario, Canada

QUALITY . . .
Quality is never an accident; it is always the result of high intention, sincere effort, intelligent direction and skilful execution; it represents the wise choice of many alternatives.

Anonymous

The purpose of this chapter is to describe an innovative family preservation program for delinquents, which exemplifies effective correctional treatment: Community Support Services of the St Lawrence Youth Association in Ontario Canada. Over 7 years, the program utilized the Teaching-Family Model's (see Chapter 7 by Dean Fixsen, Karen Blase, Gary Timbers and Montrose Wolf in this book) integrated clinical, administrative, evaluation and supervision systems to ensure quality and treatment integrity. These systems will be delineated, along with some of the challenges of implementing an integrated treatment within a fragmented children's' services delivery system. The intention is to do so from a "multilevel systems perspective"

Offender Rehabilitation in Practice. Edited by G. A. Bernfeld, D. P. Farrington and A. W. Leschied.
© 2001 John Wiley & Sons, Ltd.

(Bernfeld, Blase & Fixsen, 1990), in which four levels of analyses are used to examine the delivery of human services: client, program, agency and societal. Finally, suggestions are made for contextual supports for innovative programs, so as to foster their effectiveness, longevity and key role as catalysts for systemic change in children's services.

EMPIRICAL FOUNDATIONS

Community Support Services of the St Lawrence Youth Association was specifically developed in 1988 to offer intensive, short-term and flexible support to 12–15-year-old young offenders (juvenile delinquents) who are "at risk" of being placed in more restrictive residential settings, such as closed or secure custody. The aim was to start with the treatment orientation and procedures used by Alberta Family Support Services (Olivier, Oostenbrink, Benoit, Blase & Fixsen, 1992) with mostly child welfare clientele, and adapt them for use with young offenders. Thus, the two programs shared the same broad goal of integrating the well-researched treatment methods of the Teaching-Family Model (see Chapter 7) with the service delivery strategies of the Homebuilders Model (Whittaker, Kinney, Tracy & Booth, 1990), an exemplary family preservation program.

Other literature supporting the development of the Community Support Services model include:

- *Clinically appropriate treatment*, as defined in meta-analytic literature reviews (e.g. Gendreau, 1996; Chapter 2 by James McGuire and Chapter 4 by Friedrich Lösel, both in this book), includes behavioral systems family therapy, intensive structured skill training and structured one-on-one paraprofessional programs.
- Andrews, Leschied and Hoge's (1992) review identified a number of key risk factors for delinquency, which establish *appropriate targets for treatment*, including: cognitions (antisocial attitudes and values), family factors (low levels of affection/cohesiveness and supervision/monitoring, poor discipline, and neglect and abuse) and peer influences (association with antisocial companions and isolation from non-criminal peers).
- Patterson, Reid and Dishion (1993) provided detailed empirical support for their developmental model of antisocial or coercive behavior, in which parents are key to the early training for antisocial behavior. As well, their research targeted the teaching of appropriate *family management skills* as essential to rehabilitating delinquents.
- Christensen and Jacobson (1994) reviewed research on psychological

treatment delivered by *paraprofessionals* and concluded that paraprofessionals are usually as effective as professionals. Given that the need for mental health services exceeds the supply of professionals and the costs savings afforded by paraprofessionals, they concluded that services delivered by non-professional therapists merit wider use and further research.

- *Multisystemic therapy*, developed and carefully evaluated by Scott Henggeler (see Chapter 5 by Daniel Edwards, Sonja Schoenwald, Scott Henggeler & Keller Strother in this book) targets risk factors across the delinquents' family, peer, school and neighborhood contexts. It uses an intensive family preservation approach, combined with an eclectic mix of cognitive-behavioral services.
- Andrews et al. (1992) have continued to emphasize the importance of *treatment integrity* for programs treating delinquents. Some of the key elements of therapeutic integrity, detailed by Alan Leschied, myself and David Farrington (see Chapter 1 of this book), include: a coherent and empirically based theoretical model; an individualized approach to assessing and treating client risks/needs; a detailed program manual; structured and formal staff training; meaningful staff supervision; and monitoring of treatment process. These and other factors are incorporated in Gendreau and Andrews' (1996) Correctional Program Assessment Inventory (CPAI), which is discussed in Chapter 12 of this book by Paul Gendreau, Claire Goggin and Paula Smith.
- Paul Gendreau (Chapter 12 of this book) and others (e.g. Friedrich Lösel in Chapter 4 of this book) have also stressed the importance of *system factors*. These include: the program's careful selection of line staff for their skills and values; the efforts at disseminating knowledge to staff; the program director's credentials and skills in the area of behavioral intervention; the support for the program from the host agency; and the broader service delivery system; funding; etc.

Two annual reports on Community Support Services provide further details on the model's empirical "roots" (Bernfeld, Bonnell et al., 1995; Bernfeld, Cousins et al., 1990).

OVERALL PROGRAM

The program is delivered to young offenders and families in homes, schools and the community at large. This in-home service is designed to work in collaboration with the family to reduce the youth's offending behavior, prevent the youth's placement in a more restrictive residential setting, strengthen the emotional and psychological well-being of the youth and family and promote their self-sufficiency. Community Support Services aims to empower the young person and family with information, skill-based teaching, respect, responsibility and empathic relationships. This service is concerned with the ecology of the youth and family in the context of the community. There are two different referral routes to the program:

1. Whenever possible, the program prefers to work in a *family preservation mode*. This involves accepting younger children currently on probation in the community, who are at moderate to high risk of reoffending.
2. An alternative type of referral involves youths currently in custodial settings, who need assistance in returning to their community and families, or, in the case of older offenders, those who need preparation for semi-independent living. This reflects a *family reintegration or semi-independent living approach*.

The preference is to work with referring agents (probation officers) to identify clients who are "at risk" for the most intrusive intervention, secure custody early on, and assist their families in maintaining the young offender in the home environment. This early intervention approach (Referral Route #1) is designed not only to reduce costs by preventing future offences and residential placements, but also to maximize the impact and brevity of our services. Bernfeld, Cousins et al. (1990) provide further details on the development of Community Support Services.

HALLMARKS OF COMMUNITY SUPPORT SERVICES

Community Support Services treat young offenders who are 12–15 years of age at the time of their offence—and therefore only serve post-adjudicated youth. Referrals are made by probation officers in the six county areas around Kingston, Ontario, Canada. This area, over 200 kilometers in length and 150 in width, is largely rural, with one larger city (population 125,000) and two small urban centers. Total population is over 250,000. Travel times by car to serve rural clients range from 30 to 90 minutes or more. Electronic pagers and cellular phones are the primary means by which the staff keep in touch with clients. There is a total of six front-line staff working a 40-hour flexible workweek along with a director (the author), a supervisor and an administrative coordinator.

As noted earlier, Community Support Services integrates the *treatment methods* of the Teaching-Family Model (see Chapter 7 in this book) with the *service delivery* strategies of family preservation programs such as Home-builders (Whittaker et al., 1990). The first six hallmarks of Community Support Services listed in Table 8.1 reflect the service delivery strategies it

Table 8.1 Hallmarks of Community Support Services

FLEXIBLE
COMMUNITY-BASED
FAMILY-CENTRED
BASIC NEEDS
INTENSIVE TREATMENT/DIRECT SERVICE
FOLLOW-UP
TEACHING
GOAL-DIRECTED
EMPIRICALLY BASED
STAFF TRAINING/SUPERVISION MODEL

generally shares with family preservation programs, as well as other eco-logical programs like Multisystemic Therapy (see Chapter 5 in this book).

Overall, Community Support Services is similar to these programs in the *scope* of its services or "to whom" it is directed, the youth's social ecology, as well as in its *service delivery model* or "how" it operates. The latter refers to programs which are home based; strength-oriented and family preservation focused; intensive and time limited; individualized and client-directed; as well as combining clinical and concrete services.

However, the last four hallmarks listed in Table 8.1 underscore the differences between Community Support Services and ecological or family preservation programs in *content* or "what" interventions are offered. While others use an eclectic mix of cognitive-behavioral treatments, Community Support Services specifically organizes the implementation of these interventions within the Teaching-Family Model's standardized human service systems. Hallmarks of Community Support Services include:

1. Flexibility: The staff are on-call 24 hours a day, 7 days a week; fit the family's schedule; and are willing to work with any problem (staff are generalists).
2. Community-Based: Employees, called "specialists", work wherever they are needed (school, home, etc.), but not in an office. They work in the family's context, to decrease problems in generalization and maximize relevance and learning of the skills taught. Thus, staff are more like coaches than therapists.
3. Family-centered: The program works with the young offender and the entire family with the goal of preventing problems in the younger siblings and strengthening parenting capacity. It puts families in charge of their own service and helps them become more aware of a broader range of options available to them. The services offered "fit" the family's context and are implemented in a respectful and collegial

manner. Staff establish supportive, empathetic relationships with family members, in keeping with the philosophy that "everyone is doing the best they can with what they've got."

4. Basic needs: The family's needs for food, transportation, employment, budgeting, etc. are assessed and the focus is to teach the family skills in these areas (e.g. how to successfully apply for a job), including self-advocacy.

5. Intensive treatment/Direct service: The intensive phase of service lasts 8–12 weeks. Caseloads are of two young offenders and their families at a time. Thus, at any one time, staff serve two youths in the intensive phase of service and six to eight in the follow-up mode. On average, over 214 hours of service is provided to each case of which 35 per cent is face to face (Bernfeld, Bonnell et al., 1995). The intensive phase of service starts with three to five visits per week and fades to one direct contact per week and several phone contacts.

6. Follow-up: After the intensive phase of service ends, there is a 1-year follow-up period, during which services gradually fade to monthly phone contact. "Booster sessions" are provided on a planned basis (e.g. at the start of a new school year), or as needed during crises. The use of a 1-year follow-up period and booster sessions are unique.

7. Teaching: Community Support specialists build on strengths of families and use a cognitive-behavioral approach to counseling to teach a wide range of skills to young offenders and their entire family (e.g. anger management, positive parenting skills, effective communication, rational problem-solving, social and life skills, etc.). The service is individualized, practical and skill-oriented. Teaching is "matched" between parents and children. For example, a parent is first taught how to appropriately give an instruction, then a youth is taught how to follow one, and finally, the parent is taught how to effectively praise the youth (by being behaviorally specific and commenting on youth skills). The goal is to develop positive, self-sustaining spirals of appropriate interaction between parents and children that will be maintained long after the direct service has ended.

8. Goal-directed: Initial psychological testing which is part of the evaluation process, plus the program's intensive in-home assessment help develop the master treatment plan within the first 2 weeks of service. Thereafter, weekly and daily goals are derived and reviewed with supervisors and peers. The goals involve working with the youth's "social ecology". This is because difficulties are not conceptualized as residing solely "in" children, but in the *reciprocal, mutually impactful interactions* between the child and others in the environment (Fixsen, Olivier & Blase, 1990).

9. Empirically-based: Community Support Services was based on the

research literature on delinquency and the Teaching-Family Model, which are discussed on pp. 168–169.

10. Staff training/Supervision: These areas are critical and often under-developed in less structured community programs. This is because intensive support is needed for employees working in an intensive, crisis-oriented service. Staff are provided with a weeklong, 40 hour Pre-Service Workshop (half of which involves didactic instruction and half of which consists of behavioral rehearsals of clinical skills) along with a 500-page manual. This is followed by a 2-week orientation period, and then weekly case consultations with the supervisor, along with bi- weekly team meetings to allow for case reviews with peers, and bimonthly in-service training to develop new program technology. In addition, there are at least monthly field observations, in which the supervisor observes the employees working with families during home visits and provides the staff with written feedback. Finally, professional development plans are reviewed monthly, to guide the maturing clinical skills and judgement of the specialists. Overall, employees spend more than 20 per cent of their time in individual, group or peer supervision, and this is critical to program integrity and quality.

Taken as a whole, Community Support Services, like Alberta Family Support Services upon which it is modeled, offers *contextual therapy*. Bernfeld, Cousins et al. (1990) define this as "helping people learn to cope with their emotional and interactional issues in their own settings to maximize relevance, acquisition, and implementation and to minimize generalization problems" (p. 22). This report also provides more details on the treatment model, including an example of the treatment planning process, and case profiles. As well, it presents the extensive list of services provided by staff that are documented in case files in order to track program implementation.

The family-centered approach to treatment ensures that the treatment plan developed jointly with the family members fits their unique context. Staff also share their weekly goals and daily agendas with the family—and, most importantly, are prepared to be flexible as families' needs change. The intensity, on-call support and strength-oriented focus of the service help us build a solid relationship with family members and to facilitate behavior change. Ultimately, our ability to work in the family's home depends on how we help the family accomplish its goals.

PROGRAM EVALUATION: A SUMMARY

Bernfeld, Bonnell et al. (1995) describe the computerized Management Information System developed for Community Support Services. This system

integrates the evaluation needs of the program with supervision, management and administrative systems. This practical and cost-effective program
evaluation approach is integrated with routine service delivery. It generates
automated monthly reports of the service's processes and outcomes. As an
example of the former, time management data is collected on all members of
staff, in order to track their different activities. These range from direct work
with families (i.e. face to face and on the phone) to indirect services (e.g.
preparing for family visits, meetings, paperwork, travel, etc).

Outcome evaluation data collected at pre- and post-treatment, and at 3
month follow-up on 155 youths over 5 years is discussed in detail by
Bernfeld, Bonnell et al. (1995) and will only be briefly summarized here. A
home-based, family-centered treatment technology is evolving which seems
to reduce entry of young offenders into the residential care system. While
the results are encouraging, they should be interpreted with caution, given
the lack of a comparison group. Bernfeld, Cousins et al. (1990) discuss the
principles that guided the development of the "in-house" program evaluation model. These recognize the challenges in evaluating a flexible, strength-
oriented program, without compromising its implementation with families
in crises. In-depth analyses of these and other issues are provided by Pecora,
Fraser, Nelson, McCroskey & Meezan (1995).

Client benefits demonstrated by the program include reliable or statistic-
ally significant reductions in youth behavior problems, as measured by the
Child Behavior Checklist (Achenbach, 1991) and parent–youth communica-
tion problems, on Robin and Foster's (1989) Conflict Behavior Questionnaire.
Reliable improvements were also noted for the youths on the Social Skills
Rating System (Gresham & Elliott, 1990).

Youth recidivism after a 15-month follow-up period (55%) compared
favorably to the 67 per cent rate reported by Hoge, Leschied and Andrews
(1993) based on a 6-month follow-up for young offenders in open custody in
Ontario. Moreover, the data indicated that Community Support Services
achieved reliable reductions in the seriousness of offences, the total
number of offences, the number of multiple convictions, as well as a
longer interval between offences. Consumers (parents, youth, probation
officers, etc.) were generally satisfied with the program and provided
detailed feedback about the program's strengths and areas for improvement.

While 97 per cent of the young offenders were predicted by probation
officers at intake to the program to require residential placements, only 42
per cent were actually placed out of home in the 15 months of follow-up,
averaging less than 2 months per placement. A cost analysis indicated that
for every $1.00 spent on Community Support Services over 5 years, about
$1.48 might have been saved in residential care costs. The data suggest that
cost savings of about a quarter of a million dollars per year in residential
dollars alone could be attributed to Community Support Services. It was in

fact suggested that these modest savings are a conservative estimate of the benefits of the program, for a number of reasons.

Hoge et al. (1993) reviewed Ontario-wide young offender programs and found that they averaged a relatively low score of 0.29 on the subgroup of scales reflecting treatment on the CPAI (Gendreau and Andrews, 1996). The provincial average of 0.29 means that 29 per cent of the 56 items were present across all Ontario programs. Sector-specific averages were: probation, 0.21; open custody, 0.26; secure custody, 0.29; and the nine community support teams (including Community Support Services), 0.51. In comparison, using the scoring guide provided by Leschied, Hoge and Andrews (1993), the Community Support Services program scored above 0.70 on the scale— meaning that more than 70 per cent of the program characteristics indicative of effective treatment were present.

LINK TO THE TEACHING-FAMILY MODEL

The Teaching-Family Model (see Chapter 7 in this book) is the "heart" of Community Support Services. From its original roots in a 1968 group home for delinquent adolescents called Achievement Place, the Teaching-Family Model has developed into an integrated service delivery system. Today there are over 134 group homes serving over 1,724 children annually across the United States that serve not only delinquents but also abused, neglected, emotionally disturbed, autistic and developmentally challenged children and young adults. In addition, the Teaching-Family Model has been recently adapted for youths in treatment foster care (over 524 children annually across the USA), independent living and home-based services (over 350 families served annually across the USA). Over 100 publications on the model have researched its effectiveness and carefully evaluated its individual treatment components over the past 30+ years. In fact, over $30M of United States' government funding have supported the careful research and detailed development of the clinical, administrative, evaluation and supervision systems which ensure that the Teaching-Family Model is delivered with integrity.

Figure 8.1 provides an overview and Tables 8.2–8.5 detail the home-based version of the Teaching-Family Model, in terms of its goals as well as its treatment, program and treatment planning systems. All have been carefully *integrated* so as to support the systematic implementation of this model. Chapter 7 in this book and Bernfeld, Blase et al. (1990) present the conceptual and research basis for program development and dissemination vis-à-vis the Teaching-Family Model.

The Teaching-Family Association oversees the quality assurance evaluations that hold organizations accountable for the programs that utilize and

Figure 8.1   Overview of home-based services in the Teaching-Family Model.

Table 8.2   Goals of home-based services in the Teaching-Family Model

---

A.   *HUMANE*
    1.   Compassion
    2.   Respect
    3.   Positive regard
    4.   Cultural sensitivity
    5.   Adherence to TFA* ethical standards

B.   *EFFECTIVE*
    1.   Resolve referral issues
    2.   Achieve treatment goals
    3.   In-house evaluation validates service utility
    4.   Contribute to the systematic evolution of the Teaching-Family Model

C.   *INDIVIDUALIZED*
    1.   Service tailored to fit unique needs and strengths of family
    2.   Fit of services determined via referral issues, family goals and direct observations of staff

D.   *SATISFACTORY TO STAKEHOLDERS*
    1.   Consumers: children, family members, referral sources, allied professionals
    2.   Dimensions: cooperation, communication, effectiveness and concern of staff
    3.   Achieve treatment goals

E.   *COST-EFFICIENT*
F.   *REPLICABLE*
G.   *INTEGRATION OF ABOVE GOALS*

---

* TFA = Teaching-Family Association. Adapted from Dean L. Fixsen and Karen A. Blase (pers. comm., April, 1989). *Note:* Tables 8.2–8.4 were adapted from those developed by Fixsen and Blase during their years of consultation and Community Support Services. They are precursors to the 1994 TFA Standards for home-based services. The standards can be obtained from TFA at: 4456 Corporation Lane, Suite 120, Virginia Beach, VA 23462; phone (001) 757 497-3023; or visit their website at http://www.teaching-family-org

Table 8.3 Integrated program components of home-based services in the Teaching-Family Model

A. *PROGRAM CLARITY (guides for decision making)*
1. Philosophy
2. Goals
3. Treatment processes
4. Ethical standards

B. *STAFF SELECTION (the general "unteachables")*
1. Caring and commitment
2. Common sense
3. Intelligence
4. Background knowledge
5. Willingness to learn
6. Philosophical fit

C. *STAFF TRAINING (treatment related skills and knowledge)*
1. Pre-service and in-service training in:
    - Program goals and philosophy
    - Treatment processes and skills
    - Clinical judgements
    - Program operations
2. Emphasis on teaching of concepts and skill development
3. Opportunities for shared learning and program development

D. *STAFF SUPERVISION (putting it into practice)*
1. Assure treatment implementation
2. Develop staff skills
3. Enhance clinical judgements
4. Solve special problems
5. Create new technology
6. Support personal development

E. *STAFF EVALUATION (assessing clinical implementation)*
1. Treatment-related skills
2. Clinical judgements
3. Youth, parent and stakeholder surveys
4. Annual staff certification by TFA*

F. *PROGRAM EVALUATION (assessing service implementation)*
1. Family benefits and program costs
2. Accountability to consumers
3. Demographic information
4. Feedback for program development
5. Annual and triennial site certification by TFA*

G. *PROGRAM ADMINISTRATION (putting/keeping it all together)*
1. Facilitate treatment processes and integration
2. Support treatment staff
3. Meet operating requirements
4. Interface with other systems
5. Encourage innovation
6. Evolve effective programs

* TFA = Teaching-Family Association. Adapted from Dean L. Fixsen and Karen A. Blase (pers. comm., April 1989).

Table 8.4   Integrated treatment components of home-based services in the Teaching-Family Model

A.   *TEACHING SYSTEMS*
    1.   Proactive
    2.   Reactive
    3.   Intensive

B.   *RELATIONSHIP DEVELOPMENT*
    1.   Non-judgmental
    2.   Person-centered
    3.   Partnership

C.   *MOTIVATION SYSTEMS*
    1.   Flexible and individualized
    2.   Precise and positive
    3.   Person-centered

D.   *SELF-DETERMINATION*
    1.   Rational problem-solving
    2.   Self-control
    3.   Expressing feelings

E.   *COUNSELLING*
    1.   Empathy and concern
    2.   Support and reassurance
    3.   Feelings and relationships

F.   *SKILLS CURRICULUM*
    1.   Individualized
    2.   Appropriate alternatives
    3.   Social prosthesis

G.   *ADVOCACY*
    1.   Self-advocacy and assertiveness
    2.   "Systems" issues
    3.   Professionalism

H.   *CONTEXTUAL TREATMENT*
    1.   Relevant settings and people
    2.   Fosters acquisition and generalization
    3.   Matching skills and supports

I.   *COMMUNITY STANDARDS*
    1.   Social acceptability
    2.   Community values
    3.   Ethical standards

J.   *TREATMENT PLANS*
    1.   Interactional nature of problems
    2.   Fit the family
    3.   Implementation issues monitored

K.   *INTEGRATION OF TREATMENT COMPONENTS*
    1.   Maximize opportunities for change
    2.   Clinical judgment
    3.   Outcome oriented, process sensitive

Adapted from Dean L. Fixsen and Karen A. Blase (pers. comm., May, 1990).

Table 8.5 Treatment planning and implementation for home-based services in the Teaching-Family Model

---

A.   *REFERRAL ISSUES*
—Legal reasons
—Problem oriented

B.   *TREATMENT RATIONALE*
—Youth/Family reasons
—Solution oriented

C.   *TREATMENT GOALS*
—Focus on key issues

D.   *SKILLS RELATED TO GOALS*
—Appropriate alternatives to problems

E.   *BEHAVIORS RELATED TO SKILLS*
—How to do and say things differently

Adapted from Dean L. Fixsen, Karen A. Blase, Karen A. Olivier and Arlene C. Oostenbrink (pers. comm., June, 1990).

disseminate its model. To become a member of this association, a new organization must be formally affiliated with an already certified site for 5 years, receive systematic help in developing Teaching-Family Programs and undergo a rigorous evaluation at the service or treatment level and the organization level. The agency must meet all practice standards regarding the selection, training, supervision and evaluation of front-line staff, trainers, evaluators and supervisors. The association has established standardized procedures for how these functions are delivered in a certified organization. A *site* must be recertified annually.

In addition to maintaining records of staff supervision and training to assure the quality of the programmatic support, treatment implementation is ensured by the annual certification of individual *staff*. This involves a combination of *consumer satisfaction data*, in which staff must average a rating of "6.0" on a 7-point scale that reflects satisfaction of consumers (parents, youths, case managers and others) with various aspects of service. As well, independent reviewers assess the actual *in-home performance* of staff and a 50-page report is completed which summarizes both the consumer and on-site data and qualitative observations. Thus, the Teaching-Family Association provides a mechanism for assuring the consistency and quality of the implementation of the Teaching-Family model internationally. Note that this is a non-profit organization whose primary function is to disseminate the model and ensure its planned, databased, evolution.

What is hopefully apparent from reading the above and Tables 8.2–8.5 is that the Teaching-Family Model's vertically and horizontally integrated systems represent our "best practices" in how to translate knowledge about effective correctional treatment into practice with integrity, while ensuring quality assurance. The model addresses the previously noted treatment integrity and systems factors in the literature by Gendreau (1996) and Andrews et al. (1992). As well, it represents the only systematic, published attempt in the area of human services to develop, disseminate and evolve an integrated service delivery system.

Community Support Services worked towards site certification in the Teaching-Family Model from the early to the mid-1990s, when a change in the leadership of the provincial government drastically altered the funding arrangements and made pursuit of certification impossible. The program was about 1 year away from being certified, when the attempt had to be formally halted. Currently, Community Support Services is operating without formal implementation of all of the Teaching-Family Model systems. However, with its start-up in 1988, it represents one of the oldest family preservation programs in Canada, and the most experienced program of its kind for young offenders.

CHALLENGES TO IMPLEMENTATION

In this section, some of the challenges of implementing an integrated treatment like Community Support Services within a fragmented children's services delivery system will be described. The intention is to do so from a multilevel systems perspective (Bernfeld, Blase et al., 1990), in which four levels of analysis are used to examine the delivery of human services: client, program, organization and societal.

Client level

Clinical challenges occur at the interface of the treatment planning, program and treatment systems detailed in Tables 8.2–8.4. For example, given the intensive, home-based nature of the service, it is not surprising that the family's potential "resistance" represents a challenge to overcome. As reviewed by Ralph Serin and Denise Preston (see Chapter 10 of this book), internal treatment responsivity factors include client motivation, personality and cognitive deficits, while external factors reflect therapist, offender and setting characteristics. Treatment effectiveness depends on matching types of treatment and therapists to the types of clients.

Intensive supervision of staff in Community Support Services is critical to the matching process, so that the treatment fits the family. This is because the families of young offenders can sometimes be either difficult to engage, non-reinforcing to work with and/or reside in locations which are inaccessible or hazardous for staff. As well, the multiple problems of the target families and the intensity of the service impact directly on staff, who are immersed in the family often on a daily basis. Therefore, specialists need support from a supervisor who is intimately familiar with the staff's professional issues, so that these do not interfere with the optimal delivery of services.

Also key to the matching of treatment to family is the expectation that there be a 2-week long, in-home assessment of family issues before a con-textually sensitive master treatment plan is designed. Finally, the weekly review of this plan allows for adjustments to the intervention, as the family's needs or outside circumstances evolve. This is especially important, as optimal matching must be a dynamic process. Moreover, in order for staff supervision to successfully impact on treatment effectiveness, it has to be *intensive* (occupy about 20% of staff time), *multimodal* (occur at individual, peer and group levels) and *multi-site (office and field based)*. The latter reflects the range of supervisory activities (including regular field observations of staff interactions, and various meetings) and the various paperwork and time management systems which document program implementation.

The above examples should not imply that issues at the client level operate in isolation of the other levels that are discussed on pp. 181–186. The fact that there are interactions between multiple levels of the service delivery system underscores the importance of this perspective on treatment integrity. For example, proposals by the labor union (at the program level), which had the potential to limit service intensity, accessibility and flexibility, had to be addressed to protect the integrity of the service. Also, shifting priorities of the juvenile justice system (at the societal level) impact continually on the targeting of the service. Finally, the program's preference for working in a family preservation mode continually brought the program in conflict with systemic pressures to serve youth currently in custodial care or those being released after spending long periods of time in out-of-home placements.

Program level

The family and community-centered nature of the service was at odds with the focus of the other programs offered by the agency, which were residen-tial. It often took the creative intervention by the agency's Executive Director, Merice Walker Boswell, to solve any inter-program misunderstandings or rivalries that undermined Community Support Services. Special meetings of all agency staff and the involvement of the Community Support Services supervisor in regular meetings with her colleagues helped share information and build informal interdepartmental "coalitions". Throughout, the Executive Director reminded employees of the superordinate goal that all agency staff shared—to support, rehabilitate and advocate for children within the young offender system.

However, once again, the interactions between the multiple levels were critical to effective implementation of the service. For instance, at the organizational level, the agency's structure facilitated efforts at the program level to set up and evolve towards the Teaching-Family Model's treatment planning, program and treatment systems. This is because the agency was relatively "loosely coupled", so that individual programs like Community Support Services could set up independent systems to select, train and supervise staff, and evaluate employees individually and the program as a whole. Moreover, the program was autonomous enough to integrate these functions within its own operations and tie them directly to the Teaching-Family Model's protocols. This is quite unlike large bureaucratic organizations, like those in Corrections, which usually set up independent departments in these key areas, with differing mandates and procedures.

Moreover, because Community Support Services was positioned as a "leading edge" program by the Executive Director (a key organizational issue), it was supported in its efforts to pilot and refine new staff training and program evaluation systems, which were later exported across the agency. Elements of its computerized management information system (see pp. 173–174) were incorporated later in all other agency programs.

The personnel selection process for Community Support Services was adapted from structured interviews used in the Teaching-Family Model. Applicant ratings on similar interviews have been shown to predict on-the-job performance (Maloney et al., 1983). Our interviews included an hour-long written package requiring, among other things, answers to a series of behavioral vignettes that assess the applicant's responses to hypothetical problem situations similar to those encountered on the job. The 90-minute interview itself assessed the applicant's answers to similar questions, along with performance on behavioral role plays. The latter assessed an applicant's teaching ability at baseline, after instructions in using the teaching interaction techniques of the model, and after feedback. Three interviewers rated the applicant's performance in these and many other areas, and the comparative data was analyzed in making hiring decisions.

Organizational level

The Executive Director of this small (50 employee) non-profit agency actively encouraged innovation. This is unlike the process in large bureaucratic organizations, which supports the status quo. Due to her skilful efforts with staff and managers, the Board of Directors passed a motion committing the agency to the Teaching-Family Model. This supported the agency's work at achieving certification as a site. Resources were gathered to support this effort in a "low profile" manner, as the external zeitgeist shifted to a "punishing smarter" perspective. While Community Support Services was the focal point, the new secure custody program was set up according to some key treatment aspects of this model.

As well, the mentorship of the Community Support Services Director (the present author) by the Executive Director was essential in the development of his networking skills with other peers in the local and provincial juvenile justice system. These included the program's key consumers—the local Supervisor of Probation and senior policymakers in the provincial government. In fact, the program's interactions with the referring agency (Probation) were critical to efforts to operate in a family preservation mode, and serve youths with appropriate risk levels. As Bernfeld, Blase et al. (1990) noted, a program director's personal relationship with key administrators and policymakers continues to be critical to program survival and dissemination.

Finally, the management philosophy of the Executive Director was compatible with the Teaching-Family Model's view of administration as *integral* to effective treatment services. From this perspective, "there is no such thing as an administrative decision—every decision is a clinical decision" (D. L. Fixsen, pers. comm., 12 December 1988). This requires flexibility in the application of everything from accounting, budgeting and human resources systems, so as to support short-term, community based, crisis services. For example, there was a need to develop a unique system to calculate "flex time" while ensuring staff accountability. As well, given the highly mobile and decentralized nature of the service and the fact that staff usually worked out of their own homes, new policies governing staff travel had to be established. These are just a few of the many procedures that needed to be developed or creatively interpreted to accommodate program implementation.

Societal level

Bernfeld, Cousins-Brame and Knox (1995) comprehensively delineate the challenges of implementing an integrated treatment like Community Support Services within a fragmented children's services delivery system. The paper also describes a "sister" program for child welfare clients, operated in collaboration with another agency. The authors demonstrate how the different structural and systemic supports for the other program were essential to mitigating the impact of challenges to integrity and enhancing its implementation and effectiveness. The major types of issues identified by Bernfeld, Cousins-Brame et al. are listed below, each with an example:

1. *Referrals*. These reflect periods of scarcity, occasions when too many referrals arrive at a time when the program has only a single opening or other occasions when inappropriate types of referrals are made. An example of the latter is when a young offender is suddenly referred just a few months prior to his 16th birthday, when he will "graduate" from one government ministry's services to those run by another ministry. This has more to do with assisting probation officers in managing their workload, than in working with those most at risk of reoffending. On one occasion, Community Support Services received many simultaneous "priority" referrals that were caused by an administrative decision to save money by quickly returning many young offenders in custodial residences to their families. The local justice system's fiscal crisis necessitated our involvement to prevent family crises, irrespective of the risk level of the youths.

2. *Roles*. Government policy favouring custodial dispositions, the legal role of probation officers and their lack of extensive training in the juvenile delinquency field make it difficult for some of them to see the benefits of community-based treatment in general, and intensive family preservation treatment in particular. Not surprisingly, they favor legal sanctions (e.g. charging a youth with breaching probation), threats of punishment and reincarceration. They feel that these are the best means at their disposal to protect society—and reduce their liability—should a youth reoffend, or begin to experience non-criminal (e.g. family) problems in the community. Thus, government policy, the "hard line" political climate and the reluctance of key "gatekeepers" in the juvenile justice system to take risks impact on the autonomy and integrity of programs like Community Support Services.

3. *Communication*. Success in formal communication with probation officers is variable at best, in spite of continual efforts by managers of Community Support Services and Probation to have regular meetings or staff retreats to strengthen relationships, etc. There is little regular communication with some probation officers, lots of supportive contact with others and intermittent, crisis-oriented communication with the rest. Thus, problems can "fester" or be expressed obliquely by the officer's premature removal of a child from the home. The communication problem and the different focus of Probation vis-à-vis Community Support Services (crisis/reactive versus prevention) may also be exacerbated by the relative autonomy of probation officers.

4. *Commitment.* It was difficult to build commitment in probation officers to Community Support Services, as it was a new, pilot program. Also, the timing of its introduction in 1988 was unfortunate, as it coincided with the government's privatization of public agencies. Two other factors hindered the effort to convince probation staff that the family preservation effort was not just another temporary "fad". First was the government's history of introducing new program models with little advance planning and then dropping them shortly thereafter. Another factor was the lack of training offered to staff about the benefits of this approach. Though training in cognitive behavioral services was eventually offered years later, probation officers had little direct experience with it and little supervision in how to implement such treatments on the job.

5. *Envy and Power.* Given that probation officers are primarily concerned with case management, some of them are understandably envious of the small caseloads carried by family preservation staff, as well as their flexible working hours. This is especially true for the probation officers who preferred front-line work, or for those upset by the increasing caseloads, paperwork and office-bound nature of their work. Issues of the probation officers' blatant use of power were especially apparent in the early years, when they would tell families (sometimes inaccurately) what Community Support Services staff would do for them or would make placement decisions without consulting the specialists. More subtly, there was the above-noted power struggle over referrals and the continued pressure on the staff to "inform" on family members who were suspected of other illegal activities.

6. *Value systems and practice.* Overall, the values and practices of family preservation staff are quite different than those of traditional casework. In Community Support Services, the focus is the home and community, as well as an immediate response, flexible hours of work and a short-term, intensive orientation. These attributes, as well as the goal of empowering families by building on their strengths, often challenge the probation officer's focus on what is wrong, or on information obtained "second hand" rather than via direct observation. This is because their legal role and large caseloads do not permit an intensive, collegial approach with families. Finally, probation practice is still "punishment-oriented" and reactive, even if the theories they're being occasionally exposed to are more therapeutic. This is likely to continue until their job description permits more time for them to deliver treatment, or their supervision structures become more intense to guide this desired change in practice. Ultimately, probation practice will not change until there are major shifts in the broader government policies and the "hard line" attitude that is popular in the current political climate.

This list is a brief overview of some the challenges discussed by Bernfeld, Cousins-Brame et al. (1995) to implementing an integrated treatment like Community Support Services within a fragmented children's services delivery system. It is contended that these issues are critical to the *integrity* of any human service delivery program. As well, a program's ultimate effectiveness is a function of its ability to surmount day-to-day challenges to its implementation—no matter how strong its empirical base or its success in limited demonstration projects.

THE IMPORTANCE OF STRUCTURAL SUPPORTS

This chapter has primarily focused on delineating the challenges that one program, Community Support Services, has faced in its ongoing efforts to effectively deliver its rehabilitation services to young offenders in a disjointed service delivery system. As such, its struggles are a microcosm of others. While the use of the highly integrated treatment and program support systems pioneered by the Teaching-Family Model (see Chapter 7 by Dean Fixsen, Karen Blase, Gary Timbers & Montrose Wolf, in this book) reduced implementation problems *within* the program, it could not completely insulate the program from a variety of *external* challenges. To fully understand the nature of these challenges to treatment integrity, we need to look "outside the black box" of our correctional interventions.

An eclectic literature exists on the diffusion of innovations and the management of change in large-scale human service systems, some of which has been reviewed by Bernfeld, Blase et al. (1990), Bernfeld, Cousins-Brame et al. (1995), Fixsen et al. (Chapter 7 of this book) and by Alan Leschied, Gary Bernfeld and David Farrington (Chapter 1 of this book). This literature teaches us that the long-term survival of innovative human service programs requires a unique confluence of supportive factors at the program, organizational and societal levels. Some of these factors were already delineated in the previous section, which detailed the organizational structure of Community Support Services' host agency.

Moreover, specific suggestions can be made for contextual supports for innovative programs like Community Support Services. These include a detailed plan at the *senior levels of government* which:

- anticipates resistance to change system-wide and is prepared to support long-term implementation;
- ensures adequate numbers (or a "critical mass") of programs across the province;

- provides immediate top to bottom staff training; and
- shifts a proportion of fiscal resources from existing residential services to innovative community programs.

Overall, in order to systematically disseminate innovation, government needs to develop a comprehensive, multilevel and long-term implementation plan. For example, if such a plan was in place when Community Support Services began, it would not have allowed the program's referrals to be managed by the Probation Service. Problems arising from this situation, discussed on pp. 183–185, were a result of "the fox being in charge of the hen house". Instead, the referral structure should have resembled the system for Alberta Family Support Services. There, an independent government committee at the regional level made referrals if and only if they had already decided to remove youths from their homes. This committee was accountable to senior levels of government for reducing reliance on residential services, and could only refer youths to the family preservation program if it had an opening. This structure preserved the autonomy and integrity of the program and ensured a steady supply of referrals. In Alberta, the agency making referrals had a vested interest in the success of the innovative service and was not in competition with it. As discussed previously, the state of affairs was quite different for Community Support Services, which resulted in an ongoing struggle for integrity. This is just one way a comprehensive implementation plan by government could have worked.

It is contended that external or *contextual* supports are essential to innovative programs like Community Support Services, so as to foster their effectiveness, longevity and key role as catalysts for systemic change in children's services.

References

Achenbach, T. M. (1991). *Manual for the Child Behavior Checklist/4-18 and 1991 Profile*. Burlington: University of Vermont, Department of Psychiatry.

Andrews, D. A., Leschied, A. W., & Hoge, R. D. (1992). *Review of the Profile, Classification, and Treatment Literature with Young Offenders: A Social-Psychological Approach*. Toronto, Ontario: Ministry of Community Social Services.

Bernfeld, G. A., Blase, K. A., & Fixsen, D. L. (1990). Towards a unified perspective on human service delivery systems: Application of the Teaching-Family Model. In R. J. McMahon & R. DeV. Peters (Eds), *Behavior Disorders of Adolescents: Research, Intervention and Policy in Clinical and School Settings*, pp. 191–205. New York: Plenum.

Bernfeld, G., Bonnell, W., Cousins-Brame, M. L., Kippen, J., Knox, K., Kyte, D., Landon, B., Simmons, C., & Wright, P. (1995). *Community Support Services: Annual Report*. Kingston, Ontario: St Lawrence Youth Association. [Reprints of the entire report (90+ pp.): $10.00 to cover copying and postage.]*

Bernfeld, G., Cousins, M. L., Daniels, K., Hall, P., Knox, K., McNeil, H., & Morrison, W. (1990). *Community Support Services: Annual Report*. Kingston, Ontario: St Lawrence Youth Association. [Reprints of the text portion of this report (up to p. 32): $5 to cover copying and postage.]*

Bernfeld, G. A., Cousins-Brame, M. L., & Knox, K. (1995, May). *Contextual Challenges to Family-centered Services: Can Integrated Treatment Operate in a "Dis-integrated" Service System?* Workshop presented at the Growing '95 conference, Toronto.

Christensen, A., & Jacobson, N. S. (1994). Who (or what) can do psychotherapy?: The status and challenge of nonprofessional therapies. *Psychological Science*, **5**, 8–14.

Fixsen, D. L., Olivier, K. A., & Blase, K. A. (1990). *Home-based, Family-centered Treatment for Children*, Unpublished, Hull Child & Family Services, Calgary, Alberta.

Gendreau, P. (1996). The principles of effective intervention with offenders. In A. T. Harland (Ed.), *Choosing Correctional Options that Work: Defining the Demand and Evaluating the Supply*, pp. 117–130. Thousand Oaks, CA: Sage.

Gendreau, P., & Andrews, D. A. (1996). *Correctional Program Assessment Inventory (CPAI)*, 6th ed. Saint John, New Brunswick: University of New Brunswick.

Gendreau, P., & Goggin, C. (1997). Correctional treatment: Accomplishments and realities. In P. Van Voorhis, D. Lester & M. Braswell (Eds), *Correctional Counseling and Rehabilitation*, 3rd ed., pp. 271–279. Cincinnati, OH: Anderson Publishing Co.

Gresham, F. M., & Elliott, S. N. (1990). *Manual for the Social Skills Rating System*. Toronto, Ontario: Psycan.

Hoge, R. D., Leschied, A. W., & Andrews, D. A. (1993). *An Investigation of Young Offender Services in the Province of Ontario: A Report of the Repeat Offender Project*. Toronto, Ontario: Ministry of Community and Social Services.

Leschied, A. W., Hoge, R. D., & Andrews, D. A. (1993). *Evaluation of the Alternative to Custody Programs in Ontario's Southwest Region*. Toronto, Ontario: Ministry of Community and Social Services.

Maloney, D. M., Warfel, D. J., Blase, K. A., Timbers, G. D., Fixsen, D. L., & Phillips, E. L. (1983). A method for validating employment interviews for residential child care workers. *Residential Group Care and Treatment*, **1**, 37–50.

Olivier, K. A., Oostenbrink, A., Benoit, G., Blase, K. A., & Fixsen, D. L. (1992). *Alberta Family Support Services: Annual Report*. Calgary, Alberta: Hull Child & Family Services.

Patterson, G. R., Reid, G. D., & Dishion, T. J. (1993). *A Social Interactional Approach to Family Intervention: Antisocial boys*, Vol. 4. Eugene, OR: Castalia.

Pecora, P. J., Fraser, M. W., Nelson, K. E., McCroskey, J., & Meezan, W. (1995). *Evaluating Family-Based Services*. New York: Aldine de Gruyter.

Robin, A. L., & Foster, S. L. (1989). *Negotiating Parent-Adolescent Conflict: A Behavioral-Family Systems Approach*. New York: Guilford Press.

Whittaker, J. K., Kinney, J., Tracy, E. N., & Booth, C. (1990). *Reaching High-Risk Families: Intensive Family Preservation in Human Services*. New York: Aldine de Gruyter.

---

*Reprint requests for CSS annual reports are available from: Ms Mary Lynn Cousins-Brame, Program Director, Community Support Services, St Lawrence Youth Association, 845 Division St., Kingston, Ontario, K7K 4C4 Canada, phone (001) 613 542-6934. Please make cheque payable in Canadian funds to the St Lawrence Youth Association.

Chapter 9

"STRAIGHT THINKING ON PROBATION": EVIDENCE-BASED PRACTICE AND THE CULTURE OF CURIOSITY

Peter Raynor and Maurice Vanstone

Centre for Applied Social Studies, University of Wales Swansea, UK

The STOP program ("Straight Thinking On Probation") was one of the first systematic attempts to apply, in a British probation service, what was already being learned in other countries about the design and implementation of effective rehabilitation programs for offenders. Why this kind of program came relatively late to Britain is discussed on pp. 196–197 in the chapter, as is the relative dearth of research on the effectiveness of probation in Britain from the mid-1970s until the late 1980s. The STOP program itself was an import, based on the cognitive-behavioral "Reasoning and Rehabilitation" programs developed in Canada in the 1980s (Ross and Fabiano, 1985), and adopted by one probation service in Wales as the most likely strategy to reduce reoffending by persistent offenders and to start to introduce a new culture of effectiveness among probation staff. Both the authors of this chapter were heavily involved for about 7 years, from 1990 to 1997, in various aspects of the planning, implementation and evaluation of this

Offender Rehabilitation in Practice. Edited by G. A. Bernfeld, D. P. Farrington and A. W. Leschied.
© 2001 John Wiley & Sons, Ltd.

project, and in publication of its results (see e.g. Raynor 1998; Raynor & Vanstone, 1994, 1996, 1997). This chapter is an attempt, with hindsight, to describe and assess what has been learned from STOP: from its weaknesses and failures, as well as from its strengths and successes. Instead of the usual focus on "what works" (i.e. what can work if we do it right), we are concerned here with the process of making things work. In keeping with the general pattern of the book, we explore this theme at the levels of program development, of organizational learning in the agencies that try to deliver effective programs and at the societal level where moves towards effectiveness in criminal justice are leading to significant and rapid changes in policy. First, though, we need to consider the effects at "client level" by summarizing the impact of the program on the offenders who took part in it.

THE "CLIENT LEVEL": CHANGES IN OFFENDING, IN THINKING AND IN REPORTED PROBLEMS

The evaluation study's findings concerning the program's impact on offenders have been widely discussed in Britain, largely because of the shortage of other comparable studies. It was the first widely known and comprehensive British evaluation of a structured probation program delivered according to a design specified in advance, with arrangements to ensure program integrity. (The very few previous British studies showing a reduction in reconviction following intensive probation had involved methods of supervision that were less fully specified or less replicable: e.g. Raynor, 1988; Roberts, 1989.) As a result, the STOP findings have been widely quoted as lending substantial support for cognitive-behavioral methods of supervision, and their impact may even appear disproportionate for what are in reality fairly modest findings from a local study carried out with little research funding and, at the beginning, very little official support at government level.

Readers interested in the full details of the study's methodology and findings may wish to refer to the more comprehensive account given in Raynor and Vanstone (1997). In brief, we were able to compare actual reconviction at 12 and 24 months for the STOP program and for a number of comparison groups of male offenders with predicted reconviction rates based on static risk factors, such as age and criminal record, using the best British prediction instrument available at that time (Home Office, 1993). On this measure, several community sentences performed quite well with less serious offenders, but the nearest equivalent to the STOP group in terms of seriousness and persistence of offending was a comparison group of offenders receiving custodial sentences. The results of this comparison are set out in Table 9.1: during comparable periods at risk (i.e. from date of probation order or release from custody respectively) the STOP program

Table 9.1 Predicted and actual reconviction rates adjusted to eliminate pseudo-reconvictions ($N = 655$, sentenced during the first 10 months of the experiment)

	By 12 months		By 24 months	
	Predicted (%)	Actual (%)	Predicted (%)	Actual (%)
Started probation with STOP ($N = 107$)	44	44	63	65
Other probation ($N = 100$)	41	40	59	61
Community service ($N = 194$)	35	32	52	49
Suspended imprisonment ($N = 90$)	26	27	41	41
Imprisonment (adults <12 months) ($N = 82$)	38	44	55	56
Young offender institutions ($N = 82$)	47	54	65	73
Combined custodials ($N = 164$)	42	49	60	65
STOP completers ($N = 59$)	42	35	61	63

completers were reconvicted less. During the first 12 months, they were reconvicted at well below the predicted rate, but during the second year of follow-up they caught up with the predicted rate, though still remaining below the custodial comparison group.

Several warning notes should be sounded here. First, as is common in local evaluation studies using fairly small numbers, few of these differences satisfy conventional tests of significance (the exception is a comparison between STOP completers and people released from young offender institutions, and other comparisons of the STOP group with custodially sentenced offenders approach significance). Second, the results are nowhere near as dramatic as some of those reported for comparable programs in Canada (Ross, Fabiano & Ewles, 1988). On the other hand, we also found that Mid-Glamorgan was in general a high-reconviction area, so that predictors based on national outcomes could underpredict for the offenders in our study. Also, given the relatively poor performance of non-completers, it is important to note that the completion rate was, for this type of program, quite high at 75 per cent of those eligible to complete. This was broadly similar to completion rates for other community sentences, but clearly pointed to the maintenance and improvement of completion rates as a key component of future effectiveness.

What was rather more striking, in the case of the STOP program completers, was a study of the seriousness of reconvictions and the sentences received on reconviction. Table 9.2 shows proportions of offenders reoffending seriously (defined as violent or sexual offences or burglary) and proportions receiving custodial sentences on reconviction, which can be taken as

Table 9.2   Serious offences and custodial sentences on reconviction

	Serious offences on original conviction	Serious offences on reconviction at:		Custodial sentences on reconviction
		12 months	24 months	
Sentenced to STOP (N = 107)	42 (39%)	19 (18%)	29 (27%)	21 (20%)
Combined custodials (N = 164)	67 (41%)	34 (21%)	41 (25%)	25 (15%)
STOP completers (N = 59)	21 (36%)	5 (8%)	13 (22%)	1 (2%)

Table 9.3   Self-reported changes in thinking among program participants

	No.	%
Thinking before acting, speaking or offending	16	28
Thinking a problem through	15	26
Thinking of consequences	14	24
Talking and explaining to people	10	17
Thinking of others	8	14
Thinking about who can help/involving others	6	10
Prioritizing/Sorting out options	4	7
Understanding and/or listening to other viewpoints	4	7
Thinking positively	3	5
Dealing with a problem immediately	3	5
Thinking more clearly	2	3
More open and assertive	2	3
Less aggressive	2	3

one measure of the seriousness of reconvictions at least as perceived by sentencers. Here the differences in favor of the STOP completers are more marked, particularly the low incidence of custodial sentences on reconviction (which resembles one of the findings of Ross et al., 1988).

In earlier reports of these findings we speculated that this might indicate that some STOP group members were changing their behavior away from offences which had an obvious personal victim, rather than away from offending in general. Offences such as criminal damage or possession of drugs continued. Some support for this interpretation comes from the post-program interviews, in which many program members described ways in which they believed their thinking had changed: Table 9.3 shows the common themes in these interviews, which clustered particularly around becoming less impulsive and thinking more about other people's feelings and points of view. Several of the interviews illustrated this particularly clearly; for example: "It's made me realize ... it's learnt me to put myself in other people's places if they'd been burgled ... guilty's the word ... it's

Table 9.4 Changes in CRIME-PICS scores and reconvictions within 12 months

Component and direction of change	Proportion (%) reconvicted
Attitudes and beliefs become more procriminal ($N = 40$)	38%
Attitudes and beliefs become more prosocial ($N = 55$)	27%
Self-reported problems increase ($N = 31$)	48%
Self-reported problems decrease ($N = 45$)	22%

out of order"; "I sit down and work things out whereas before I'd just drink. I sit down and look at my options and work it out that way instead of rushing off and doing something stupid."

Some other aspects of the study contributed to this general picture. Questionnaires designed to measure the extent of attitudes and beliefs favorable to crime and the level of self-reported social and personal problems (the CRIME-PICS instrument: Frude, Honess & Maguire, 1990) were administered before and after the program, and to comparison groups of offenders on "standard" probation orders or community service (Table 9.4). Both the STOP program and "standard" probation appeared to have a positive effect on attitudes, and the STOP program in particular was associated with a marked reduction in self-reported problems. The latter was especially associated with lower reconviction rates ($p < 0.05$).

Overall, a fair summary of our findings in relation to the STOP program's impact on its members would be that we found some evidence of fairly short-term reductions in offending and rather more persistent reductions in more serious offending among those who completed the program. These were associated with reported changes in attitudes, thinking and behavior consistent with the rationale of a cognitive-behavioral program, and offered a more effective and constructive sentencing option than other likely sentences for this group of relatively serious and persistent offenders. However, the findings also pointed to a need to improve the matching of offenders to the program and the proportion completing it: some program members were clearly selected on a tariff basis, being at high risk of a custodial sentence, rather than on the basis of assessed needs appropriate to the program. Most importantly, our findings highlighted a need to reinforce what was learned during the program by appropriate follow-up during the remainder of the period of supervision. The context created by other methods and practices in the organization was of fundamental importance, and later in the chapter we turn to what was learned about the impact on the agency and its staff, and how decisions and practices at the organizational level contributed to what worked and what didn't work. First, however, it is important to consider the historical context, the process of innovation which led to these results, the reasons for the choice of this type of program and the special measures needed to ensure its delivery and integrity.

THE "PROGRAM LEVEL": DEVELOPMENT, DELIVERY AND INTEGRITY

Accounts of the development of what has been described as "what works" (McGuire, 1995) usually relate it to the history of the "nothing works" research of the 1970s. A central premise of this version is that the largely pessimistic findings of that research had a significant and negative influence on the practice of probation officers and other criminal justice workers throughout the late 1970s and 1980s. This orthodox account associates the reason for a loss of faith in the minds of both practitioners and policy makers about the possibility of influencing offenders away from crime, with the research of Lipton, Martinson and Wilks (1975) in North America and Folkard, Smith and Smith (1976) in Britain. According to this account, managers within the probation service changed the direction of policy away from rehabilitative effort to diversion from custody. Further credence is lent to this argument by the growth in the use of probation with additional conditions, day centers and community service during the same period (Bottoms, 1987; Pease, Billingham & Earnshaw, 1977; Pointing, 1986; Vass, 1990). However, in a challenge to this line of argument one author (Vanstone, 2000) has argued that the "nothing works" research went largely unheeded by practitioners who, within the framework of diversionary policies, continued to maintain a focus on the attempt to help people stop offending and to use innovative methods of work.

The STOP experiment in Mid-Glamorgan, therefore, was not simply a response to the elusiveness of the goal of reducing offending but rather was a culmination of a process of practice development and initiatives that can be traced from the mid-1970s, as well as being directly influenced by the research of Robert Ross and his colleagues in Canada (Ross et al., 1988; Ross & Fabiano, 1985). However, the story is incomplete without surveying the wider picture and giving recognition to the influence of two particular theoretical initiatives developed in Britain on the practice culture not only of the Mid-Glamorgan Service but also other criminal justice practitioners.

The first, the social skills and personal-problem solving model, was inaugurated in Britain in 1975 when a Home Office research unit funded experiment was established in Ashwell and Ranby prisons and the Sheffield Day Training Center. As a part of the experiment, prison officers and probation officers were trained in the use of what were largely cognitive-behavioral methods and then applied them, using a 4-stage framework of assessment, objectives, learning and evaluation (McGuire, 1978; Priestley, McGuire, Flegg, Hemsley & Welham, 1978). Significantly, as it seems with hindsight, the methods used in this experiment were drawn primarily from life skills work undertaken in Canada (Saskatchewan Newstart, 1969). The model provided practice methods that were both tangible and usable, and as a result of widespread short training courses it became the fulcrum of a significant proportion of probation officers' practice throughout England and Wales (Raynor, Smith & Vanstone, 1994).

The anatomy of that impact is worth some examination. The experiment took place at a critical time in the history of probation theory because not only the effectiveness of probation intervention but also its theoretical paradigm was under challenge (Bottoms & McWilliams, 1979). As with other forms of social work, the professionalization of probation practice had been linked closely to particular theories of individual psychology (McWilliams, 1983) and to a psychotherapeutic model (Golding, 1959). "Casework", as it was called, attained its position as a badge of professional expertise in the 1950s and 1960s, and permeated much of the professional discourse in the *Probation Journal* (Aylwin, 1961; Garrett, 1961; Thornborough, 1960). The emphasis was put on "the understanding of human relationships and the modification of personality and attitudes" (Sanders, 1961, p. 142). Bottoms and McWilliams (1979) challenged not only the efficacy of probation practice but also argued that the treatment (or casework) model was theoretically faulty because of the inappropriateness of the "analogy made with individual medical treatment".

The Social Skills and Problem-Solving model, therefore, had an impact on probation at a time of unique vulnerability in the history of community supervision of offenders. Its influence was reinforced in the mid-1980s by the evolution of the Offending Behavior model, which stemmed from a recognition that the Social Skills and Problem-Solving model was deficient in so far as it compounded a historical neglect of the offense as a focus for work (McGuire & Priestley, 1985). The Offending Behavior model involved a particular focus on the offence and encompassed methods and materials that facilitated the exploration of offending and patterns of behavior. Again, the dissemination of these ideas through training courses established the approach as the second major influence on probation practice in Britain.

Both models offered exciting, concrete programs that compared favorably with the elusiveness and mystique of casework. It can be argued, therefore, that the openness of practitioners to these new models was more to do with skepticism about, and dissatisfaction (or even boredom) with the casework model than a considered response to the pessimism of research findings. Indeed, there is evidence that officers had already discarded that model in favor of more practical work on the day-to-day problems of those they supervised (Willis, 1983).

The receptivity of Mid-Glamorgan's officers to the new approaches, and ultimately to the "Reasoning and Rehabilitation" program was increased by the history of that service's involvement in the Day Training Center experiment (McGuire, 1978; Smith, 1982; Vanstone, 1986: Vanstone 1993). From the late 1970s the Mid-Glamorgan Center had implemented a program based on the social skills and personal problem solving model and throughout the 1980s the program was modified in response to the lessons learnt from the Offending Behavior model. Both models, however, had a broader impact on the service and as elsewhere in Britain various programs, such as anger management, and offending behavior groups were set up. From the onset of the STOP experiment, therefore, practitioners had considerable experience of the kinds of methods used in the "Reasoning and Rehabilitation" program. Moreover, the incumbent Chief Probation Officer had been the instigator of an innovative approach to the supervision of offenders based on the idea of induction, assessment and groupwork programs (Brown & Seymour, 1984).

Despite the fact that the Mid-Glamorgan Service was better placed than others to engage in such change it remained a difficult and complex process. So, how was that change made? First, the service set the following objective:

> that we should systematically apply an agreed challenging program of social work inputs which are drawn from proven best practice and which are applied by staff who are enthusiastic and well trained in the delivery of that program. Any such program will be rigorously monitored to enable us to evaluate its effectiveness regarding either reducing or slowing down re-offending.
>
> (Sutton, 1990)

The process of implementation then involved discussion of the proposal with the management group and the probation committee; consultation with practitioners; the negotiation of training and research consultancies; the creation of a commissioning group with overall responsibility for establishing the project and cross-grade working parties on training, targeting, research and external marketing; and the building of a collaborative relationship with the University of Wales, Swansea. This initial phase was completed with the selling of the program to the courts. Following the approval of the project by the Probation Committee, the work of the various working groups was disseminated at a staff conference, public relations work with the various local probation liaison committees was undertaken and the training program for staff began. An awareness of the principles emerging from effectiveness research informed the planning and management of the process of change as well as the experiment itself. This influenced the appointment of research and project consultants; the revision of the Canadian manuals (Ross, Fabiano & Ross, 1986) so that they were appropriate to the local cultural context; the appropriate resourcing of the project; delivery of a 5-day training program for 45 officers and training for managers; the development of a research and evaluation design; and the production of an agreed format for the delivery of the program and provisions to ensure program integrity. Program integrity was critical to the success and evaluation of the program and was ensured, first, by the examination (using a checklist) by one of the authors of a random sample of nearly 100 hours of visually recorded group sessions; second, through supervision of officers by their line managers; and, third, by a group of practitioners and a specialist manager who discussed and monitored the running of the programs.

THE ORGANIZATIONAL LEVEL: STAFF, MANAGEMENT AND AGENCY

Unavoidably, the rigorous implementation of the program had a significant impact on the whole of the organization. Probably the most potent aspect of that impact resulted from the decision to involve all the teams in the Service in the program. At the time, this gave uniqueness to the STOP experiment, and merits further discussion. First, however, it is important to explain the motivation for that decision.

The history of innovative development in probation practice in Britain is characterized by a practitioner-led effort insufficiently supported by the organization as a whole, or by what we describe as the specialist project syndrome. The Day Center in Mid-Glamorgan was an example of this, having been set up as part of an inconclusive national experiment and having survived for nearly a decade in a "penal limbo" (Vanstone & Raynor, 1981). As such, it experienced many of the problems associated with specialist projects: these include detachment and isolation from mainstream activity within the organization; inconsistent levels of commitment from other staff; low rates of referral; charges of elitism; and the development of a separate and sometimes exclusive culture that misfits the broader organizational culture.

These problems minimized its influence on that broader culture and ensured that its survival depended, not on being an integral part of the organization but rather on its status as a separate institution. In turn, this perpetuated the existence of small groups of practitioners, detached from the rest of an organization which had a limited sense of ownership. More importantly, perhaps, like so many innovative projects in the history of probation, its theoretical and practice bases emanated more from the skills and particular interests of the staff group than from evidence about effectiveness. One of the principal goals of the STOP experiment, therefore, was to change the culture of the organization so that practitioners became committed to evidence-based practice, and "believers" in their ability to influence those they supervised (Humphrey & Pease, 1992). The management group attempted to achieve that by learning from the lessons of the specialist project syndrome.

Some evidence of the impact on the culture of the organization can be discerned in the results of a survey of staff views conducted as part of the research. This was undertaken at the end of the 12-month experimental period, and involved interviews with all the officers who had run at least one STOP group and a sample of officers and managers who had been working in the Service during the experiment. The full details of the results have been published elsewhere (Lucas, Raynor & Vanstone, 1992); here, a summary of the main findings will suffice. Officers were positive about the approach, and expressed an increased confidence in their knowledge and skills; also they indicated an increased belief in the capacity of probation intervention to reduce offending, and reported an enhanced interest in research and evaluation issues. The level of change was less discernible in the group which had not been involved in the running of groups, thus suggesting that practical involvement in the project was of greater significance in stimulating change in officers' views than simply working in an organization which was going through a process of change. This finding also lent support to the management's strategy of involving as many staff as possible in the delivery of the program.

Further evidence of change in the culture was provided by the development of a range of group programs alongside the STOP experiment, but that change was also the result of the simultaneous creation of a unit responsible for the development of those programs. The aim of the Resource and Policy Unit was to create, deliver and evaluate effective programs for people being supervised by the Mid-Glamorgan Probation Service. The influences that underpinned the STOP experiment also impinged on the unit. So, it worked in partnership with colleagues in the field teams, based the programs on the prerequisites of effectiveness and set evaluation criteria which enabled them to assess the impact of the programs not only on the participants but on the organization itself. The template for these additional programs which focused on, for example, violence and car-related crime, was the available knowledge base about "what works" in community sentences (e.g. Lipsey, 1995; Andrews et. al., 1990; Antonowicz & Ross, 1994), and the STOP program itself. They were overseen by groups of practitioners (program action groups) which acted as catalysts for ideas; opportunities for the discussion of evaluation and research and the refinement of programs; and networks of support. The cooperation of groups of practitioners in this way reinforced the impact of the STOP experiment on the organization; but what was its broader impact?

THE SOCIETAL LEVEL: FROM EFFECTIVE PRACTICE TO CRIME REDUCTION

Since the 1-year reconviction results of STOP were first disseminated in 1994 (Raynor & Vanstone, 1994) and in a contribution to James McGuire's influential collection "what works" (Knott, 1995), the study has been widely cited as lending support to a series of initiatives in and around the Probation Service, known at various times as the What Works project, the Effective Practice Initiative and Evidence-based Practice. There were, of course, many sources of these initiatives in addition to STOP; together, they represent a developing awareness among practitioners, managers, academics and policy makers in Britain of an international trend in criminal justice towards applying the lessons of evaluative research. Some of the key stages in this development were a Home Office conference for chief probation officers and probation committee chairs in May 1995 on "managing what works", addressed among others by Friedrich Lösel, another contributor to McGuire's book, and followed by a circular (Home Office, 1995) drawing probation managers' attention to "critical success factors" and giving notice that the Probation Inspectorate would be looking for evidence that these were being embodied in probation programs. An inspection of probation orders with additional requirements (e.g. requirements to attend programs) found little evidence of this (HMIP, 1996), and in January 1996 the Chief Probation Inspector, Graham Smith, launched the What Works project to address the problem. What had originally seemed a fairly simplistic approach (identify the 'success factors' and require managers to implement them) was increasingly being seen as a much more fundamental program of organizational learning and cultural change. Eventually this was to lead to an unprecedented degree of cooperation between the Probation Inspectorate, civil servants and Home Office researchers in driving forward the agenda for change. After the election of a new government in 1997, this also fitted well with politicians' commitment to more effective public services and, in particular, a more effective criminal justice system.

Throughout this process the STOP experiment was regularly cited (along with developments in other areas such as Greater Manchester and Hereford and Worcester) as evidence not only that probation could be effective, but that the required cultural changes could occur. For example, the first stages of the What Works project sought to identify and disseminate examples of effective practice and invited chief probation officers to submit examples of effective practice from their own areas; subsequent analysis showed that out of the 267 projects submitted by chief officers, only 210 met the criteria for inclusion in the survey (e.g. they were current or recent), and only 109 of these claimed to have carried out even basic evaluation. Further enquiry yielded only 33 actual evaluation reports; examination of these eventually found only four (including STOP) which used adequate evaluation methodology and showed some positive results, and another seven which showed "promising approaches to some aspects of evaluation". Clearly one of the major cultural changes needed was for managers to become interested in evidence of effectiveness, instead of simply making claims of effectiveness. The report singles out STOP for special comment: "Of all the returns made in this study, STOP was the most extensively evaluated" (Underdown, 1998, p. 109).

Since then, there has been progress on a number of fronts. The Chief Probation Inspector's Annual Report for 1998 describes the establishment of the Effective Practice Initiative, in which the Inspectorate, the Home Office Probation Unit, the Association of Chief Officers of Probation and the Central Probation Council (the employers of probation services) are working together to establish a "national curriculum" of effective programs across the spectrum of different types of offender; "pathfinder" programs are being developed and piloted with the support of the Probation Studies Unit in Oxford (Home Office, 1998); a common system of risk and need assessment for offenders is being developed for adoption in both prisons and probation services; a research-based guide to Evidence-based Practice has been published and widely disseminated in probation services (Chapman & Hough, 1998), and a panel of experts has been appointed to scrutinize and accredit the effective programs which prisons and probation services are now expected to implement. The initiative, now known again as What Works, is described in a glossy booklet introduced by a Home Office minister of state (Home Office, 1999) and has a budget of £21 million over 3 years, including provision for external evaluation of key parts of the program. Even this is only part of a wider evidence-driven "crime reduction strategy" with a budget of £250 million. With investment and evaluation on this scale, it should not be long before we have far more comprehensive and reliable evidence to guide us than can be provided by pioneering local programs such as STOP.

There are also, of course, some anxieties. Forthcoming reforms of the Probation Service will see it restructured as a more centralized national service, more responsive to direction from central government. This is seen as part of the process of making services more effective, and certainly it should reduce the parochialism which has sometimes delayed progress, but STOP itself was a local initiative which ran well ahead of Home Office thinking in 1990. Also, Probation Service funds have been cut for the past few years, which may make it more difficult to mount new projects effectively. We believe that it will be essential to strike a balance between central direction and local initiatives: the necessary cultural changes will not come from the managerialist approach which tells people "we know what works: now you do it". One of the lessons of STOP is that change is not driven only by knowledge, skills and determination, but also by curiosity: "Can this work? What will happen if we do this?" Curiosity drives the spirit of experiment which allows organizations to learn. After all, "What works?" is a question not a statement.

References

Andrews, D. A., Zinger, I., Hoge, R. D., Bonta, J., Gendreau, P., & Cullen, F. T. (1990). Does correctional treatment work? A clinically relevant and psychologically informed meta-analysis. *Criminology*, **28**, 369–404.

Antonowicz, D., & Ross, R. (1994). Essential components of successful rehabilitation programs for offenders. *International Journal of Offender Therapy and Comparative Criminology*, **38**, 97–104.

Aylwin, G. D. L. (1961). Personality in probation work. *Probation Journal*, **9**, 178–179.

Bottoms, A. E. (1987). Limiting prison use: The experience of England and Wales. *Howard Journal*, **26**, 177–202.

Bottoms, A. E., & McWilliams, W. (1979). A non-treatment paradigm for probation practice. *British Journal of Social Work*, **9**, 159–202.

Brown, A., & Seymour, B. (Eds) (1984). *Intake Groups for Clients: A Probation Innovation*. Bristol: University of Bristol.

Chapman, T., & Hough, M. (1998). *Evidence-based Practice*. London: Home Office.

Folkard, M. S., Smith, D. E., & Smith, D. D. (1976). *Impact*, Vol. II, Home Office Research Study 36. London: HMSO.

Frude, N., Honess, T., & Maguire, M. (1990). *CRIME-PICS Handbook*. Cardiff: Michael & Associates.

Garrett, A. C. (1961). Casework. *Probation Journal*, **9**, 134.

Golding, R. R. W. (1959). A probation technique. *Probation Journal*, **9**, 47–49.

HMIP (Her Majesty's Inspectorate of Probation) (1996). *Probation Orders with Additional Requirements: Report of a Thematic Inspection 1995*. London: Home Office.

Home Office. (1993). *The National Risk of Reconviction Predictor*. London: Home Office Research and Planning Unit.

Home Office. (1995). *Managing What Works: Conference Report and Guidance on Critical Success Factors for Probation Supervision Programmes*, Circular 77/1995. London: Home Office.

Home Office. (1998). *Effective Practice Initiative. National Implementation Plan for the Supervision of Offenders*, Circular 35/1998. London: Home Office.

Home Office. (1999). *What Works: Reducing Re-Offending: Evidence-Based Practice*. London: Home Office.

Humphrey, C., & Pease, K. (1992). Effectiveness measurement in the probation service: A view from the troops. *Howard Journal*, **31**, 31–52.

Knott, C. (1995). The STOP programme. In J. McGuire (Ed.), *What Works: Reducing Reoffending*. Chichester: John Wiley.

Lipsey, M. (1995). What do we learn from 400 research studies on the effectiveness of treatment with juvenile delinquents? In J. McGuire (Ed.), *What Works: Reducing Reoffending*. Chichester: John Wiley.

Lipton, D., Martinson, R., & Wilks, J. (1975). *The Effectiveness of Correctional Treatment*. New York: Praeger.

Lucas, J., Raynor, P., & Vanstone, M. (1992). *Straight Thinking on Probation One Year On: The Second Report of the Evaluation Study*. Bridgend: Mid-Glamorgan Probation Service.

McGuire, J. (1978). *Sheffield Day Training Centre Programme Development Report*. Sheffield: South Yorkshire Probation Service.

McGuire, J. (Ed.) (1995). *What Works: Reducing Reoffending*. Chichester: John Wiley.

McGuire, J. & Priestley, P. (1985). *Offending Behaviour: Skills and Stratagems for Going Straight*. London: Batsford.

McWilliams, W. (1983). The mission to the English police courts 1876–1936. *Howard Journal*, **22**(3), 129–147.

Pease, K., Billingham, S., & Earnshaw, I. (1977). *Community Service Assessed in 1976*, Home Office Research Study 39. London: HMSO.

Pointing, J. (Ed.) (1986). *Alternatives to Custody*. Oxford: Blackwell.

Priestley, P., McGuire, J., Flegg, D., Hemsley, V., & Welham, D. (1978). *Social Skills and Personal Problem Solving*. London: Tavistock.

Raynor, P. (1988). *Probation as an Alternative to Custody*. Aldershot: Avebury.

Raynor, P. (1998). Attitudes, social problems and reconvictions in the STOP probation experiment. *Howard Journal*, **37**, 1–15.

Raynor, P., Smith, D., & Vanstone, M. (1994). *Effective Probation Practice*. Basingstoke: Macmillan.

Raynor, P., & Vanstone, M. (1994). *Straight Thinking On Probation: Third Interim Evaluation Report*. Bridgend: Mid-Glamorgan Probation Service.

Raynor, P., & Vanstone, M. (1996). Reasoning and rehabilitation in Britain: The results of the Straight Thinking On Probation (STOP) programme. *International Journal of Offender Therapy and Comparative Criminology*, **40**, 279–291.

Raynor, P., & Vanstone, M. (1997). *Straight Thinking on Probation (STOP): The Mid-Glamorgan Experiment*, Probation Studies Unit Report No. 4. Oxford: Centre for Criminological Research.

Roberts, C. (1989). *Hereford and Worcester Probation Service Young Offender Project: First Evaluation Report*. Oxford: Department of Social and Administrative Studies.

Ross, R. R., & Fabiano, E. A. (1985). *Time to Think: A Cognitive Model of Delinquency Prevention and Offender Rehabilitation*. Johnson City, TN: Institute of Social Sciences and Arts.

Ross, R. R., Fabiano, E. A., & Ewles, C. D. (1988). Reasoning and rehabilitation. *International Journal of Offender Therapy and Comparative Criminology*, **32**, 29–35.

Ross, R. R., Fabiano, E. A., & Ross, R. D. (1986). *Reasoning and Rehabilitation: A Handbook for Teaching Cognitive Skills*. Ottawa: University of Ottawa.

Sanders, H. (1961). A time of re-birth. *Probation Journal*, **9**, 141–144.

Saskatchewan Newstart (1969). *Life Skills Coaching Manual*. Prince Albert, Saskatchewan: Training Research and Development Station, Department of Manpower and Immigration.

Smith, L. (1982). Day training centres. *Research Bulletin* (Home Office) **14**, 34–37.

Sutton, D. (1990). Memorandum to senior probation staff. Mid-Glamorgan Probation Service, Unpublished.

Thornborough, M. M. (1960). What are we doing, and why? *Probation Journal*, **9**, 89– 90.

Underdown, A. (1998). *Strategies for Effective Offender Supervision: Report of the HMIP What Works Project*. London: Home Office.

Vanstone, M. (1986). Moving away from help?: Policy and practice in probation day centres. *Howard Journal*, **24**, 20–28.

Vanstone, M. (1993). A "missed opportunity" reassessed: The influence of the Day Training Centre experiment on the criminal justice system and probation practice. *British Journal of Social Work*, **23**, 213–229.

Vanstone, M. (2000). Cognitive-behavioural work with offenders in the UK: A history of influential endeavour. *Howard Journal*.

Vanstone, M., & Raynor, P. (1981). Diversion from prison—a partial success and a missed opportunity. *Probation Journal*, **28**, 85–89.

Vass, A. A. (1990). *Alternatives to Prison*. London: Sage.

Willis, A. (1983). The balance between care and control in probation: A research note. *British Journal of Social Work*, **13**, 339–346.

Chapter 10

DESIGNING, IMPLEMENTING AND MANAGING TREATMENT PROGRAMS FOR VIOLENT OFFENDERS

Ralph C. Serin* and Denise L. Preston[†]

* Research Branch, Correctional Service of Canada, Kingston, Ontario, Canada
[†] Department of Psychology, Collins Bay Institution, Kingston, Ontario, Canada

THEORETICAL MODEL

Although this chapter is focused on our experience in implementing a program for persistently violent offenders, upon reflection it seems to us that the process and guidelines vary very little across programs. Although there may be some specialized assessment issues that are linked to admission criteria and measurement of treatment gain in violent offenders, other domains (e.g. sex offenders) have idiosyncrasies as well. For this reason, we do not consider our experience to be unique and believe that our lessons learned apply to a broad range of offender programming initiatives.

The importance of theory to program development and evaluation has been well described by Elliott (1980). Less clear, however, has been the role of a conceptual framework to facilitate program implementation. The theory dictates the specific intervention strategy, which includes the identification of treatment targets, the procedures for use within the actual

Offender Rehabilitation in Practice. Edited by G. A. Bernfeld, D. P. Farrington and A. W. Leschied.
© 2001 John Wiley & Sons, Ltd.

program and the evaluation protocol. Therefore, it is critical that consumers of the program (prison administrators, clinical staff, security staff and offenders) consider the components and theory reflected in the "new" program to have face validity. Furthermore, it is necessary for the program to appear to be value-added in order that staff consider changing the way they currently do business. Mandates from headquarters down are far less compelling than agreement by consumers that the program appears to make sense. With this in mind, successful program implementation must translate the theory into practical levels for all staff. Too often, theory is considered the purview of academics living in ivory towers, rather than a road map to inform assessment and treatment efforts.

Two concerns that typically describe organizations are inertia and chaos. The former describes the situation where an organization or facility is comfortable with their current practices and is resistant to change. Within this situation, clearly any new program must appear to make sense and be value-added. The latter situation describes an organization that experiences constant change, without apparent direction in terms of vision, mission statements or policy. For such an organization, the implementation of a new program must appear to address or resolve problems. Ideally, the program model should build on existing work within the organization. In this manner, the program development and implementation can be viewed as iterative, rather than disconnected, to previous initiatives. Additionally and ideally, then, staff training becomes more one of fine tuning than major conceptual shifts every few years. A similar argument can also be made regarding the value of utilizing existing assessment procedures, where appropriate, at least for referral purposes, so that there is limited duplication of effort by staff for each new initiative. For example, the Correctional Service of Canada has an intake assessment strategy (Motiuk, 1997) that has proved useful in identifying the distinct treatment needs of persistently violent offenders (Serin & Preston, in press). Furthermore, by using the assessment protocol instead of a more limited approach, such as index offense, the prevalence of persistently violent offenders in federal custody drops from 78 to 35.4 per cent.

These data suggest that it is possible to identify chronic or persistently violent offenders who have greater treatment needs and a higher likelihood of recidivism (Serin & Preston, 2001). Relative to other offenders, they show significantly greater need in the areas of employment, family, associations, substance abuse, community functioning, personal/emotional skills and criminal attitudes.

Finally, the conceptual model must inform the derivation of treatment targets and the preferred mode of delivery (Andrews & Bonta, 1998). For instance, if the theoretical model hypothesizes that deficits in social-information processing skills are related to offenders' violent behaviour, the components of these skills must be represented in the treatment targets. In this manner, the program will look very different from a program that considers arousal management and anger difficulties as antecedents to violent offending. Presumably, the referral criteria will also differ between these programs, even though both purport to address violent offending.

SITE SELECTION

A primary consideration in the selection of site(s) for a new program is the identification of a treatment need. Specifically, there must be an adequate referral base to sustain the program for its intended duration. Depending on the evaluation methodology, the referral base may also need to provide for one or more control groups, thus substantially increasing the potential number of offenders required at a site. Furthermore, the program must have the support of senior management, program and security staff, and the offender population. Site visits are important to ascertain the degree of support before the final decision of a site is made. This may avoid possible pitfalls in the future. Additionally, the physical requirements are important when making a site selection. For instance, if the available space is too small, too isolated or otherwise unsuitable, it may be a poor choice, notwithstanding the stated support. If the program has management support this should extend to physical space. Otherwise, support is simply provided to get the program implemented without a clear commitment for its overall success.

Depending on the magnitude of the program, the issue of the representativeness of the population must also be considered. If the goal is to eventually expand the program to other sites, it is important to ensure that the sites have similar populations. Otherwise the experiences and evaluation results from one site cannot reliably inform efforts in another new site. Furthermore, some consideration must be given at the onset regarding the scope of the project in terms of the anticipated number of sites required. Needs analyses, focus groups and site visits can all be instructive in this matter, but from an implementation perspective it is preferable to begin with a pilot and consider expansion carefully. The greater the number of sites, the greater the likelihood of program drift and the more likely is diminished program integrity. Also, an increase in the number of sites dictates the need for someone to oversee the programs. This resource issue must be built into the design as early as possible. All too often the interest is to fund direct services, only to unwittingly compromise the quality of the program evaluation.

Similarly, it is not uncommon for the site to wish to select their staff to deliver the new program. Even if such a strategy is well intentioned, such a decision is probably best left to the program development and implementation team. Otherwise the very backbone of the program, the staff, may not be a good fit with the program model. Increasingly, evidence is being accumulated that describes the characteristics of effective staff in programming (Dowden, 1998) and their impact on outcome (Fernandez, Serran & Marshall, 1999).

STAFF SELECTION AND TRAINING

Perhaps the single most important factor contributing to the successful implementation of any program is staff selection. In recruiting staff for program delivery, three factors must be considered: education, experience and personal suitability.

Education

While education includes relevant upgrading efforts and in-house training, it refers most obviously to academic credentials. These should be commensurate with the expectations of the job. Ideally, staff should have completed either a college or university level program in the behaviour sciences.

In the case of intensive violent offender programs, groups should be co-facilitated and at least one of the program delivery staff should be a registered, doctoral level psychologist. Co-facilitation is preferable because it reduces the likelihood of a shift or decline in performance and increases the likelihood that staff remain objective. It enables staff to learn from each other and to benefit from ongoing feedback. It also allows them to pay attention to both content and process issues in the group. Finally, it provides additional security to staff when working with a difficult and potentially violent population. The inclusion of a registered psychologist is advantageous as violent offender programming entails tasks that are psychological in nature, from assessment and diagnosis to intervention for co-occurring mental health problems. As well, given the risk and need levels of this population, it is possible that staff will end up in court as part of an inquest or inquiry. Having a registered professional associated with the program likely enhances the credibility of the program, its documentation and related testimony.

Experience

Because therapist experience appears to be positively related to treatment outcome (Gerstley et al., 1989), staff should bring a variety of relevant experiences to the program: experience with the population in question or with related populations, preferably in a therapeutic context; experience with program delivery, especially those that have a similar theoretical basis to the proposed program; and experience working in the proposed setting of the program. This will ensure that staff are knowledgeable about principles and techniques germane to intervention with the population and able to attend to systemic obstacles to effective implementation.

Staff should have previous experience working with offenders, preferably sexually or non-sexually violent offenders. They should also have experience delivering programs to groups of offenders and working in a correctional setting. All of this increases the likelihood that they will be familiar with the nature of violent offenders and the dynamics of working with them in a group setting. This will also ensure that staff attend to risk, need and responsivity issues (Andrews & Bonta, 1998) in working with them. Finally, all of this will facilitate a safer working environment.

Personal suitability

While academic credentials and relevant experience are important staff selection criteria, personal suitability is critical. This is true for both non-forensic and forensic clinical settings, including those focused on interventions for violent offenders (Preston & Murphy, 1997). Effective program delivery staff should be perceptive, sensitive, empathic, enthusiastic, friendly and trustworthy. They should also be flexible, tolerant and supportive, and have good oral and written communication skills.

In working with violent offenders, many of whom are treatment-resistant, staff must believe in rehabilitation and be genuinely motivated to work with a very difficult population. They must be both confident and competent in order not to react defensively to inevitable personal or professional attacks by clients and to minimize the likelihood of being manipulated by them. They must have a strong sense of their professional identities and boundaries and ascribe to a "firm but fair" approach in order to develop therapeutic relationships with offenders while at the same time being able to set and enforce reasonable limits on behaviour (Andrews & Bonta, 1998). They must also be intrinsically motivated as treatment gains, intermediate and long-term, often seem minimal in this population.

Recruitment process

After careful consideration of the desired education, experience and personal suitability of potential program delivery staff, it is necessary to develop a selection process to recruit such candidates. The selection process should be both knowledge and performance-based and have an explicit scoring protocol. For example, knowledge can be assessed through a structured interview that makes specific inquiries about violent offenders and intervention strategies. The structured interview can also be used to assess personal suitability by, for example, asking candidates how they would deal with pertinent clinical and security scenarios. Performance can be assessed in several ways (e.g. by having potential candidates participate in a role play or complete a written assignment). These performance measures will also allow an evaluation of knowledge and personal suitability.

Whatever selection process is developed, the program manager should have control over staff selection. If this falls down, unsuitable staff may not be identified and then recruited, which could seriously undermine the effective implementation of the program.

Staff training

Staff should be trained according to an explicit training module. The module should provide comprehensive coverage of the program to be implemented. This assumes, of course, that a therapist manual has been developed. Each group should be discussed in detail such that staff have an understanding of the content to be imparted and the dynamics that may arise. This will allow staff to anticipate and prepare for difficulties or opposition. Staff could practice delivering parts of specific groups through brief role plays. This provides a mechanism for feedback and evaluation of staff knowledge and skills.

The module should also involve training on the administration, scoring and interpretation of any assessments conducted in the program. This includes pre- and post-treatment psychometric assessments, in-program knowledge or content "quizzes", and any performance-based measures or staff ratings. Staff should practice test administration and scoring with a previously completed assessment protocol. Again, this will provide a mechanism for evaluation and feedback and will help to ensure inter-rater reliability.

In addition to the program and assessments conducted, the module should include training on the content and format of any reports produced by program staff. There should also be a report template to guide report-writing.

Finally, the training module should include coverage of relevant theoretical and clinical topics such as the theoretical context for the program, risk and need assessment, treatment resistance and treatment engagement, psychopathy, confidentiality, and personal and institutional security. This should include copies of or a reference list for seminal articles and books.

In addition to formal training upon being selected, staff should be supported in their efforts to participate in further relevant training through workshop and conference attendance. Topics of relevance could include conducting cognitive therapy with personality disordered clients, dealing with difficult populations and attention deficit disorder throughout the lifespan. Supporting such efforts should not only ensure more knowledgeable and better-trained staff, but also likely increase their commitment to the program and mitigate against stress and burnout.

MARKETING OF THE PROGRAM

Under site selection, we stressed the importance of support for the program at all levels of the organization. To garner that support, a program must be marketed. This is made easier by developing a program that has the appearance of meeting existing program needs of both the site and the offender population. Tailoring the program to the characteristics of the setting, while maintaining its integrity, also facilitates its acceptance.

While it may be relatively easy to gain the support of specific individuals in the organization, particularly those who have managerial, clinical or functional responsibility for the program's implementation, it is more difficult to gain support from some operational staff and offenders. In the case of operational staff, lack of support may stem from cynicism about rehabilitative efforts. However, lack of support frequently stems from a lack of understanding about the program. In the case of offenders, lack of support typically stems from general and specific cynicism about, for example, the "system's" motives for providing the program or the staff's motives in delivering it. Suggested marketing strategies for each of these groups follow.

To operational staff

In order to sell a program to operational staff, it is necessary to inform as many as possible about the existence of the program, its mandate, content and target population, and the referral process. It is also necessary to introduce the program staff to as many of these as possible. To accomplish this, program staff should utilize existing forums such as regularly scheduled departmental and operational meetings. This should include attendance at meetings for every department represented by operational staff because, although some operational groups will have regular contact with staff or offenders in the program, all staff will eventually have contact with offenders participating in the program. Program staff should also make presentations on any scheduled staff training days. In addition to presentations, staff should write about the program in any available forum; local and regional newsletters are options as are memos or e-mail messages. Because of shiftwork, it is not always possible to reach all staff in one appearance at a departmental meeting, for example. For this reason, it is desirable to repeat presentations several times. It may also be necessary to schedule brief meetings at different times of the day to maximize exposure to as many staff as possible. Similarly, because of staff turnover and inattentiveness, it is necessary to market the program on an ongoing basis.

Another and perhaps more fruitful way of marketing the program is through informal mechanisms. Program staff should take every opportunity to promote the program to operational staff by, for example, discussing it in the lunchroom or during coffee breaks. They should also spend time on the units talking to operational staff. This accomplishes several things. First, it ensures that the program is marketed to as many staff as possible. Second, it allows a smaller learning environment that typically invites more questions. Third, it helps to establish staff credibility, which facilitates better working relationships and program credibility.

To offenders

Offender support for the program is arguably most important to successful program implementation. This is because offenders can easily "shut down" a program by refusing to attend and by pressuring others not to attend. Prior to marketing to offenders, staff should clearly define the referral process and implications to offenders of both participation and refusal. Any implications must, of course, be defensible according to governing legislation.

Meeting with the Inmate Committee, the offenders' elected representatives, is an important first step. In this meeting, staff should briefly discuss the impetus for the program to illustrate how the organization is attempting to be responsive to offender needs. They should stress the advantages of the program to the offender population and solicit the committee's assistance with marketing strategies. If this meeting is successful, staff can then approach the rest of the population with somewhat more credibility and confidence. To advertise to the offender population at large, staff could place an explanatory notice in a visible place on a bulletin board. They should also produce a more detailed brochure to provide to all offenders, through the institutional mail or by leaving them in high traffic areas, such as on each living unit, at the canteen, in the library or in the visiting room. As well, they should ensure that the program is described in the information package provided to newly admitted offenders. A final strategy is to provide brochures to staff in reception units or facilities. This serves to inform reception staff about the program such that they can consider this information in deciding where to place offenders and what programs to recommend. This also serves to inform offenders about the program, right from the start.

PROGRAM REFERRAL ISSUES

For ease of implementation and to maintain program integrity, it is critical to have clear program referral criteria. While the attributes of the intended target population must be specified by program staff (e.g. the requisite number of previous convictions or the level of risk and need), the referral process should be co-developed by referral agents, program delivery staff and program department staff. This will ensure that the referral process is consistent with existing referral processes at the site and that it is accepted and easily implemented by referral agents. However, it should be clearly specified that program delivery staff maintain control over admissions to the program, regardless of the type, number and perceived urgency of referrals.

Although the referral process should be specified in the marketing strategies described earlier, most importantly it must be communicated to potential referral agents. As with marketing to operational staff, this could be accomplished in regularly scheduled departmental or operational meetings, or at staff training sessions. However, it is essential to describe the referral process in writing and disseminate it to referral agents. This allows them something to refer to in deciding whether or not to refer particular offenders.

Again, as with marketing to operational staff, it will be necessary to meet with referral agents on an ongoing basis, or to re-issue the written description of the referral process. It may even be necessary to reiterate the limits of the program and expected outcomes. This is partly because of staff turnover and partly because of a tendency on the part of referral agents to become less stringent in applying referral criteria over time. This highlights the need for program staff to maintain ongoing quality control of referrals.

CREDIBILITY ISSUES—CORPORATE

Critical to the successful development and implementation of a new program is the designation of a corporate champion. Such an individual must be reasonably senior in the organization, well respected and passionate about the initiative. At key points during the development and implementation this individual will be called upon to defend the new program. Criticisms could surface in terms of costs, theoretical approach, resistance to change (investment in the status quo) and unreasonable demands for premature demonstration of program effectiveness. Several strategies can assist the program champion to withstand such challenges and sustain the program. First, the program must reflect the corporate objectives and be consistent with the guiding principles or mission of the organization. Second, the program must attend to a demonstrable need both corporately and for the selected site(s). Third, it is likely preferable if the program "fits" within an existing intervention framework within the agency. For instance, if the new program is very behaviorally based and the organization has long supported more general psychotherapeutic intervention, this could cause difficulties. Similarly, if the organization has widely accepted relapse prevention as an overarching framework for viewing intervention, the implementation of a program that disputes these principles will have greater implementation difficulties. Minimally, staff and offenders will be unfamiliar with the new vocabulary and unclear as to how to integrate the new program into the existing intervention strategy. Finally, in terms of corporate credibility, it is critical to have the support of all stakeholders at headquarters for successful implementation and sustenance of the program. Without such support, issues such as territorial fights, budgetary disputes, recruitment and staffing problems, and general sabotage in the boardroom will erode the potential contribution of any new program. Corporate credibility is therefore essential if the program is to survive long enough for its long-term evaluation.

CREDIBILITY ISSUES—SETTING-SPECIFIC

Setting-specific credibility encompasses credibility of the program at the institutional level and professional and personal credibility of the program staff. To some extent, the marketing strategy begins the establishment of program credibility as staff and offenders are informed of the ways in which the program will meet their various needs. Program credibility is further established by successfully integrating into the existing culture, structure and routine of the institution. The more a program is at odds with these pre-existing conditions, the more difficult the implementation.

Program staff must establish professional and personal credibility with other staff and with offenders. Two factors that facilitate this are having prior correctional and program experience and being known to and respected by the institutional management team, other key staff and key offenders. Failing this, they will have to earn it over time through continued competence and professionalism. Another way to facilitate this is by anticipating and preparing for initial resistance to the program or to themselves on the part of staff or offenders.

RESPONSIVITY—GENERAL AND SPECIFIC

Within the arena of correctional programming, there is consistent evidence that certain models of intervention and characteristics of staff are related to improved outcomes (Andrews & Bonta, 1998). In general, programs that direct services in terms of need and risk will yield enhanced effects. In addition, more intensive services should be provided to higher risk offenders. Notably, the targeting of criminogenic needs is related to the development of theory as discussed on pp. 206–207. For violent offenders it may be useful to consider the role of certain characteristics in either inhibiting or facilitating the expression of violence (Serin & Preston, in press-a). Also, with respect to violent offenders, it is important to further note that they are a heterogeneous group, with distinctions using offense information proving to be quite limited for programming purposes (Serin & Preston, in press-b). Finally, the most effective model of service delivery for offender samples has proved to be cognitive behavioral. Meta-analytic findings have demonstrated that considerable gain can be made by simply considering these principles in the development of a program for offenders. More recently, this issue of general responsivity of attending to risk, need and mode of program delivery has been expanded to address specific responsivity factors (Kennedy & Serin, 1999). These authors propose that further gains in the effectiveness of correctional programming are possible by attending to these specific factors. This work includes the development of an assessment protocol to evaluate treatment readiness, interpersonal variables and treatment performance variables (Serin & Kennedy, 1998). In this manner, treatment gain is distinguished from generalization effects. Furthermore, they recognize the interaction between general and specific responsivity factors to inform differential treatment effectiveness.

RESPONSIVITY

Responsivity factors must be taken into consideration in developing and implementing any program (Andrews & Bonta, 1998). These are characteristics of the site, program, offender and staff that influence program implementation and efficacy. To maximize responsivity, as many of these characteristics as possible should match. For example, program content, duration, and style of delivery should be tailored to the cognitive functioning and treatment needs of participants. Program duration, specifically hours of operation, should also be tailored to the institutional routine. Assuming that responsivity factors have been incorporated into program development, the content, duration, frequency and style of program delivery should be consistent with the needs of the target population and only slight modifications should be necessary to integrate into existing institutional cultures and routines. Suggestions for how a violent offender program can address site, offender and staff responsivity will be considered in turn.

Site responsivity

A number of site-related factors contribute to responsivity.[1] As stated on p. 207 in this chapter, the site must demonstrate support for the program. Institutional managers should provide a solid infrastructure and consistently convey a strong pro-program message to staff and offenders. They should promote an environment that is supportive of the program; this includes ongoing efforts to maintain staff awareness. They should ensure that the program is adequately and stably resourced. The site should provide suitable space for staff offices and program delivery as well as the necessary supplies for program operation.

The site should also provide support, feedback and supervision to program staff. As well, the site should ensure proper control of the referral process and related issues such as data management and offender payment. Program managers must also recognize that program delivery is physically, intellectually and emotionally taxing and should, therefore, set realistic expectations with respect to the time between programs or other responsibilities in addition to program delivery. Finally, the site should allow for creativity and innovation on the part of program staff in their efforts to improve program efficacy.

Offender responsivity

At the heart of maximizing offender responsivity is recognizing the heterogeneity of violent offenders. They vary not only in level of risk and treatment need, but also in cultural beliefs, language skills and cognitive ability. An efficacious program must endeavor to address these differences by matching program features to offender characteristics as much as possible.

Perhaps the most important variable that affects offender responsivity is lack of motivation for treatment or behaviour change. When compared to other offenders, violent offenders, particularly those who are persistently violent, tend to be less motivated for treatment, more resistant or non-compliant while in treatment, have higher attrition rates, demonstrate fewer positive behavioral changes while in treatment and demonstrate

---

[1] These form the basis of site accreditation efforts currently underway by the Correctional Service of Canada.

higher recidivism rates post-treatment. This is particularly true for those who are also psychopaths (Ogloff, Wong & Greenwood, 1990). See Preston (in press) for a detailed discussion of strategies to reduce treatment resistance.

Therapist responsivity

The staff selection and training section of this chapter (pp. 208–211)) describes the preferred academic credentials, experience and personal characteristics of program staff. It also describes how staff should be trained. In addition to these qualifications, staff should be cognizant of research on the relationship between therapist style and program performance (Fernandez, Serran & Marshall, 1999; Murphy & Baxter, 1997) and modify their behaviour accordingly.

In delivering a violent offender program, it is critical that staff presents a united front. Ongoing communication is the best way to ensure that they remain united. They should also be consistent, both between each other and across situations.

Staff should expect to be tested by offenders, both early and often, in obvious and subtle ways. Thus they should be prepared to handle all forms of resistance. Setting clear limits with clear consequences at the outset of the program, and enforcing the limits consistently, will help them in their efforts. Staff should be innovative in dealing with this population. At times, it might be necessary to step outside of traditional bounds to motivate these offenders to consent to treatment and to remain in treatment. For example, given the lack of motivation inherent in this population, it is typical that they fail to attend interviews to discuss program admission or they are ambivalent during interviews. Consequently, staff must be persistent and persuasive in their efforts to make and maintain contact by, for example, going to their cells or telephoning them at their work location. It has been our experience that such persistence has led to increased agreement to consent to take the program.

Similarly, also because of their lack of motivation, regular attendance to the program can be problematic. While one option is to discharge them from the program after missing a certain number of sessions, this fails to accomplish the broader objective of protecting public safety by reducing the risk posed by these offenders. Developing a reinforcement schedule based on group attendance rate can be a powerful way to increase attendance, because those with good attendance or those who want to receive the specified reward will exert influence over those with poor attendance.

Finally, staff must be both patient and realistic when providing programs for violent offenders. Often, persistently violent offenders have such an overwhelming number and severity of treatment needs that expectations of outcome must be moderate. As well, providing programs in an institutional setting, with its attendant milieu, subcultural norms and legal ramifications, sometimes entails a moderation of expectations. In some cases, offenders often know what they "should" do, but cannot because of potential physical or legal consequences. For example, offenders often see the benefit of discussing their histories of violence in detail in order to maximize treatment gains, but they choose not to do so for fear of being charged for additional offenses.

Staff survival

Various sections of this chapter have indicated, explicitly or implicitly, how difficult it is for staff to work with violent offenders on an ongoing basis. At best, fluctuations in motivation, energy and hence skills is an inevitability. At worst, staff could burn out. Obviously, both of these possibilities will undermine program integrity; thus it is essential to take steps to maintain healthy, productive staff.

The program director should maintain regular meetings with program delivery staff. This provides a forum for the resolution of program-related issues and for the provision of encouragement and emotional support. The development of a peer support system could also be beneficial. To some extent, this exists by virtue of having a co-facilitated program as staff provides an ever-present source of support for each other both inside and outside of the group.

Managers should allow sufficient time between programs for rejuvenation and for the completion of non-program related tasks. The latter is often a necessity as such tasks typically get postponed until program completion, but it is also a welcome break for staff. Professional development should be incorporated into the program delivery schedule. This allows staff to increase their knowledge and skills, but, more importantly, it allows them a break from program delivery. In addition, it can facilitate greater commitment to the manager, department and program.

PROGRAM EVALUATION

Given the time, energy and financial investment in the development and implementation of a new program, it is obvious that we would like to be able to demonstrate that it is effective and yields improved effects over existing programs. Our experience is that evaluation is greatly facilitated by key decisions made during program implementation. First, wherever possible evaluation should be prospective. Second, in the same way it takes time to deliver programs of high integrity, so too does program evaluation. Stakeholders must be convinced of the importance of agreed-upon assessments or their reliability will be low. Third, a priori hypotheses that are testable should be generated, and specific strategies and measures should be developed for the purpose of program evaluation. Fourth, methodological issues—such as type of control or comparison group(s), matching variables (e.g. age, criminal risk, program need, motivation) and intermediate indices of program effectiveness—must be determined at the time of program implementation. Fifth, some consideration of the required power for the statistical analyses should inform decisions about sample size, number of comparisons and necessary follow-up time for an adequate base rate.

Without falling into the trap of searching until we find an effect, there are additional considerations in terms of program evaluation. In some cases where programming is common, it may be impossible to have a randomized design or no-treatment comparison. In such a situation the essential question becomes one of programming sequencing. The permutations quickly become alarming with the co-existence of three or more programs. Alternative strategies may need to be developed to tease out the effects of one program relative to another (Dowden, Serin & Blanchette, in press). Earlier the distinction between treatment gain and generalization was made. We consider gain to be an intermediate effect, best measured by multi-method assessments of a particular deficit or skill that was addressed in the program. In this manner, recidivism becomes an index of the failure to generalize treatment gain. When assessing treatment gain, it may be instructive to consider both change scores and threshold scores. For instance, an offender who begins a program with significant treatment needs and demonstrated poor skills may make significant gains (change scores), but fail to reach a sufficient level of competence (threshold score) to effect sustained behavior change, particularly in novel situations. Although recidivism is the *raison d'être* for correctional programming, it may not be the preferred index of treatment effectiveness (Elliott, 1980). Specific to recidivism, there are several considerations (e.g. the length of follow-up time will affect base rates). The absence of a standard follow-up period makes comparisons across programs problematic. For violent offenders it seems most probable that reductions in violent reoffending would be viewed as the most desirable outcome, yet even then there could be debate, since violence defined by conviction is a poor proxy to actual behaviour. Also, if a violent offender recommits a violent crime, but relative to their history it involves a less serious incident, less victim injury or longer time to reoffense, is this a clear indication of program failure? Defining outcome only dichotomously, then, limits our understanding about program effectiveness.

SUMMARY

Our understanding about effective correctional interventions has increased markedly over the past decade, and there has been an exponential growth of community and institutional programs for offenders. Interestingly, however, the *process* of effective programs or looking into the "black box of treatment" is less well understood. The purpose of this chapter has been to highlight various issues that relate to program implementation and evaluation that will impact on program integrity. We believe that theory and a sound program, then, are necessary but not sufficient ingredients for program success. Attending to implementation issues appears an important additional consideration in the search for effective programs.

References

Andrews, D. A., & Bonta, J. (1998). *The Psychology of Criminal Conduct*, 2nd ed. Cincinnati, OH: Anderson Publishing Co.

Dowden, C. (1998). *A Meta-analytic Examination of the Risk, Need and Responsivity Principles and Their Importance within the Rehabilitation Debate*, Unpublished master's thesis, Department of Psychology, Carleton University, Ottawa.

Dowden, C., Serin, R., & Blanchette, K. (in press). *A Follow-up of the CSC Anger Management Program for Federal Male Inmates: Dropouts*, Research report. Ottawa: Correctional Service of Canada.

Elliott, D. S. (1980). Recurring issues in the evaluation of delinquency prevention and treatment programs. In D. Schichor & D. Kelly (Eds), *Critical Issues in Juvenile Delinquency*, pp. 237–262. Lexington, MA: D. C. Heath.

Fernandez, Y., Serran, G., & Marshall, W. L. (1999). *The Reliable Identification of Therapist Features in the Treatment of Sexual Offenders*, Paper presented at the Association of Treatment of Sexual Abusers Annual Conference, Orlando, Florida, October 1999.

Gerstley, L., McLellan, A. T., Alterman, A. I., Woody, G. E., Luborsky, L., & Prout, M. (1989). Ability to form an alliance with the therapist: A possible marker of prognosis for patients with antisocial personality disorder. *American Journal of Psychiatry*, **146**, 508–512.

Kennedy, S., & Serin, R. (1999). Examining offender readiness to change and the impact on treatment outcome. In P. M. Harris (Ed.), *Research to Results: Effective Community Corrections*, pp. 215–230. Lanham, MD: American Correctional Association.

Motiuk, L. L. (1997). Classification for correctional programming: The Offender Intake Assessment (OIA) process. *Forum on Corrections Research*, **9**(1), 18–22.

Murphy, C. M., & Baxter, V. A. (1997). Motivating batterers to change in the treatment context. *Journal of Interpersonal Violence*, **12**, 607–619.

Ogloff, J. R. P., Wong, S., & Greenwood, A. (1990). Treating criminal psychopaths in a therapeutic community program. *Behavioral Sciences and the Law*, **8**, 181–190.

Preston, D. L. (in press). Treatment resistance, treatment engagement. In L. Motiuk & R. Sirin (Eds), *Compendium on Effective Correctional Programming*. Ottawa: Correctional Service of Canada.

Preston, D. L., & Murphy, S. (1997). Motivating treatment-resistant clients in therapy. *Forum on Corrections Research*, **9**(2), 39–43.

Serin, R. C., & Kennedy, S. (1998). *Assessment Protocol for Treatment Readiness, Responsivity, and Gain: Guidelines for Clinician Ratings*, Unpublished research report. Ottawa: Correctional Service of Canada.

Serin, R. C., & Preston, D. L. (in press). Programming for violent offenders. In L. Motiuk & R. Serin (Eds), *Compendium on Effective Correctional Programming*. Ottawa: Correctional Service of Canada.

Serin, R. C., & Preston, D. L. (2001). Managing and treating violent offenders. In J. B. Ashford, B. D. Sales & W. Reid (Eds), *Treating Adult and Juvenile Offenders with Special Needs*, pp. 249–272. Washington, DC: American Psychological Association.

PART III: IMPLEMENTING GENERAL PROGRAMS

PROLOGUE

This final section focuses on implementing general programs. In addition to the evidence on issues with implementation of specific programs, there is now mounting evidence documenting the experience of large-scale dissemination of program factors such as assessment, correctional treatment and the work of consultants.

In Chapter 11, James Bonta, Brad Bogue, Michael Crowley and Laurence Motiuk report on experiences gained from large scale implementation of offender classification systems. In a previous report, Bonta (1996) noted that the advent of risk assessment with offenders represents the third generation of classification for use with correctional clients. It is a development based on the empirical evidence from the prediction literature that suggests there is now a science of criminal conduct that allows for classification for use in case management and clinical decision-making. This chapter focuses on the strategic factors necessary for successful implementation that include confronting the "ideological, political and practical" issues that get in the way of successful implementation. The use of consultants, trainers and research are also reviewed in the context of successful offender classification implementation.

Chapter 12 by Paul Gendreau, Claire Goggin and Paula Smith focuses on treatment implementation from the perspective of the major findings from the meta-analyses and the principal factors emerging from those findings. Based primarily on the work of Paul Gendreau and Don Andrews in the development of the *Correctional Program Assessment Inventory* (CPAI), organizational, programmatic and staff characteristics form the basis of effective program implementation. This chapter reports on the CPAI as an instrument that measures the nature and extent of the presence of these factors that assist organizations in both developing and monitoring the extent of the presence of the known factors for effect correctional service.

Finally, Chapter 13 by Clive Hollin discusses the role of the consultant in the implementation of effective correctional intervention. Based on the considerable evidence reported by Hollin, the role of an outside change agent is considered critical in both conveying current knowledge and providing direction for staff training and evaluation of promising efforts in delivering effective correctional interventions. Given the current context of an increasing emphasis on accreditation of criminal justice programs, Hollin concludes by suggesting that consultants can be among the very important driving forces behind the promotion of evidence-based practice within the criminal justice system.

References

Bonta, J. (1996). Risk–needs assessment and treatment. In. A. T. Harland (Ed.), *Choosing Correctional Options that Work*, pp. 18–32. Thousand Oaks, CA: Sage.

Chapter 11

IMPLEMENTING OFFENDER CLASSIFICATION SYSTEMS: LESSONS LEARNED

JAMES BONTA,* BRAD BOGUE,[†] MICHAEL CROWLEY[‡] AND LAURENCE MOTIUK[§]

* Solicitor General Canada, Ottawa, Canada
[†] Justice System Assessment and Training, Boulder, Colorado, USA
[‡] National Parole Board of Canada, Kingston, Ontario, Canada
[§] Director General, Research Branch, Correctional Service of Canada, Ottawa, Ontario

The foundation for effective correctional practice is good offender classification. Within the correctional context, "effective" means providing a humane, cost-efficient service that maximizes public safety. Good offender classification contributes to these goals by ensuring that offenders are differentiated in ways that direct correctional resources to those offenders who are most in need of those resources. This chapter describes our experiences with introducing and maintaining new offender classification practices. Our experiences vary from state (Bogue) and provincial (Bonta) implementation projects, to national (Motiuk) and private-sector correctional agencies (Crowley). Not all of our efforts ended favorably, but most did. Our intention in this chapter is to prepare those who are interested in revitalizing their offender classification system for what lies ahead. We hope that our "lessons learned" will help correctional staff deal more effectively with the inevitable obstacles that arise.

Offender Rehabilitation in Practice. Edited by G. A. Bernfeld, D. P. Farrington and A. W. Leschied.
© 2001 John Wiley & Sons, Ltd.

The chapter begins with a summary of the "state of the art" in offender classification; that is, how well can we assess offenders in order to maximize public safety and reintegrate offenders into their communities? We then describe what we see as the common steps (given our varied experiences) in successful implementation. In this section we will also note some of the specific challenges faced by non-governmental agencies. Third, once a new classification system is introduced, attention must be given to maintaining the integrity of the system. Finally, we close with a summary of the core requirements for the implementation and maintenance of a new offender classification model.

THE STATE OF OFFENDER CLASSIFICATION

One of the primary purposes of offender classification is to construct groups of offenders who differ in their risk to violate rules. By classifying offenders according to their risk for rule violation, correctional resources can be distributed in a reasonable manner. Low-risk offenders are allotted more freedom (e.g. community placement) and less supervision. Higher risk offenders are subjected to more intensive, and expensive, controls (e.g. maximum security placement, intensive monitoring). The assessment of offender risk is perhaps the single most important function of any correctional agency.

Many, but not all correctional agencies, also have an interest in assessing the needs of offenders. This interest is particularly strong when those needs may reduce the risk of reoffending. At a certain moral, humane level, we can argue that society has a responsibility to address the unfortunate social and personal situations many offenders experience. The assessment of offender needs then leads to interventions and programs to address their needs. For correctional organizations that assume this responsibility, it could be a demanding undertaking. Whereas the low-need offender may require relatively few services, the high-need offender could drain considerable resources. Whether or not a correctional organization has a responsibility to address offender needs will be discussed on p. 230. For now, it is sufficient to say that the assessment of offender needs is a concern for many correctional agencies.

How risk or needs are assessed can vary considerably. On one hand, the assessment can be highly unstructured, idiosyncratic and subjective. The factors considered important in the assessment of risk or needs may vary from assessor to assessor. At times, the same assessor may consider different factors from one day to the next. Furthermore, the factors considered in the assessment may not have been validated by systematic research. This approach to assessment is often referred to as the clinical approach. On the other hand, the assessment of risk and needs can be based upon the objective measurement of factors that have demonstrated an empirical relationship to rule violation and criminal behavior. This approach is referred to as the objective, actuarial approach (Bonta, 1996).

Today, very few correctional agencies would disagree with the statement that structured, actuarial approaches to assessing offenders are preferred to clinical, non-actuarial approaches. Not only does the need for public accountability support objective, actuarial assessments but the research evidence clearly shows the superiority of actuarial assessment over clinical assessment (Dawes, Faust, & Meehl, 1993). Although almost everyone agrees upon the importance of objective, actuarial assessments, not all agencies employ this approach. Many correctional organizations still classify offenders using a subjective, clinical approach taking false comfort in the ability of their staff to recognize a high-risk criminal "when they see one". Those correctional systems that do use actuarial assessments tend to use them for the assessment of offender risk (Champion, 1994). Relatively few jurisdictions assess offender needs with research-based actuarial scales (Clements, 1996).

The typical actuarial offender risk instrument consists of a few quantifiable factors cobbled together to form a scale. The factors or items comprising the scale are almost exclusively criminal history variables—prior convictions, type of offence, juvenile delinquency, etc. Sometimes a few non-criminal history variables are thrown in to give a bit of variety. Examples of this type of actuarial offender risk scale, labeled by Bonta (1996) as "second generation" risk scales, are shown in Table 11.1

Table 11.1 Second-generation offender risk scales

Item	SFS	GSIR	ROR
Offence type	Yes	Yes	Yes
Criminal history	Yes	Yes	Yes
Age	Yes	Yes	Yes
Prior parole	Yes	Yes	No
Gender	No	No	Yes
Prison security level	No	Yes	No
Sentence length	No	Yes	No
Prior time in community	No	Yes	No
History of drug abuse	Yes	No	No
Unemployed*	Yes	Yes	No
Single*	No	Yes	No
Dependents*	No	Yes	No

Notes: SFS is the Salient Factor Score (US), GSIR is the General Statistical Information on Recidivism (Canada) and ROR is the Risk Of Reconviction (UK).
*Symbolizes dynamic items.

There are a few important observations regarding second-generation offender risk scales. First, many of the items are static in nature. This static quality presents practical, theoretical and ethical concerns. With respect to practice, once an offender is assessed at a certain risk level, correctional staff are given precious little guidance as to what could be done to decrease the offender's risk of reoffending. Historical variables do not disappear and the few dynamic variables that may appear in these risk scales provide a limited menu for intervention (find employment, get married). Theoretically, there is no coherent rationale as to *why* these items are important (they predict recidivism and that is all we need to know). Moreover, the assessment of static risk factors subtly promotes the view that offenders are somehow different from you and me—they cannot change. The immutable image of criminals drawn by second-generation risk scales raises ethical concerns. Do we view offenders as hopeless creatures who are a constant thorn to society? Do we accept such an image that allows us to ignore efforts to reintegrate them into society? The static, second-generation risk scales leave much to be desired.

It is true that static risk factors, similar to those displayed in Table 11.1, predict recidivism (Gendreau, Little & Goggin, 1996) and that the second-generation risk scales do differentiate lower risk offenders from higher risk offenders (Bonta, 1996). If our value system, for whatever reason, is not concerned about offender needs then static risk scales are sufficient. Correctional agencies are obligated to minimize the risk that offenders pose to the public, at least while under sentence. However, the public has increasing expectations that corrections should reach beyond end of sentence to reduce recidivism. In order to attain this goal, interventions must be introduced to decrease offender risk. These public expectations force a change in correctional philosophy that embraces the idea that offenders can change. The large literature on the effectiveness of offender rehabilitation programs (Andrews & Bonta, 1998a; see Chapter 4 in this book by Friedrich Lösel) has been very influential in promoting a shift away from the view that all offenders are incorrigible. From the offender rehabilitation literature we now know that for treatment programs to be effective, they must decrease the criminogenic needs of offenders (Andrews, Bonta & Hoge, 1990). Consequently, the first step in effective treatment is to assess criminogenic needs in an objective, empirically based manner.

Criminogenic needs or dynamic risk factors are characteristics of the offender and the offender's situation that when changed are followed by changes in criminal behavior. The past decade has accumulated a wealth of information as to which needs are related to criminal behavior and which needs are non-criminogenic. For example, self-esteem and feelings of uneasiness and anxiety are poor predictors of criminal conduct (Gendreau et al., 1996) and improving self-esteem or reducing anxiety does not lead to reductions in recidivism (Andrews et al., 1990). In contrast, examples of criminogenic needs are *current* substance abuse (not history of substance abuse) and *present* associations (not who your friends were 10 years ago).

To the best of our knowledge, there are only three empirically validated offender classification instruments that assess static and dynamic risk factors. These instruments are referred to as risk–needs instruments. They are the Level of Service Inventory-Revised (LSI-R; Andrews & Bonta, 1995), the Community Risk/Needs Management Scale (Motiuk & Porporino, 1989) and variations of the Wisconsin classification risk and needs instruments (Baird, 1981; Bonta, Parkinson & Barkwell, 1994). The LSI-R is perhaps the most widely used of the risk–needs instruments (e.g. used in Canada, the United States, United Kingdom, Australia and New Zealand). The Community Risk/Needs Management Scale is used by the Correctional Service of Canada to assist in the community supervision of offenders. Finally, the Wisconsin system is used in some states and in three Canadian provinces.

Our experience has been with assisting correctional agencies in introducing, implementing and maintaining risk–needs classification systems. All of us have had experience with the LSI-R, but some of us have also been involved in implementing the Community Risk/Needs Management Scale (Motiuk) and variations on the Wisconsin system (Bonta). Many of our examples will be drawn from our work in introducing the LSI-R, although we will make reference to the implementation of other systems.

CHALLENGES ENCOUNTERED

Correctional organizations differ in their level of commitment to offender rehabilitation. However, public demands for reductions in recidivism have persuaded some correctional systems, sometimes reluctantly, to enhance their rehabilitative efforts. Bringing an organization to this commitment is often the first challenge when introducing risk–needs classification. Some agencies do not see their role as providing treatment services to offenders and view offender programs as unnecessary frills.

The obstacles to committing to offender rehabilitation are ideological, political and practical. Staff and managers may hold the view that the purpose of corrections is to administer the punishment imposed by the courts and that punishment will deter offenders from further crime. Politically, decisions that look soft on crime come with peril. Consequently, particularly in the United States, responding more severely to crime through mandatory sentences and lengthier prison terms has considerable currency.

There is, however, a moderating force to the "get tough" movement for dealing with crime. In Canada and the United Kingdom there are various legislative and policy documents that have appeared voicing a commitment to offender rehabilitation. Canada's Corrections and Conditional Release Act (Canada, 1992), the legislation governing the federal corrections system, lists the "rehabilitation of offenders and their reintegration into the community" as a goal of the system. In the United Kingdom, the report of the HMIP What Works Project calls for a national framework on how risk and "offender-related need should lead to the use of more intensive programmes" (Underdown, 1998, p. 145). Legislative and policy support for offender rehabilitation is also making inroads in the United States. For example, Colorado's legislation (HB91-1173) calls for the standardized assessment of needs for the purpose of treatment.

From a practical perspective, the financial costs associated with treatment programs are seen as prohibitive for many organizations. Staff need to be trained with special skills, services purchased and sufficient time allotted to deliver services. The question becomes whether the significant financial investment is cost effective.

Overcoming the ideological, political and practical obstacles can be approached in two ways. First, the ideology and political obstacles can be fought by relaying the evidence on the effectiveness of offender rehabilitation to policy-makers and senior managers. The evidence shows that not only can treatment reduce recidivism but that deterrence and imprisonment have little effect on recidivism (Andrews & Bonta, 1998a; Gaes, Flanagan, Motiuk & Stewart, 1999; Gendreau, Goggin & Cullen, 1999). Opportunities to convey this message can be through publications and conferences as well as facilitating meetings between experts in offender rehabilitation and senior correctional managers. There are also some recent studies that demonstrate that the treatment of offenders is more cost effective than imprisonment (Aos, Phipps, Barnoski & Lieb, 1999; Cohen, 1998). Cohen (1998) has estimated that approximately $2 million can be saved for each high-risk youth who is diverted from a criminal career. This information can be very important for influencing politicians and senior managers.

A second approach that encourages agencies to adopt a rehabilitative agenda is to capitalize on the front-line staff's desire to assume a more professional and rehabilitative role. Quality of work life and level of job satisfaction are important in any job and perhaps more so in corrections where staff must deal with a very difficult clientele. Front-line workers often see first hand the ineffectiveness of deterrent policies. They see the multitude of problems presented by offenders and recognize a need to do something about these problems. In our own experiences, there have been many instances of a "grass roots" offender rehabilitation movement. Those who work directly with offenders have expressed their dissatisfaction with deterrent policies to their supervisors who in turn have influenced senior managers and the system to change the way they do business.

Once senior management makes the decision to place offender treatment

Table 11.2   The desired characteristics of risk–needs classification

Characteristic	Description
Objective	Items described with publicly observable referents; structured administration and scoring rules.
Internal reliability	Items relate to each other and the total score.
Inter-rater reliability	High agreement among test administrators; items are scored the same way producing similar results.
Meaningful	Information makes sense; items consistent with the research on the prediction of recidivism.
Predictive validity	Scores predict relevant outcomes (e.g. recidivism, prison misconduct, parole violation).
Dynamic validity	Changes in scores predict changes in outcome.
Socially unbiased	Items do not violate constitutional/charter rights (e.g. ethnicity, gender).
Generalization	Instrument applies well to other groups and settings beyond the initial construction sample.

on the correctional agenda, the agency needs to develop programs and train staff to deliver them. Many organizations do have programs in place, but they are sorely weak in their potential to influence recidivism. One large private-sector agency undertook a review of its services using the Correctional Programs Assessment Inventory (CPAI; Gendreau & Andrews, 1996). The CPAI provides an objective assessment of correctional programs and their potential to reduce recidivism. The results of the CPAI found that the agency could provide more effective services if it adopted a standard needs assessment for guiding the delivery of treatment programs. Consequently, the LSI-R was adopted for use. Another advantage of risk–needs assessment is that it would provide an estimate of the prevalence of the problems offenders present, and thus anticipate the types of programs required.

One of the early decision points for correctional managers is to select a risk–needs classification instrument. Table 11.2 presents many of the desirable characteristics of a risk–needs classification instrument. Whether the instrument is developed by the agency or chosen from existing instruments, these features should be present.

At this point, many correctional agencies find themselves in a quandary over whether or not to develop their own risk–needs assessment instrument(s) or to select one "from the shelf". Developing a risk–needs instrument has some appeal. It maximizes confidence in the instrument having relevance to the organization. After all, the items and procedures can be specifically tailored to the organization. Developing a new instrument engages staff through consultations surrounding item selection and administration procedures. Testing the new instrument also involves staff with the new classification procedures. Gradually, these activities can foster staff commitment to the instrument.

As with anything, there are disadvantages. First, and foremost, the agency must have the expertise and resources to launch a research development project. This requires staff knowledgeable of the research on the prediction of criminal behavior and the methodology required for evaluating the psychometric and predictive attributes of an assessment scale. Many agencies, particularly non-governmental agencies, are too small to have their own in-house research capabilities. Larger agencies may have research units, but not necessarily the expertise in risk prediction and test construction. Often, in-house researchers have their expertise in the areas of program evaluation and population analysis and forecasting.

Outside consultants may be used to develop and validate a risk–needs classification instrument. This option, in our experience, has produced mixed results. To benefit from consultants, the agency must be able to recognize who is an "expert" in the area. Private consulting firms rarely have experts in risk prediction since to maintain a viable business more generic researchers are preferred. University consultants bring with them another set of dangers. There are similar problems in selection (tenure does not make an expert). But, more problematic is the need to give clear direction to the consultant. The miscommunication between policy and practical oriented correctional managers and academic consultants sometimes results in products that fail to meet expectations. In one situation where one of us (Bonta) was conducting an evaluation for a large probation department, the department had hired a university-based consultant to develop an offender assessment instrument. The consultant came from *another* state and had *no* research publications in the area of offender risk assessment. Needless to say, the resulting classification instrument was despised by staff (not meaningful to them), it completely ignored dynamic risk factors and the scale did not cross-validate to the new setting.

Related to the resource issue is the fact that developing and validating a risk–needs scale takes time. Considerable thought and consultations with staff must be invested in the selection of items for the instrument, their wording and how the information will be collected. Guiding this process requires an expert, or group of experts (in-house and/or outside consultants), who lead the project and conduct the evaluation. In the development of the LSI-R, Don Andrews (university-based consultant), James Bonta and Laurence Motiuk (in-house) conducted numerous consultations and validation studies that produced revisions to the instrument. It was not until the fourth revision of the LSI-R that the instrument was implemented in probation and three more revisions before implementation across the prison system. It took nearly 15 years for the instrument to become the standard classification instrument in Ontario corrections.

The Correctional Service of Canada also developed their classification system using internal expertise. The organization had the financial resources to develop the system and, more importantly, it had the necessary in-house expertise on risk–needs assessment (e.g. Laurence Motiuk and Frank Porporino) along with easy access to the writings of other Canadian experts in the field (e.g. Andrews, Bonta, Gendreau). Even with these advantages, full-scale implementation of the Offender Intake Assessment (OIA) system took 3 years (1992–1994). Consultation, pilot testing and validation studies that require a follow-up of released offenders for at least 6 months and preferably a year or more are time-consuming activities.

One final note about the development of risk–needs instruments. There is no guarantee that the final version of the scale will work as well as expected. Much goes into the development of an offender assessment instrument and many things can go wrong. Items can be poorly selected and inappropriate validation procedures used. Thus, there is always the risk that after years of development a correctional system may not have advanced any further.

Many correctional agencies find that choosing a risk–needs classification instrument "off the shelf" is their most practical option. Using the criteria listed in Table 11.2, the state of Colorado followed this option. A committee reviewed a number of risk–needs instruments and chose the LSI-R as an instrument that appeared to be suited to their needs. Colorado's shift to standardized assessment was also driven by legislation (HB91-1173) specific-ally mandating standardized assessment across the criminal justice system. A major concern for Colorado, and for any jurisdiction that selects a risk–needs instrument developed outside their jurisdiction, is that of generaliza-tion; that is, does the instrument produce valid classifications of its own offender population? The problem of generalization may also influence staff acceptance of the new assessment tool. Staff are almost always skeptical about something that is not "home grown". They see their offenders, their system and their context as different from the jurisdiction where the scale was originally developed.

The likelihood of an instrument generalizing to another sample and cor-rectional context depends upon many factors. First, the more replications of the instrument, the more likely that the instrument will "work" in other settings. Even in the development of the LSI-R, suspicions were voiced that the LSI-R would not be valid for inmates in Toronto because the early prison research was done in Ottawa! It was only after numerous replications in different locations across the Province of Ontario that staff accepted the instrument for province-wide use.

A second factor that increases generalization is item content. Many of the items in the LSI-R were selected from the recidivism prediction literature demonstrating a relationship with recidivism. Who would argue that a history of criminal behavior, drug abuse and employment problems would not be associated with recidivism for their offenders? Finally, the LSI-R has its theoretical basis in the general psychology of criminal conduct (Andrews & Bonta, 1998a) and therefore, independent of territorial boundaries and citizenship. Replications, items consistent with the prediction literature and theory were influential in Colorado's decision to select the LSI-R. However, before widespread implementation, a pilot study was conducted to evaluate the suitability of the LSI-R for Colorado.

Pilot testing of a new classification instrument permits an organization to assess how well the instrument "works", staff reactions and training requirements. Pilot testing eases the worries associated with premature, system-wide implementation and can help prepare staff to accept a new procedure for assessing offenders. A successful pilot test serves as a model for other sites within the organization showing that implementation is feasible. Staff from a successful site become advocates for the instrument and encourage others as they adapt to the new classification procedures. The pilot testing in Colorado indicated that the LSI-R was worth pursuing and state-wide implementation in probation was initiated, followed by community corrections and institutions. Since then, replications on the predictive validity of the LSI-R have been reported in Colorado (O'Keefe, Klebe & Hromas, 1998) and other US jurisdictions (Kirkpatrick, 1999). The applicability of the LSI-R has also been extended to other parts of the world including the United Kingdom (Raynor, 1999) and Australia (Cumberland & Boyle, 1997).

Once a classification instrument is chosen, the next challenge is persuading staff that the new way is better than the old way. Behavioral habits do not change easily and yet, there is clearly a need to socialize staff into the new behaviors and roles expected by the agency. Shifting staff behaviors and attitudes can be hindered by a number of factors. Staff may have grown quite accustomed to the way things were done in the agency. They know what is expected, may value their present role and they have developed the skills necessary to carry out their duties. Staff may have been originally hired for certain abilities and psychological characteristics. For example, an organization with a custodial/supervision orientation may seek staff who are authoritarian and tough minded. Perhaps physical strength rather than "book smarts" may be more valued. Non-governmental agencies are often hampered by their very limited resources. They may be forced to hire staff with inadequate educational backgrounds that poorly prepare them for assuming a rehabilitation role.

Persuading staff of the value of risk–needs assessment requires knowing the attitudes and abilities of the staff. Some organizations may undertake a staff survey to collect information that could be helpful when implementing a new initiative. For example, the Correctional Service of Canada surveyed nearly 7,000 correctional officers, administrative staff and managers in 1994 and again in 1996 during a period when the Service was implementing risk–needs assessments and treatment programs on a national scale (Correctional Service of Canada, 1997). Information from the surveys was used in the development of a strategy to align staff attitudes and behaviors to new policy and procedures.

Regardless of whether or not a staff survey is conducted, the process of attitudinal and behavioral realignment involves nourishing a respect for research and valuing the role of offender rehabilitation in public safety. It is important to show staff that research is the basis for the implementation of a new classification system rather than something that the agency head heard at a conference. For this reason, an explanation of the research should be part of the staff training program (discussed later in more detail). In some situations, the introduction of new classification models begins with conferences outlining the research and theory. For example, prior to the implementation of the LSI-R in the Department of Corrections for Washington State, a conference was held where one of the authors of the LSI-R presented the relevant research. Similarly, the Correctional Service of Canada held 17 single-day professional development workshops for 550 parole officers during the implementation of the Community Risk/Needs Management scale.

In our view, one of the most important messages to convey to staff is that risk–needs assessments professionalize their work. As noted earlier, many front-line staff have become disenchanted with the policing, security-oriented focus of their work. They see the difficulties encountered by many offenders and recognize that assistance is needed more than monitoring. Moreover, staff have become increasingly frustrated by referring offenders to mental health or substance abuse services with long waiting lists, that leave them "out of the loop" or simply refuse to deal with criminals. More and more, correctional staff are asking to assume a more active, interventionist role. Training in risk–needs assessment gives staff added skills and confidence in dealing with the problems offenders face. Using validated risk–needs assessment helps the supervisor understand better the offender and opens the door for more effective case management.

There are other benefits to risk–needs assessment that should be conveyed to staff. The comprehensive and objective nature of many risk–needs instruments can be comforting. If supervision decisions are ever challenged in court or questioned by supervisors, the officer can say that s/he conducted a reasonable review of the relevant factors in a fair and objective manner. The dynamic quality of risk–needs assessment also permits the supervising officer to monitor changes in the offender's situation. Changes in risk–needs scores can alert staff of the need to intervene or change supervision practices. When retest scores decrease, the information reassures the supervisor that things are going right. When scores increase, it is time to do something quickly and, if necessary, restrict the offender's freedoms. This feedback is vital for managing offender risk and maximizing public safety.

From a system perspective, allocating services to those who require the services is simply good correctional management. There is evidence that leaving classification decisions to professional judgment leads to overclassification. Most people, left to their own devices, tend to err on the side of caution. One study (Bonta & Motiuk, 1992) estimated that prison over classification could be reduced by up to 38 per cent with the introduction of objective risk–needs assessment.

There is one more important organizational consideration when introducing a new classification model. There needs to be either a management oversight committee or at least an individual identified by senior management responsible for implementation. When the LSI-R was first developed in Ontario, it was implemented in probation and parole services and a senior management committee oversaw the implementation. It took another 10 years to introduce the LSI-R into institutions and this delay was due in part to the fact that there was no senior manager responsible for implementation. It was only after a position was created that the LSI-R was implemented in the institution division.

Similarly, the state of Colorado had an oversight committee. One of the roles of the committee was to follow up and make sure that procedures were being followed and to maintain field consultations to deal with problems as they arise. Within the private sector, such committees are rare. If the non-governmental agency is large enough, there may be an oversight committee, or the CEO may take a direct interest. However, most of the time, there is no one except a program director or an individual who takes on the work himself or herself. In this case, implementation occurs at a very local level and the use of a new classification instrument continues as long as the individual remains with the organization.

Staff training issues

There are a number of issues related to the training of staff. First, the agency must have clear expectations for their staff. Preferably, the expectations on when to use the risk–needs instruments and how to use professional override, for example, should be written down.

Next, there are the questions of whether staff are qualified to use the new instrument and whether they are able to learn how to administer the instrument. Most risk–needs classification instruments are relatively easy to learn. Their administration usually does not require advanced university training. Some other offender assessment instruments, such as the Psychopathy Checklist-Revised (Hare, 1990) require specialized expertise. Even though risk–needs instruments do not require extensive training, they are more sophisticated than the brief, static risk scales that are familiar to corrections. In our experience, college educated staff learn the rationale and procedures quite readily. Staff with high school education, however, have more difficulties grasping the concepts and require more extensive training and support. A basic prerequisite for the administration of risk–needs scales is to have some interviewing skills. Staff graduating from colleges may already have some interviewing skills, and if they do not most learn them quickly.

Finally, we highly recommend that managers attend at least the first day of training and for smaller agencies that managers attend all of the training. The active participation of managers in the risk–needs assessment training helps them better understand what their staff will be doing and the reasons for the new classification procedures. Moreover, exposure to the training facilitates supporting staff during implementation and giving them good-quality supervision.

A typical training program should have the following features. Time must be devoted to summarizing the research supporting the instrument and the concept of offender rehabilitation. Workshop participants need to know that the new classification procedures are reasonable and empirically defensible. The research information must be conveyed in a non-technical manner but the trainer must be prepared to answer questions with knowledge and authority. All too often, agencies pay little attention to the training of trainers. We have seen trainers who had only superficial knowledge of the literature and who had not even used the instrument themselves! Trainers should be *intensively* trained and they should have direct experience working with the instrument and offenders. These two requirements would give trainers credibility when they conduct training sessions.

Enough time must be devoted to staff to allow staff to be reasonably skilled and confident in administering the risk–needs instrument. This requires a minimum of 2 days. At least 3 days is needed when staff require training in some basic interviewing skills (e.g. how to ask non-leading questions, establishing rapport). The training sessions must include practice test administrations preferably using videotaped offender interviews. After viewing videotaped interviews, participants can practice scoring, ask questions and refine their skills. Time should also be devoted to theoretical explanations of criminal behavior. Administration manuals cannot cover all the scoring possibilities that arise everyday. Theory allows test administrators to score the unusual and exceptional cases. Structured training programs are available that can be used to guide trainers (Bonta, 1997).

Finally, the training program must include a follow-up session. We have never found workshop participants to be error-free at follow-up. At the end of a 2 or 3 day training session, participants have grasped the main ideas and can score the "practice" interviews without error. However, once they return to their offices and deal with their own clientele, it is easy to make some errors. Left uncorrected, errors continue and sometimes multiply. For this reason, there should be a mechanism whereby corrective feedback is given. This can be accomplished by having the trainers return to conduct "booster" training sessions with participants who have gathered experience with the instrument. Another method is to have peer review sessions where participants can case conference and discuss their scoring and problems encountered.

Once a training program has been implemented, steps must be taken to ensure that the instrument is administered accurately. Implementation integrity is crucial for maintenance of the new classification system.

MAINTAINING INTEGRITY

As already mentioned, booster training sessions are important for ensuring that the instrument is delivered in a standardized, error-free manner. Other steps can be taken to ensure integrity of the system. One step is to introduce some form of computerization in the risk–needs classification (Andrews & Bonta, 1998b). The advantage of computerization is that software programs can be written to check for internal consistencies. For example, if the offender abuses drugs then the item having criminal associates should be scored. Computers can also check for errors resulting from adding items to calculate a total score.

Colorado has taken the results from the LSI-R, entered them into a databank and periodically analyzes the data looking for state-wide uniformity. Figure 11.1 shows the variation in LSI-R scores across five districts in the state. Scores varied with some districts having higher scores than other

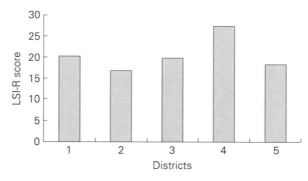

Figure 11.1 Variation in LSI-R scores across districts (Colorado).

Table 11.3 Errors rates in LSI-R scoring acoss implementation sites

Agency site		Error rate	Sample size
1.	Probation	0.18	64
2.	Probation and Sheriff's	0.08	42
3.	Court Support Services	0.12	110
4.	Community Corrections	0.06	218
5.	Community Corrections	0.15	210
6.	Department of Corrections	0.14	95
7.	Department of Corrections	0.10	36
8.	Probation	0.14	152
9.	Probation	0.15	700
Average		*0.13*	*336*

districts. The variation, in a relatively small state, suggested that the instrument was not being used in a standard way. The results then prompted trainers to return to those sites to identify the problems and correct them.

The use of videotaped offender interviews has been used effectively with both state implementation and smaller private agencies. Test administrators submit a videotaped offender interview along with their scored risk–needs classification form to expert trainers. The trainers review the videotape and corrective feedback is provided to the test administrators. The use of videotapes is very advantageous to small agencies that cannot afford to have expert trainers on site. The videotape reviews can be done from a distance with reasonable costs.

Colorado has invested significantly in the use of videotapes to monitor risk–needs classification. Hundreds of videotapes conducted by probation officers have been reviewed and feedback given. The interviews are coded for a variety of behaviors ranging from general interviewing styles to scoring errors. Table 11.3 summarizes the scoring error rates from nine sites across the United States. Note that on average, errors occur with approximately 13 per cent of LSI-R interviews. However, with corrective feedback, significant improvements are found. For Site 5, a review of LSI-R interviews after feedback found the error rate to decrease from 0.15 to 0.01.

In the private sector, we have had success with the use of quality assurance teams to monitor the implementation of risk–needs classification. Staff review and comment on each other's interviews and, to facilitate the discussion, an interview appraisal scale is completed. The interview appraisal scale rates the interview along the following five dimensions:

(1) accuracy of scoring;
(2) rapport with the offender;

(3)   concreteness and specifity in obtaining information;
(4)   ability to probe and challenge; and
(5)   use of a time context (e.g. from focusing only upon historical events to a comparison between present situation and events leading to it).

The role of research

Finally, when possible, research and evaluation should be conducted. As noted earlier, staff is always suspicious when a risk–needs instrument is used that did not originate locally. Although some reassurances on the generalizability of an instrument may be offered, there remains a hint of skepticism. Research can address the generalization of the instrument to the jurisdiction. Evaluation studies can also identify ways of improving the use of the instrument and making modifications. An important modification with any risk–needs instrument is altering the cut-off scores.

The cut-off scores that define levels of risk are a function of resources and community/political tolerance. Correctional systems do not want to place too many offenders into the highest risk–needs classification level because it may stress program resources. Some jurisdictions may also tolerate more risk and are willing to place offenders into minimum risk–needs classification levels. When selecting a risk–needs instrument from the shelf, cut-off scores were established for the jurisdiction where the instrument was developed and the cut-off criteria may not apply to the new jurisdiction. Research can guide the selection of appropriate cut-off scores.

A SUMMARY AND A CHECKLIST

In the past 20 years there has been considerable progress in the assessment of offenders. The debate over actuarial versus clinical assessment is now a historical footnote. The actuarial approach to the assessment of offender risk is widely accepted and there is widespread recognition of the value of assessing dynamic risk factors or criminogenic needs. The development of risk–needs classification instruments has arisen from our accumulated knowledge on the effective components of offender rehabilitation programs and, surely, these classification instruments contribute to further advances in our understanding of interventions that reduce recidivism.

Our knowledge about risk–needs assessment and offender rehabilitation has blossomed relatively recently. We are now only turning our attention to how best to apply this knowledge into real settings. Certainly we need systematic research on this "technology transfer", but, for now, we hope that our shared experiences will shed some light on how to best introduce

Table 11.4   Implementing risk–needs classification: a checklist of issues and suggested strategies

Goal	Strategic approach
1. Commit to offender rehabilitation	Exposure to publications, conferences and meetings with researchers.
2. Select an instrument	Use criteria listed in Table 11.2.
(a) Develop in-house	Requires experts, resources and time
(b) Chose extant instrument	Research and development work is done but need to test for generalization and engage staff commitment.
3. Obtaining staff acceptance	Recruit staff who are predisposed to the new policy and procedures, provide staff training on the research basis to practice.
4. Maintaining classification integrity	Booster sessions; computerized assessments; videotapes; quality assurance teams.
5. Research	Monitor and improve instrumentation.

risk–needs classification into correctional organizations. Between the four of us, we have assisted over 50 agencies with implementing risk–needs assessment. We hope that this experience is worth something although we realize that sooner or later our knowledge will be replaced by empirical, actuarial evidence.

Table 11.4 provides a summary and checklist of the major goals for implementing a new classification system and suggestions for dealing with the issues faced. Given that risk–needs classification identifies criminogenic needs, the door to offender programming is opened. Thus, before an organization incorporates offender risk–needs classification it must be prepared to invest in treatment programs. Commitment to offender rehabilitation is the necessary groundwork prior to introducing a risk–needs instrument.

Deciding whether to develop a risk–needs instrument or to choose one that has already been developed has advantages and disadvantages. We have no simple advice to give on this dilemma, only to outline the various resource and procedural demands required by either choice. Whichever route is taken, we hope that the instrument meets the criteria set out in Table 11.2.

Although staff commitment to risk–needs instrumentation may be more elusive when an instrument is chosen that was developed outside of the jurisdiction, in-house instruments are not invulnerable to staff suspicions. For example, it took years before most staff in Ontario corrections accepted the LSI-R even though it was developed within its own jurisdiction by their own researchers. A risk–needs instrument developed in-house may fail to be accepted by staff if the research results are not positive, and especially if the predictive validity of their instrument does not match the predictive validity of other instruments. Therefore, considerable training effort is required in any case.

The most serious oversight that any organization can make when introducing a new classification system is to ignore the maintenance of the system. We have evidence that the error rate is approximately 15 per cent after training. Staff make errors in interpretation, scoring and simple calculations. Left unchecked, error rates cannot decrease and we have suggested a number of approaches to decreasing errors and ensuring a classification system that has a high degree of integrity (see Table 11.4). Research may not only help monitor the integrity of the system but it can play a vital role in making improvements. It is only through research that advances are made.

In closing, correctional systems are adopting a more proactive, interventionist approach to dealing with offenders. Prison warehousing and intensive supervision practices are seen by more and more correctional systems as ineffective in increasing community safety. The introduction of risk–needs classification instruments is viewed as one tool for achieving the goal of enhanced public safety through reductions in offender recidivism. Implementing the new risk–needs instruments is not an easy task without risk to the organization but it is a risk worth taking.

References

Andrews, D. A., & Bonta, J. (1995). *The Level of Service Inventory-Revised*. Toronto: Multi-Health.

Andrews, D. A., & Bonta, J. (1998a). *The Psychology of Criminal Conduct*, 2nd ed. Cincinnati, OH: Anderson Publishing Co.

Andrews, D. A., & Bonta, J. (1998b). *LSI-R Level of Service Inventory-Revised Software Manual*. Toronto: Multi-Health.

Andrews, D. A., Bonta, J., & Hoge, R. D. (1990). Classification for effective rehabilitation: Rediscovering psychology. *Criminal Justice and Behavior*, **17**, 19–52.

Andrews, D. A., Zinger, I., Hoge, R. D., Bonta, J., Gendreau, P., & Cullen, F. T. (1990). Does correctional treatment work? A clinically-relevant and psychologically informed meta-analysis. *Criminology*, **28**, 369–404.

Aos, S., Phipps, P., Barnoski, R., & Lieb, R. (1999). *The Comparative Costs and Benefits of Programs to Reduce Crime: A Review of National Research Findings with Implications for Washington State*. Olympia, WA: Washington State Institute for Public Policy.

Baird, C. (1981). Probation and parole classification: The Wisconsin model. *Corrections Today*, **43**, 36–41.

Bonta, J. (1997). *Trainer's Manual for the Level of Service Inventory-Revised (LSI-R)*. Toronto: Multi-Health.

Bonta, J. (1996). Risk–needs assessment and treatment. In A. T. Harland (Ed.), *Choosing Correctional Options that Work*, pp. 18–32. Thousand Oaks, CA: Sage.

Bonta, J., & Motiuk, L. L. (1992). Inmate classification. *Journal of Criminal Justice*, **20**, 343-353.

Bonta, J., Parkinson, R., & Barkwell, L. (1994). *Revising the Wisconsin Classification System*, Paper presented at the Annual Meeting of the American Society of Criminology, Miami, Florida, November.

Canada (1992). Corrections and Conditional Release Act. *Criminal Code of Canada*. Ottawa, Canada.

Champion, D. J. (1994). *Measuring Offender Risk: A Criminal Justice Sourcebook, 1994*. Westport, CN: Greenwood Press.

Clements, C. B. (1996). Offender classification: Two decades of progress. *Criminal Justice and Behavior*, **23**, 121–143.

Cohen, M. A. (1998). The monetary vale of saving a high-risk youth. *Journal of Quantitative Criminology*, **14**, 5–33.

Correctional Service of Canada (1997). *Staff Survey 1996 Final Report*, Vol. 1. Ottawa: Research Branch, Correctional Service of Canada.

Cumberland, A. K., & Boyle, G. J. (1997). Psychometric prediction of recidivism: Utility of the risk needs inventory. *Australian and New Zealand Journal of Criminology*, **30**, 72–86.

Dawes, R. M., Faust, D., & Meehl, P. E. (1993). Statistical prediction versus clinical prediction: Improving what works. In G. Karen & C. Lewis (Eds), *A Handbook of Data Analysis in the Behavioral Sciences*, pp. 351–367. Hillsdale, NJ: Erlbaum.

Gaes, G. G., Flanagan, T. J., Motiuk, L., & Stewart, L. (1999). Adult correctional treatment. In M. Tonry & M. Moore (Eds), *Crime and Justice: A Review of Research*, pp. 85–150. Chicago: University of Chicago Press.

Gendreau, P., & Andrews, D. A. (1996). *Correctional Programs Assessment Inventory (CPAI)*, 6th ed. Saint John, New Brunswick: Department of Psychology, University of New Brunswick.

Gendreau, P., Goggin, C., & Cullen, F. T. (1999). *The Effects of Prison Sentences on Recidivism*, Report to Corrections Research and Development. Ottawa: Solicitor General Canada.

Gendreau, P., Little, T., & Goggin, C. (1996). A meta-analysis of the predictors of adult recidivism: What works! *Criminology*, **34**, 401–433.

Hare, R. D. (1990). *The Hare Psychopathy Checklist-Revised*. Toronto: Multi-Health.

Kirkpatrick, B. (1999). Exploratory research of female risk prediction and LSI-R. *Corrections Compendium*, **24**(1-3), 14–17.

Motiuk, L. L., & Porporino, F. (1989). *Offender Risk/Needs Assessment: A Study of Conditional Releases*, Report R-06. Ottawa: Correctional Service of Canada.

O'Keefe, M. L., Klebe, K., & Hromas, S. (1998). *Validation of the Level of Supervision Inventory (LSI) for Community Based Offenders in Colorado*. Denver, CO: Colorado Department of Corrections.

Raynor, P. (1999). *Risk, Needs and Effectiveness in British Probation Services*, paper presented at the Annual Meeting of the American Society of Criminology, Toronto, Canada, November.

Underdown, A. (1998). *Strategies for Effective Offender Supervision: A Report of the HMIP What Works Project*. London: Home Office Publications Unit.

Chapter 12

IMPLEMENTATION GUIDELINES FOR CORRECTIONAL PROGRAMS IN THE "REAL WORLD"

Paul Gendreau, Claire Goggin and Paula Smith

Centre for Criminal Justice Studies, University of New Brunswick, Saint John, Canada

It is ironic that the fundamental component in the delivery of effective offender treatment services, that of program implementation, has traditionally received the least attention. Only a dozen or so studies exist in the corrections literature which address this topic, in contrast to at least a thousand studies on offender assessment and treatment. In this chapter we begin to seek redress for this omission by outlining a number of guidelines that, in our opinion, are crucial for the successful implementation of correctional programs. Particular attention is paid to two of these guidelines, namely, needs assessment and knowledge cumulation. Second, the issue of evaluating the quality of correctional treatment programs is addressed, focusing on the application of the *Correctional Program Assessment Inventory (CPAI)* (Gendreau & Andrews, 1996) to that end. The available evidence regarding program quality in the "real world" is reviewed and areas that require remediation are noted.

With the rejuvenation of the rehabilitative ideal in corrections during the last decade, attention turned to the development of reliable risk assessment

Offender Rehabilitation in Practice. Edited by G. A. Bernfeld, D. P. Farrington and A. W. Leschied.
© 2001 John Wiley & Sons, Ltd.

protocols and effective treatment paradigms (see Gendreau, Smith & Goggin, 2001). Consequently, some 50 comprehensive narrative and quantitative reviews of the offender assessment and treatment literatures have identified which offender needs are appropriate treatment targets, which are the most reliable risk assessment measures in that regard, and what are the most effective offender treatment strategies.[1] Notwithstanding the adequacy of any assessment and intervention initiatives, however, failure to attend to issues of program implementation unwittingly attenuates treatment effectiveness (Gendreau & Andrews, 1979; Harris & Smith, 1996).

It is our contention that the topic of program implementation, generally subsumed under the rubric "technology transfer", has largely been ignored in the corrections literature (Gendreau, Goggin & Smith, 1999b), in part due to the *borné* nature of many corrections professionals (Gendreau, 1995; 1996).[2] To what else can we attribute the general ignorance of several thousand studies (Backer, David & Soucy, 1995) in the technology transfer literature, or the failure to incorporate lessons learned from research in "neighbouring" fields, such as mental health (e.g. Backer, Liberman & Kuehnel, 1986; Fairweather, Sanders & Tornatzky, 1974; Shadish, 1984)?

We have initiated a modest attempt at redressing this imbalance by developing a set of useful program implementation guidelines for correctional policy-makers and program managers (Gendreau et al., 1999b). In this chapter we propose to revisit these guidelines while examining in detail two pivotal implementation issues, needs analysis and knowledge cumulation, neither of which, in our view, have heretofore received the attention they merit. We then turn to the issue of post-implementation program monitoring through the use of measures that assess program quality.

GUIDELINES FOR IMPLEMENTING PROGRAMS

When the senior author (Paul Gendreau) and Donald Andrews began to evaluate their efforts at implementing programs 20 years ago (Gendreau & Andrews, 1979) they were aware of the value of a priori comprehensive needs analyses and literature searches, but no more so than they were of a variety of other implementation factors. Some 20 years later, the need to attend specifically to these two factors has been reinforced by the rather

---

[1] Representative narrative summaries of these literatures are detailed in Andrews (1995), Andrews and Bonta (1998), Bonta (1996), Cullen and Gendreau (2000), Gendreau (1996) and Gendreau, Goggin & Paparozzi (1996).

[2] Lest we appear too harsh on our colleagues, the problem is a longstanding one and crosses many disciplines. A quarter of a century ago Williams (1976) remarked that the "lack of concern for implementation is currently the crucial impediment to improving complex operating programs, policy analysis and experimentation" (p. 267).

disconcerting results of several recent program audits conducted by the senior author. At first glance, we might be inclined to demur. After all, what could be simpler than conducting a needs assessment and reviewing the relevant literature? In truth, these issues have not routinely been credited with a measure of importance commensurate with their impact on program outcome. At the very outset of the implementation process, a poorly done needs assessment and/or inadequate literature review can seriously compromise the implementation process which, in turn, can jeopardize program quality.

Needs assessment

A needs assessment may be instigated by an agency or government department in response to demands by personnel or the public for a particular service or program. Of the various methods for assessing needs we will make only a passing comment on key informant, focus groups or community forum methods. While recognizing their utility in some circumstances (see Posavac & Carey, 1997), we rarely rely on them. It may be that our experiences in this regard have been unusual or perhaps it is because of the controversy characteristic of criminal justice issues, but we have found that these processes are too easily hijacked by ideological agendas (e.g. get tough on crime), resulting in needs being greatly exaggerated or misrepresented.

Rather, our focus has been on social indicators of need which are readily available and frequently employed by program planners to determine the nature and degree of social problems in specific areas or within particular target populations. Social indicators are intuitively appealing as they have immediate face validity. They give the appearance of objectivity as they are usually based on extensive survey data collected by various "official" government and/or private-sector organizations.

Yet, social indicators can also provide an inaccurate estimation of a particular need. While they may highlight the incidence and prevalence of an existing problem, social indicators do not necessarily identify its fundamental causal factors nor the solutions best suited to mediate them (Posavac & Carey, 1997). Where needs assessments often go awry is when they cite statistics based on rates and averages, or aggregate data, as persuasive evidence that a specific need exists within a particular population. The mistake most commonly made when interpreting aggregate statistics is known as the ecological fallacy, or the assumption that the aggregate or ecological correlation (also referred to as a correlation of averages, Zajonc & Mullaly, 1997) between a predictor and criterion implies knowledge of the correlates of individual behaviour (see Andrews & Bonta, 1998; Robinson, 1950). A clear exposition of this point can be found in Freedman, Pisani, Purves & Adhikari (1991). They summarized a study which had produced a sizeable correlation ($r = 0.70$) between aggregate rates of smoking and lung cancer deaths in each of 11 countries. As Freedman et al. (1991) noted, however, "... it is not countries which smoke and get cancer, but people. To measure the strength of the relationship for people, therefore, it is necessary to have data relating smoking and cancer for individual people" (p. 140). Coincidentally, the magnitude and direction of the ecological correlation in this study were supported by the results from individual level data but, as we shall see, ecological correlations can very often be inflated.[3]

How does this inflation occur? Returning to the smoking example, if we examine the correlation between individuals who smoke and the incidence of lung cancer in each country, even with an $r = 0.20$ (a correlation considered "large" in medical research of this sort), the scatter plots would be relatively heteroscedastic. If, on the other hand, we represent each country by an aggregate index of the smoking–cancer relationship and then compute a correlation across the countries, the considerable variability between individuals is eliminated, in effect "smoothing out" the points in the scatter plot (see Freedman et al., 1991, p. 141, fig. 6 for a clear graphical representation of this inflation effect).[4] Thus, comparisons of predictor–criterion relationships using individual versus aggregate data almost always inflate the latter values, especially as the units being aggregated become larger (e.g. IQ relative to birth order), where aggregate correlations of ($r \approx 0.90$ are not unknown even when individual level correlations are actually in the order of $r \approx 0.10$ (see Zajonc, 1962; Zajonc & Mullaly, 1997).

Within the criminal justice field we have found some glaring examples of this inflation effect. Hsieh and Pugh's (1993) meta-analysis reported that the aggregate correlations between indices of social class of origin and crime were in the $r \approx 0.40$ range, a result supportive of traditional sociological theory, whereas a meta-analysis of this relationship at the individual level found an $r = 0.06$ (Gendreau, Little & Goggin, 1996).

Our second example illustrates the danger of relying exclusively upon aggregate data when public policy decisions are being considered. There is a pervasive public sentiment that crime is a serious social problem and that

---

[3] Ecological correlations in the range 0.70 are not uncommon. It should be noted that there may be instances where ecological correlates might not be overstated but "... the conditions under which this can happen are far removed from those ordinarily encountered in data" (Robinson, 1950, p. 357)

[4] Ecological correlations are commonly used in economics, political science and sociology. We suspect that when aggregate date is used in these disciplines it is widely interpreted in the same way as would be the results derived from individual-based correlations. Now, there is an interesting thesis topic!

the most effective means of reducing criminal behaviour is the application of severe sanctions such as more frequent and lengthier periods of incarceration (see DeJong, 1997; Doob, Sprott, Marinos & Varma, 1998; Wood & Grasmick, 1999). One study, that of Fabelo (1995), is often highlighted as conclusive proof that prisons deter criminal behaviour (Reynolds, 1996). Fabelo (1995) summarized data on the percentage increases/decreases in incarceration rates in each state with their respective changes in crime rates over a 5 year period. He reported that a 30 per cent increase in incarceration rates led to a 5 per cent decrease in the crime rate which, according to our calculations, results in an aggregate correlation of $r = 0.41$. Contrast this conclusion with the results of a recent meta-analysis of the comparative effects of longer versus shorter periods of incarceration and brief periods of prison versus probation on individual offender recidivism. This study, which encompassed 325 effect sizes from studies involving 398,300 offenders (Gendreau, Goggin & Cullen, 1999), yielded an overall mean effect size of $r = 0.02$, or a 2 per cent increase in recidivism!

In conclusion, with regard to program implementation, when dealing with the effects of a particular intervention for individuals, offender needs assessment should be based on individual not aggregate data.[5]

Cumulating knowledge

Even assuming an appropriate and adequate needs assessment has been conducted, we must still attend to the quality of the knowledge cumulation process (i.e. literature search) as it can be tainted by various factors. These include ideology, management style and the choice of literature review technique. We will limit our present discussion to the third factor; for a review of how ideology and management practices affect knowledge cumulation, the reader is referred to Gendreau, Goggin and Smith (2000).

When the senior author began working in corrections 40 years ago the literature review process was a relatively easy task as there was less than a handful of requisite books or journals to consult in order to stay informed regarding the development of new programs (Gendreau, 1996). Given the

---

[5] There is no reason to be concerned about the fact that individual level correlations are most often smaller than their aggregate counterparts. The former, which typically lie within the 0.10–0.40 range, are not inconsequential. We have addressed this issue elsewhere (Gendreau, Goggin et al., 1996) and are in the process of expanding our arguments in this matter. In one meta-analysis the correlation between criminogenic needs and recidivism was $r = 0.18$ (Gendreau, Little et al., 1996). Behavioural programs that target the criminogenic needs of higher risk offenders produce reductions in recidivism in the 25% range, which translates into a dramatic result from a cost-effectiveness perspective (see Cohen, 1998; Cullen & Gendreau, 2000).

voluminous amount of information now available on specific topics, most of which is highly variable or even contradictory, the development of new programs has become a much more onerous undertaking.

Historically, decision-makers have relied upon narrative reviews[6] to make sense of a given literature and decide what types of programs to implement. Although this method may be appropriate when a literature base is relatively small (e.g. five to ten studies) or purely qualitative in nature, critics of this approach have noted several limitations (Glass, McGaw, & Smith, 1981). Among the most troublesome shortcomings of the narrative review are its relative imprecision and its tendency to omit key data. As such, the scope of a literature to be summarized is often subject to the prejudices of the reviewer (Meehl, 1990). In addition, essential concepts are often poorly operationalized. Redondo, Sánchez-Meca & Garrido (1999) have also pointed out that the mind has a limited capacity for accurately processing a multitude of methodologies, outcomes, study characteristics and potential moderators.

Faced with the daunting task of summarizing the results of large numbers of quantitative studies (i.e. 30–200), the narrative reviewer tends to rely on only a small subset in order to generate conclusions about large and sometimes complex literatures (e.g. Gendreau & Ross, 1987). As a result, narrative reviews are virtually impossible to replicate. Glass et al. (1981) provided one of the most compelling examples of this phenomenon. When five leading scholars conducted narrative reviews of the same literature (the effectiveness of psychotherapy versus drug therapy) they differed as to which studies qualified for the review, disagreed as to which studies should be placed in the treatment categories and disputed the consistency and magnitude of the results.

One means by which narrative reviews have tried to be more precise is to utilize the box score analysis. This method tabulates the frequency of statistically significant versus non-significant effects within a given body of studies, the "winner" being the condition with the greater frequency of statistically significant results. Although this technique appears straightforward, the issue becomes complicated when the values of some statistically significant results are larger than others, or, worse, when the values of some non-significant results are larger than those designated as significant (determination of significance, of course, being inherently wedded to sample size). As Meehl (1992) has commented, this "... is a scientifically preposterous way to reason" (p. 541).

---

[6] In a typical narrative review, the author attempts to establish the truth of a matter by reading a few influential theoretical articles, sifting through the readily available evidence and generating conclusions that substantiate possibly pre-existing perspectives on the issue.

Reliance on significance testing has, generally, severely hindered the process of knowledge cumulation (Schmidt, 1996). Schmidt (1996) has cited several common misinterpretations accruing from statistical testing:

(a)   a result that is statistically significant indicates whether the findings are reliable and can be replicated;
(b)   the significance level provides an estimate of the importance of the effect (i.e. $p < 0.01$ is better than $p < 0.05$); and
(c)   if we fail to reject the null hypothesis ($p > 0.05$), then the results are due to chance alone and are likely zero.

Each of these statements is incorrect, and can lead to serious misinterpretations about the nature and utility of a given literature.

At this point we would not be surprised if some of our readers were slightly incredulous. Denigrating the narrative review is one thing, but rejecting the hallowed icons of statistical instruction is, seemingly, heretical. Our recommendations, however, are neither radical nor, for that matter, original. In fact, their foundations were laid years ago. Standardizing and quantifying the results from a research literature using a simple statistical technique had its origins in the 1930s (Rosenthal, 1991). It was only much later that the process became known as meta-analysis.[7] This review strategy has now become so important to some fields (e.g. medicine) that it is recommended that decisions regarding "best-practice" treatments should be based on the results of meta-analytic literature reviews once the particular need has been identified (Horton, 1993). While meta-analysis may sound forbidding—it can be a complex, arduous process (see Cooper, 1997)—when it comes to the needs of clinicians and policy-makers, most "bare bones" meta-analyses (i.e. points estimates, confidence intervals) will readily suffice (Rosenthal, 1995). In corrections, as in most applied fields, we are rarely concerned with subtle effects and higher order interactions, the meanings of which are often uninterpretable. Instead, what is needed is empirical data to guide informed policies on elementary but crucial issues such as which type of treatment is more effective in reducing recidivism or which risk measure is the more accurate in predicting reoffending.

Table 12.1 reinforces a few points about the utility of a basic meta-analysis.[8] Hypothetical data from six cognitive treatment studies with

---

[7] Of interest, quantitative summary techniques have been used in the "hard" sciences for years (Hedges, 1987).
[8] Readers unfamiliar with meta-analysis can consult Gendreau, Goggin & Smith (in press) for a policy-maker "friendly" summary.

Table 12.1   The relationship between treatment and recidivism across a sample of studies

Study No.	Risk	Quality	N	r	CI_r
1	L	L	52	−0.09	−0.36 to 0.18
2	L	L	180	0.02	−0.13 to 0.17
3	H	H	42	0.34*	0.07 to 0.61
4	H	L	82	0.22*	0.01 to 0.43
5	H	H	30	0.29	−0.04 to 0.62
6	L	H	68	0.06	−0.18 to 0.30
Total			*454*	*0.14*	*0.05 to 0.23*

Note: Risk = offender risk level; Quality = study design quality; N = study sample size; r = correlation coefficient (or effect size) between treatment and recidivism; CI_r = confidence interval about r.
*$p < 0.05$.

offenders are presented with two commonly coded moderators (at least vis-à-vis corrections): offender risk level and quality of research design.[9]

The studies, which are typical of the offender treatment literature, vary considerably as to sample size (n_{range} = 30 to 180) and effect size (r_{range} = −0.09 to 0.34).[10] Recall our discussion about box score summaries and significance testing. Only two of the six studies in Table 12.1 (#3, #4) produce a statistically significant effect on recidivism. Using a box score tabulation of significant effects, we would inevitably conclude that the treatment is ineffective. Yet the 95 per cent confidence intervals (CI_r) of each of the six studies overlap, indicating that they are, indeed, sampling from the same population parameter.

The use of the CI in meta-analysis is crucial. Many people erroneously think that null hypothesis significance testing equally limits the probability of Type I (incorrectly concluding there is an effect) and Type II errors (incorrectly concluding there is no effect). Rather, what happens with significance testing is that, while Type I errors may be held at the 5 per cent level (i.e. $\alpha = 0.05$), no equivalent control of the Type II error rate can be assumed. The rate may commonly, in fact, be very high, often in the 50 per cent range

---

[9] Important study characteristics that are routinely coded in a meta-analysis include: (a) study context— country of study, author's discipline, source of funding and year and type of publication; (b) sample characteristics—age, gender, race and offender risk level; (c) variables specific to treatment studies—type of treatment, treatment dosage, "who" administers the treatment, treatment setting, program sponsorship, age of program, theoretical foundation of program and role of evaluator; (d) method—comparability of treatment-control groups, rate of attrition, type of outcome and length of follow-up.

[10] The effect sizes are expressed as correlations which can, in most cases, be interpreted at face value (Cullen & Gendreau, 2000). Here, they range from a 9% increase to a 34% decrease in recidivism.

(Cohen, 1988), especially among studies with low power due to small sample sizes. Confidence estimates, on the other hand, provide a great advantage to knowledge cumulation in that they hold the overall error rate at 5 per cent (Schmidt, 1996). That is, in only 5 per cent of confidence intervals would we *not* expect to find the population parameter or "true" effect size.

Besides quantitatively demonstrating the degree of agreement there is within a given body of literature, meta-analysis also provides an estimate of certainty about an obtained effect. When the *CI* is very wide it tells the program implementer to be cautious, that conclusions about a particular relationship should be regarded as tentative; more research is required before embarking upon establishing a new program. When the interval is very narrow, as in recent studies on the lack of effectiveness of intermediate sanctions on recidivism (Gendreau, Goggin, & Fulton, 2000), the decision-maker can place much more confidence in the conclusions of a literature review and, therefore, in his/her recommended course of action.

Returning to Table 12.1, the average effect size is $r = 0.14$, or a 14 per cent reduction in recidivism with an associated *CI* of 0.05 to 0.23. Furthermore, following a useful procedure generated by Hedges and Olkin (1985), the effect sizes from studies can be weighted by sample size and the number of effect sizes involved which, in this case, produces a mean value of 0.10 with a *CI* bounded by 0.01 and 0.19.

Now we have a much more accurate notion of the utility of the cognitive treatments in our example. Furthermore, we can examine moderators of interest within the database (i.e. offender risk or quality of program design), and repeat the procedures noted above to determine if these produce differential effects on recidivism. In this case, risk level appears to be an important moderator (i.e. $r_{\text{high risk}} = 0.28$) in that our hypothetical treatment results in a 28 per cent decrease in recidivism among high-risk offenders versus a negligible effect ($r_{\text{low risk}} = -0.003$) on recidivism among the low-risk group.[11]

Recently, "new" statistics have appeared that can measure how "solid" the evidence from a literature review may be. One group includes the fail-safe indicators (Gendreau, Gupta, Smith & Goggin, 2001; Orwin, 1987; Rosenthal, 1991) which determine the degree of confidence one can attribute to the mean effect of a given set of studies; that is, they specify how many additional studies averaging null effects would be required to counter the conclusions of a given meta-analysis.

We also favour the common language (CL) effect size indicator (McGraw & Wong, 1992). In a forthcoming meta-analysis[12] we report on which of two

---

[11] This result is similar to what we find in recent meta-analyses of the treatment literature (Andrews, Dowden & Gendreau, 1999).
[12] For a preliminary report see Gendreau, Goggin & Smith (1999a).

risk measures is the most useful for predicting offender recidivism. This is an extremely important issue within corrections. And clearly, a statement of statistical significance is not particularly helpful to the policy-maker or clinician in this regard as it gives no indication of the "practical" size of the effect. The CL indicator, on the other hand, is both an easily calculable and comprehensible statistic that can be of immediate utility to administrators by providing them with a probabilistic statement of the relative performance of each of a pair of variables with outcome. In this instance, the CL indicated that one of the two risk measures produced higher correlations with recidivism 78 per cent of the time. This is an example of the limitations of significance testing and the benefits of having available more probative information in order to make informed programming decisions.

In conclusion, no matter how skilled programmers may be in identifying needs and adhering to the ensuing implementation guidelines, an *inadequate* literature review, upon which all subsequent treatment decisions are predicated, places the entire enterprise at risk.

Implementation guidelines

As noted at the outset, we have previously presented the following guidelines (Gendreau et al., 1999b, pp. 182–184). In reiterating them, the reader should be aware that none were founded on well-designed experimental or quasi-experimental research. They were initially developed by looking through the "retrospectroscope" at past attempts at program implementation and selected readings in the technology transfer literature (see Gendreau & Andrews, 1979; Gendreau, 1996). Obviously, the availability heuristic and the vagaries of clinical wisdom affected the validity of these authors' observations. Having said this, on those few occasions where programmers were sensitive to implementation issues (e.g. Byrne & Kelly, 1989; Fagan, 1990; Paparozzi, 1994),[13] reductions in recidivism ranging from 15 to 30 per cent were associated with better quality implementation procedures. Thus, we are confident that the utility of more than a few of these guidelines will eventually be confirmed by fellow programmers in the future.[14]

---

[13] Paparozzi (1994) used an implementation inventory drawn up by the senior author which contained most of the items listed below.

[14] HM Inspectorate of Probation is undertaking a massive implementation of "effective offender supervision" strategies in the UK (Underdown, 1998). Preliminary indications from sources in that organization suggest items from our list are considered to be quite crucial to their efforts: Organizational—item #7; Program—item #9; Change agent—item #7; Staff—item #6.

The presentation of our guiding principles for effective implementation falls within four general categories:

- organizational factors;
- program factors;
- change agent; and
- staffing activities.

Organizational factors

These items concern the host agency where the program will be implemented.

1. The agency has a history of adopting new initiatives.
2. The agency is efficient in putting into place new initiatives.
3. The bureaucratic structure is moderately decentralized thus allowing for a flexible response to problems.
4. Issues are resolved in a timely fashion.
5. Issues are resolved in a non-confrontational manner.
6. There is little task/emotional–personal conflict within the organization at the interdepartmental, staff, management and/or management–staff levels.
7. Staff turnover at all levels has been less than 25 per cent during the previous 2 years.
8. The organization offers a formal program of instruction in the assessment and treatment of offenders on a biannual basis.
9. The agency has formal links with educational institutions or consultants for the purpose of developing guidelines and receiving training on clinical/service matters.

Program factors

1. The need for the program has been empirically documented (e.g. surveys, focus groups, etc.).
2. Stakeholders (i.e. community sources, management and staff) agree that the program is timely, addresses an important matter and is congruent with existing institutional and/or community values and practices.
3. Funding originates with the host agency.
4. The fiscal aspects of the program: (a) are cost-effective, (b) do not jeopardize the continued funding of existing agency programs and (c) are sustainable for the near future.

5. Stakeholders agree the program matches the needs of the clientele.
6. The program is designed to: (a) maintain current staffing levels, (b) support professional autonomy, (c) enhance professional credentials and (d) save staff time/effort.
7. The program is based on credible scientific evidence.
8. The program does not overstate the gains to be realized (e.g. recidivism reductions).
9. The program is being initiated during a period when the host agency is free of other major problems/conflicts.
10. Program initiation proceeds: (a) incrementally, (b) has a pilot/transitional phase and (c) initially focuses on achieving intermediate goals.

Change agent

The change agent is the person primarily responsible for initiating the program and can be an external consultant or someone within the organization.

1. The change agent has an intimate knowledge of the agency and its staff.
2. The change agent has the support of senior agency officials as well as that of line staff.
3. The change agent's professional orientation and values are compatible with the agency's mandate and goals.
4. The change agent has professional credibility.
5. The change agent has a history of successful program implementation in the agency's program area.
6. In bringing about change, the change agent employs: (a) central routes of persuasion, (b) motivational interviewing techniques (e.g. empathy, discrepancy, non-confrontational, self-efficacy support), (c) reciprocity, (d) authority (but does not use threats), (e) reinforcement (e.g. praise), (f) modelling, (g) systemic problem solving and (h) advocacy/brokerage.
7. The change agent continues until there are clear performance indices that management and staff are able to maintain the delivery of the program with a reasonable degree of competence.

Staff factors

In this context, "staff" refers to both those who deliver the service and the program directors who have direct line authority over treatment staff.

1. The staff have frequent and immediate access to the change agent.
2. The staff understand the theoretical basis of the "program".
3. The staff have the technical/professional skill to implement the program. They have taken applied courses on the assessment and treatment of offenders.
4. The staff think or believe (i.e. self-efficacy) they can run the program effectively.
5. The staff participate directly in designing the new "program".
6. In order to run the program efficiently, the staff are: (a) given the necessary time, (b) given adequate resources and (c) provided with feedback mechanisms (e.g. focus groups and workshops).

MEASURING PROGRAM QUALITY

Even when most of the above criteria have been satisfied and the program has been successfully implemented, steps must be taken to ensure its therapeutic integrity is maintained. To our knowledge the only measurement tool available for this purpose in corrections is the *Correctional Program Assessment Inventory (CPAI)* (Gendreau & Andrews, 1996). According to Van Voorhis and Brown (1996) the tool has become the standard for "evaluability assessments" in corrections and it would appear that the CPAI assists in meeting the 13 evaluation goals delineated by those authors.

Correctional Program Assessment Inventory (CPAI)

The CPAI is designed to assess how well various aspects of an offender treatment program (i.e. client risk assessment, treatment targets, etc.) correspond with known principles of effective programming for offenders (Gendreau & Goggin, 1997). The latest version consists of 75 items, 65 of which are scoreable (i.e. 1 = meets criteria, 0 = does not meet criteria), representative of six key program components:[15]

1. Program implementation: the previous experience of the program's initiators, their qualifications, whether a community-needs assessment and/or pilot has been conducted, etc.
2. Client pre-service assessment: the types of offenders and presenting problems accepted in the program, the assessment of risk, need and responsivity, etc.

---

[15] At this writing, the CPAI is currently being revised by the senior author and Donald Andrews (Gendreau & Andrews, 2001). About two dozen additional items will be included giving greater emphasis to the correctional treatment practices of staff. Sections on organizational culture and inter-agency communication are also being added.

3. Program characteristics: the types of treatment offered by the program and how they are delivered, the quality of collateral program documentation, etc.
4. Staff characteristics: the types of professional discipline found among staff as well as their training, experience, etc.
5. Evaluation: the types of quality assurance mechanisms in place, including content of client files, details of program follow-ups, process and outcome measures, methodological quality, etc.
6. Other: the program's ethical guidelines, funding and community support issues, etc.

A number of program assessments have been conducted using the CPAI and they provide sobering insight into the quality of correctional programs in the "real world".[16] Some of the results described below are summarized in more detail in Gendreau and Goggin (1997).

Three series of large-scale reviews of correctional treatment programs using the CPAI have been conducted. In addition, a number of single program reviews have also been carried out. The former can be summarized as: Gendreau and Goggin (1991) assessed 101 federally funded offender substance programs across Canada, 80 per cent of them prison based. Hoge, Leschied and Andrews (1993) reviewed 130 juvenile offender programs in Ontario, equally split between open/secure correctional facilities and community support teams or probation settings. Latessa and Holsinger (1998, 1999) have evaluated 51 programs of all types (e.g. adult, juvenile, prison based, community residential centers, etc.) across the US.

While some excellent individual programs were discovered through these surveys, the blunt truth is that 70 per cent of all programs (summing across the three surveys) "failed" according to the CPAI.[17] Some of the major programming deficits are outlined in the following sections.

---

[16] Cynics of rehabilitation have claimed, with some justification, that the published evaluation literature is abysmal and unrepresentative of the state of correctional programming in the "real world". Thus, we might as well abandon efforts at providing effective treatment (Lab & Whitehead, 1990). Our response has been to meet this challenge by identifying program weaknesses in the field so as to *improve* upon matters (Gendreau & Goggin, 1991).

[17] Recall that the CPAI is based on the principles of effective treatment literature. The ultimate validity, based on correlations between CPAI scores and the recidivism rates associated with the programs being assessed, is a long way off. It is quite uncommon, in our experience, for programs to collect recidivism data and rarer still for any of them to publish evidence of their success (or failure) using comparison groups. Gray (1997) has reported on a kind of proxy validity of the CPAI. As part of his research on the influence of coercion in offender treatment programs, he scored 93 "successful" published treatment programs (success was defined as reductions in recidivism of at least 10%) on an abbreviated version of the CPAI. Despite an attendant restriction of range and the fact that many reports neglected to include important information in their program descriptions, an $r = 0.41$ was reported between the CPAI and program recidivism outcome.

Implementation

1. Program directors and staff were not adequately familiar with the literature in their field. Moreover, they did not conduct thorough reviews of the literature of the effectiveness of the proposed treatments prior to implementing the program. As a result, they may have found themselves "following a hunch", repeating the mistakes of others or chasing the latest panacea.
2. The professional credibility (i.e. training, experience with successful programs) of program designers is suspect.
3. Notwithstanding the paucity of corrections-specific program implementation information, there is an extensive literature in this regard within other social science/services and management fields that demonstrates how to effectively establish programs and it is rarely referred to by corrections program designers.

Client pre-service assessment

1. Somewhat surprisingly, given all that has been written about actuarial risk assessment (e.g. Bonta, 1996), the traditional clinical subjective/intuitive format persists. This seems to be particularly endemic within juvenile corrections. There is virtually no recognition of the classic literature concerning the inadequacy of this assessment approach (e.g. Little & Shneidman, 1959; Meehl, 1954).
2. Among the programs that use actuarial systems (or tests) to assess offenders, it is not unusual to find a preoccupation with static factors (e.g. previous criminal history, type of offense) while the assessment of dynamic criminogenic risk factors (e.g. attitudes, values and behaviours) is generally overlooked. It is impossible to monitor treatment effectiveness unless the latter are considered because they represent key targets for behavioural change.
3. There is still confusion as to which dynamic factors should be appraised. Programs continue to focus on the assessment of self-esteem, anxiety or depression, which are among the weakest predictors of recidivism.

Program characteristics

1. Programs either do not use an "appropriate" treatment (those known to be effective) or they dilute the overall effectiveness of the program by marrying appropriate and inappropriate strategies. In some cases, it was found that the most frequently used interventions were empirically

established failures (Gendreau & Goggin, 1991) (see Hester & Miller's, 1995, comprehensive analysis of the alcoholism treatment literature for similar findings).

2.   The dosage level (i.e. intensity) of treatment is often insufficient (e.g. several hours per week). In other words, offenders simply do not spend enough time in treatment.

3.   The responsivity principle is almost totally ignored. This lack of attention to individual differences is striking; it reflects a long-standing bias in theory development in criminology (Andrews & Bonta, 1998) and the evolution of management practices in corrections that emphasize a macro-level "input–output" orientation which takes little account of the needs of the individual offender. In these instances, offenders are treated as if they are all alike.

4.   Very few programs incorporate a meaningful system of reinforcers.

5.   Relapse prevention strategies are underutilized.

6.   A sound index of therapeutic integrity in a program is a treatment manual that outlines, in ample detail, the theory underlying the treatment, the daily treatment task schedule (i.e. lesson plans, homework exercises, teaching aid materials, etc.), as well as the process evaluation assessment tools. The manual should be of sufficient quality that an "external" therapist could attend the program and conduct a class session with relative ease. Such manuals are, in our experience, quite rare. Furthermore, few programs monitor, in any quantifiable way, the quality of instruction *per se*. We are aware of only one measure developed in this regard (Mitchell & Egan, 1995).

7.   Many programs experience problems finding any relevant/useful community-based services to which clients may be referred.

Staff characteristics

The following should be read as more of an indictment of the lack of quality control exhibited by employers and the paucity of relevant training programs in academic settings than a general critique of program staff. For the most part, we have found treatment staff to be dedicated and eager to upgrade their skills when the opportunity avails itself.

1.   It is not unusual to find staff hired for a treatment program based on characteristics other than clinical experience and training relevant to the task at hand. Program staff commonly have less than a university degree; postgraduate training is rare. In addition, we have not discovered one hiring protocol that employed an actuarial assessment of

the staff characteristics (e.g. clarity, honesty, empathy, fairness) that have been found to be associated with effective counselling skills.

2. Time and again, when questioning staff, we have encountered large gaps in knowledge regarding: (a) The criminological theories of criminal behaviour and the psychological theories of personality and their relevance to offender treatment, and (b) basic concepts of classical and operant conditioning without which it is impossible to undertake any sort of effective counselling. These are, admittedly, strong comments, but with respect to this last point, how can it be otherwise when some programs have difficulty identifying a sufficient variety of and ratio of reinforcers and punishers let alone a demonstrated awareness of the principles of behavioural reinforcement and punishment? Seldom have we seen the seminal behaviour modification texts referenced by programmers (Masters, Burish, Hollon & Rimm, 1997; Spiegler & Guevremont, 1993). Therefore, in our opinion, much of what goes on under the guise of cognitive therapy is virtually non-directive "chats" with no guarantee that prosocial behaviour is being reinforced and that antisocial behaviour is not, or is at least being punished. Recommended reading on how counselors should function as competent role models can be found in Van Voorhis, Braswell and Lester (2000) and Andrews and Bonta (1998, pp. 283–288).

3. Not surprisingly, given some of the working conditions and salary levels we have seen, the staff turnover rate in many programs is often unacceptably high.

Evaluation

1. Systematic and thorough evaluation practices are, for all intents and purposes, non-existent. Process evaluations, or how the client is progressing during treatment, are sporadic at best, and post-program outcome (i.e. at follow-up) is rarely assessed.

2. Consumer satisfaction surveys are infrequent.

While the aforementioned list of "deficits" in program quality seem discouraging, in our opinion it is more instructive to appreciate the true nature of the situation than to delude ourselves as to its quality, as was the case with many rehabilitation aficionados in the heyday of that agenda (see Cullen & Gendreau, 2000). Thus, rather than bemoan our fate, there are two avenues to pursue in order to alleviate these shortcomings, and these are better education and training, and more knowledge dissemination. This topic has been discussed in detail elsewhere (Gendreau, 1996). Unfortunately, there are few opportunities for training in offender assessment and treatment. There are, at best, only a handful of academic psychology/criminal justice programs in the United States that have an in-depth curriculum in the offender treatment area. We are hopeful, however, that more opportunities for training will be developed.[18] As for fostering knowledge dissemination, it is essential that the leaders[19] in the field take every opportunity to provide workshops and training courses, and to initiate demonstration projects of worthwhile programs. In conclusion, in this chapter we have made a modest attempt at furthering the development of effective service delivery for offenders. It is acknowledged that the implementation guidelines outlined herein need further refinement and clarification. Nevertheless, we are confident many of them will prove useful in the short term. Moreover, we are slowly filling in the gaps in our knowledge about "what works" in correctional programming and how it does so.

Acknowledgment

We would like to thank Angela Taylor, BA (Hons) for her assistance in the preparation of this manuscript.

References

Andrews, D. (1995). The psychology of criminal conduct and effective treatment. In J. McGuire (Ed.), *What Works: Reducing Reoffending: Guidelines from Research and Practice*, pp. 35–61. New York: John Wiley.

Andrews, D., & Bonta, J. (1998). *The Psychology of Criminal Conduct.* Cincinnati, OH: Anderson Publishing Co.

Andrews, D. A., Dowden, C., & Gendreau, P. (1999). *Clinically Relevant and Psychologically Informed Approaches to Reduced Re-offending: A Meta-Analytic Study of Human Service, Risk, Need, Responsivity, and Other Concerns in Justice Contexts,* Unpublished manuscript, Carleton University, Ottawa, Ontario.

Backer, T. E., David, S. L., & Soucy, G. (1995). *Reviewing the Behavioral Science Knowledge Base on Technology Transfer,* NIDA Research Monograph 155. Rockville, MD: US Department of Health and Human Services, Public Health Services, National Institute of Health.

Backer, T. E., Liberman, R. P., & Kuehnel, T. (1986). Dissemination and adoption of innovative psychosocial interventions. *Journal of Clinical and Consulting Psychology,* **1**, 111–118.

---

[18] The Correctional Service of Canada has provided seed money for funding academic positions in the area. In our province the Solicitor General has funded academic programs in applied corrections.

[19] Two examples who come readily to mind in the juvenile area are Scott Henggeler and Alan Leschied.

Bonta, J. (1996). Risk–needs assessment and treatment. In A. T. Harland (Ed.), *Choosing Correctional Options that Work: Defining the Demand and Evaluating the Supply*, pp. 18–32. Thousand Oaks, CA: Sage.

Byrne, J. M., & Kelly, L. M. (1989). *Restructuring Probation as an Intermediate Sanction: An Evaluation of the Massachusetts Intensive Probation Supervision Program*, Research program on the punishment and control of offenders. Washington, DC: National Institute of Justice.

Cohen, J. (1988). *Statistical Power Analysis for the Behavioral Sciences*, 2nd ed. Hillsdale, NJ: Erlbaum.

Cohen, M. A. (1998). The monetary value of saving a high-risk youth. *Journal of Quantitative Criminology*, **14**, 5–32.

Cooper, H. (1997). Some finer points in meta-analysis. In M. Hunt (Ed.), *How Science Takes Stock: The Story of Meta-Analysis*, pp. 169–181. New York, NY: Russell Sage Foundation.

Cullen, F. T., & Gendreau, P. (2000). Assessing correctional rehabilitation: Policy, practice, and prospects. In J. Horney (Ed.), *NIJ Criminal Justice 2000: Vol. 3, Changes in Decision Making and Discretion in the Criminal Justice System*, pp. 109–175. Washington, DC: US Department of Justice, National Institute of Justice.

DeJong, C. (1997). Survival analysis and specific deterrence: Integrating theoretical and empirical models of recidivism. *Criminology*, **35**, 561–575.

Doob, A. N., Sprott, J. B., Marinos, V., & Varma, K. N. (1998). *An Exploration of Ontario Residents' Views of Crime and the Criminal Justice System* (C98-931656-4). Toronto, Ontario: University of Toronto, Centre of Criminology.

Fabelo, T. (1995). *Testing the Case for More Incarceration in Texas: The Record So Far*. Austin, TX: Criminal Justice Policy Council.

Fagan, J. (1990). Treatment and reintegration of violent juvenile offenders: Experimental results. *Justice Quarterly*, **7**, 233–263.

Fairweather, G. W., Sanders, D. H., & Tornatzky, L. G. (1974). *Creating Change in Mental Health Organizations*. Elmsford, NY: Pergamon.

Freedman, D., Pisani, R., Purves, R., & Adhikari, A. (1991). *Statistics*, 2nd ed. New York: W. W. Norton.

Gendreau, P. (1995). Technology transfer in the criminal justice field. In T. E. Backer, S. L. David & G. Soucy (Eds), *Reviewing the Behavioral Science Knowledge Base on Technology Transfer*, NIDA Research Monograph 155. Rockville, MD: US Department of Health and Human Services, Public Health Services, National Institute of Health.

Gendreau, P. (1996). Offender rehabilitation: What we know and what needs to be done. *Criminal Justice and Behavior*, **23**, 144–161.

Gendreau, P., & Andrews, D. (1979). Psychological consultation in correctional agencies: Case studies and general issues. In J. Platt & R. Wicks (Eds), *The Psychological Consultant*, pp. 177–212. New York: Grune & Stratton.

Gendreau, P., & Andrews, D. A. (1996). *Correctional Program Assessment Inventory (CPAI)*, 6th ed. Saint John, New Brunswick: University of New Brunswick.

Gendreau, P., & Andrews, D. A. (2001). *Correctional Program Assessment Inventory (CPAI-2000)*. [Available from the authors.]

Gendreau, P., & Goggin, C. (1991). *Evaluation of Correctional Service of Canada Substance Abuse Programs*, Research Report No. 16. Ottawa, Ontario: Research and Statistics Branch, Correctional Service of Canada.

Gendreau, P., & Goggin, C. (1997). Correctional treatment: Accomplishments and realities. In P. Van Voorhis, M. Braswell & D. Lester (Eds), *Correctional counseling and Rehabilitation*, 3rd ed., pp. 271–279. Cincinnati, OH: Anderson Publishing Co.

Gendreau, P., Goggin, C., & Cullen, F. T. (1999). *The Effects of Prison Sentences on Recidivism*, Cat. #J42-87/1999E. Ottawa, Ontario: Public Works and Government Services Canada.

Gendreau, P., Goggin, C., & Fulton, B. (2000). Intensive supervision in probation and parole. In C. R. Hollin (Ed.), *Handbook of Offender Assessment and Treatment*, pp. 195–204. Chichester: John Wiley.

Gendreau, P., Goggin, C., & Paparozzi, M. (1996). Principles of effective assessment for community corrections. *Federal Probation*, **60**, 64–70.

Gendreau, P., Goggin, C., & Smith, P. (1999a). Predicting recidivism: LSI-R vs. PCL-R. *Canadian Psychology Abstracts*, **40**(2a).

Gendreau, P., Goggin, C., & Smith, P. (1999b). The forgotten issue in effective correctional treatment: Program implementation. *International Journal of Offender Therapy and Comparative Criminology*, **43**, 180–187.

Gendreau, P., Goggin, C., & Smith, P. (2000). Generating rational correctional policies: An introduction to advances in cumulating knowledge. *Corrections Management Quarterly*, **4**, 52–60.

Gendreau, P., Goggin, C., & Smith, P. (in press). *Cumulating Knowledge: Some Ways in which Meta-Analysis Can Serve the Needs of Correctional Clinicians and Policy Makers*, Compendium of Effective Correctional Programs. Ottawa, Ontario: Solicitor General of Canada; Correctional Service of Canada, Research Division.

Gendreau, P., Little, T., & Goggin, C. (1996). A meta-analysis of the predictors of adult offender recidivism: What works? *Criminology*, **34**, 575–607.

Gendreau, P., & Ross, R. R. (1987). Revivification of rehabilitation: Evidence from 1980s. *Justice Quarterly*, **4**, 349–407.

Gendreau, P., Gupta, R., Smith, P., & Goggin, C. (2001). *Catching Up is Hard to Do: Fail Safe Statistics to Overturn Conclusions regarding the Utility of Prediction and Treatment Research*. Unpublished manuscript, University of New Brunswick, Saint John.

Gendreau, P., Smith, P., & Goggin, C. (2001). Treatment programs in corrections. In J. Winterdyk (Ed.), *Corrections in Canada: Social Reaction to Crime*. Scarborough, Ontario: Prentice-Hall.

Glass, G., McGaw, B., & Smith, M. L. (1981). *Meta-Analysis in Social Research*. Beverly Hills, CA: Sage.

Gray, G. (1997). *Does Coercion Play a Significant Role in Community Treatment Programs that Reduce Offender Recidivism?* Unpublished master's thesis, University of New Brunswick, Saint John, New Brunswick, Canada.

Harris, P., & Smith, S. (1996). Developing community corrections: An implementation perspective. In A. T. Harland (Ed.), *Choosing Correctional Options that Work: Defining the Demand and Evaluating the Supply*, pp. 183–222. Thousand Oaks, CA: Sage.

Hedges, L. V. (1987). How hard is hard science, how soft is soft science: The empirical cumulations of research. *American Psychologist*, **42**, 443–455.

Hedges, L. V., & Olkin, I. (1985). *Statistical Methods for Meta-Analysis*. New York: Academic Press.

Hester, R., & Miller, W. (1995). *Handbook of Alcoholism Treatment Approaches: Effective Alternatives*, 2nd ed. Needham Heights, MA: Simon & Shuster.

Hoge, R., Leschied, A., & Andrews, D. A. (1993). *An Investigation of Young Offender Services in the Province of Ontario: A Report of the Repeat Offender Project*. Toronto, Ontario: Ministry of Community and Social Services.

Horton, R. (1993). Data-proof practice. *Lancet*, **342**, 1499.

Hsieh, C.-C., & Pugh, M. D. (1993). Poverty, income equality, and violent crime: A meta-analysis of recent aggregate data studies. *Criminal Justice Review*, **18**, 182–202.

Latessa, E. J., & Holsinger, A. (1998). The importance of evaluating correctional programs: Assessing outcome and quality. *Corrections Management Quarterly*, **2**, 22–29.

Latessa, E. J., & Holsinger, A. M. (1999). *Evaluation of the Ohio Department of Youth Services' Community Correctional Facilities (CCFs)*, Subgrant number 96-JJ-SI1-0697. Cincinnati, OH: Division of Criminal Justice.

Lab, S., & Whitehead, J. (1990). From "nothing works" to the "appropriate works": The latest step in the search for the secular grail. *Criminology*, **28**, 405–417.

Little, K., & Shneidman, E. (1959). Congruencies among interpretations of psychological test and anamnestic data. *Psychological Monographs: General and Applied*, **73**, 1–42.

McGraw, K. O., & Wong, S. P. (1992). A common language effect size statistic. *Psychological Bulletin*, **111**, 361–365.

Masters, J., Burish, T., Hollon, S., & Rimm, D. (1997). *Behavior Therapy: Techniques and Empirical Findings*, 3rd ed. New York: Harcourt Brace Jovanovich.

Meehl, P. (1954). *Clinical versus Statistical Prediction*. Minneapolis, MN: University of Minnesota Press.

Meehl, P. E. (1990). Appraising and amending theories: The strategy of Lakatosian defense and two principles that warrant it. *Psychological Inquiry*, **1**, 108–141.

Meehl, P. E. (1992). Theoretical risks and tabular asterisks: Sir Karl, Sir Ronald, and the slow progress of soft psychology. In R. B. Miller (Ed.), *The restoration of Dialogue: Readings in the Philosophy of Clinical Psychology*, pp. 523–555. Washington, DC: American Psychological Association.

Mitchell, C., & Egan, J. (1995). *Quality of Instruction Inventory*. Boston, MA: Department of Corrections, Program Services Division.

Orwin, R. G. (1987). A fail-safe N for effect size in meta-analysis. *Journal of Educational Statistics*, **8**, 157–159.

Paparozzi, M. A. (1994). *A Comparison of the Effectiveness of an Intensive Parole Supervision Program with Traditional Parole Supervision*, Unpublished doctoral dissertation, Rutgers University, Brunswick, NJ.

Posavac, E. J., & Carey, R. G. (1997). *Program Evaluation: Methods and Case Studies*, 5th ed. Upper Saddle River, NJ: Prentice-Hall.

Redondo, S., Sánchez-Meca, J., & Garrido, V. (1999). The influence of treatment programmes on the recidivism of juvenile and adult offenders: A European meta-analytic review. *Psychology, Crime and Law*, **5**, 251–278.

Reynolds, M. O. (1996). *Crime and Punishment in Texas: Update*, NCPA Policy Report No. 202. Dallas, TX: National Center for Policy Analysis.

Robinson, W. S. (1950). Ecological correlations and the behavior of individuals. *American Sociological Review*, **15**, 351–357.

Rosenthal, R. (1991). *Meta-Analytic Procedures for Social Research*. Newbury Park, CA: Sage.

Rosenthal, R. (1995). Writing meta-analytic reviews. *Psychological Bulletin*, **8**, 183–192.

Schmidt, F. (1996). Statistical significance testing and cumulative knowledge in psychology: Implications for training of researchers. *Psychological Methods*, **1**, 115–129.

Shadish, W. R. (1984). Lessons from the implementation of deinstitutionalization. *American Psychologist*, **39**, 725–738.

Spiegler, M., & Guevremont, D. (1993). *Contemporary Behavior Therapy*, 2nd ed. Pacific Grove, CA: Brooks/Cole.

Underdown, A. (1998). *Strategies for Effective Offender Supervision: Management Summary*. London: Home Office Publication Unit.

Van Voorhis, P., Braswell, M., & Lester, D. (2000). *Correctional Counselling and Rehabilitation*, 4th ed. Cincinnati, OH: Anderson Publishing Co.

Van Voorhis, P., & Brown, K. (1996). *Evaluability Assessment: A Tool for Program Development in Corrections*, Monographs for the National Institute of Corrections. Washington, DC: U S Department of Justice.

Williams, W. (1976). Implementation analysis and assessment. In W. Williams & R. Elmore (Eds), *Social Program Evaluation*, pp. 267–292. New York: Academic Press.

Wood, P., & Grasmick, H. (1999). Toward the development of punishment equivalencies: Male and female inmates rate the severity of alternative sanctions compared to prison. *Justice Quarterly*, **16**, 19–50.

Zajonc, R. B. (1962). A note on group judgements and group size. *Human Relations*, **15**, 177–180.

Zajonc, R. B., & Mulally, P. R. (1997). Birth order: Reconciling conflicting effects. *American Psychologist*, **52**, 685–699.

Chapter 13

THE ROLE OF THE CONSULTANT IN DEVELOPING EFFECTIVE CORRECTIONAL PROGRAMMES

CLIVE R. HOLLIN

Centre for Applied Psychology, University of Leicester, Leicester, UK

Alongside death and rising taxes, one of life's certainties is that crime will always be with us. For as long as records have been kept, crime has been recorded as one of the problems that any society must face. Taking a long, historical perspective, it is clear that for centuries the most favoured crime reduction policies were based on the simple premise of incapacitation. At different times, such legally sanctioned incapacitation took various forms, ranging from imprisonment and transportation to mutilation and execution. It is only comparatively recently, around the turn of the 20th century, that the ethos of *treating* offenders began to emerge. Based on the application of emerging psychological theories of human behaviour, innovative attempts at therapeutic interventions with offenders began to appear. The changing face of these interventions, from psychodynamic therapies to behaviour modification, reflected the growth and development of psychology as a discipline (Hollin, 2001).

Offender Rehabilitation in Practice. Edited by G. A. Bernfeld, D. P. Farrington and A. W. Leschied.
© 2001 John Wiley & Sons, Ltd.

Moving closer in time to the present day, there has been a remarkable upsurge in the popularity of the treatment ethos. After a period covering the 1970s and 1980s when the idea that "nothing works" held sway, the current, pragmatic emphasis is on "what works". Set against the backdrop of an emerging climate of evidence-based practice, a string of meta-analyses published throughout the 1980s and 1990s underpinned the argument that treatment with offenders could be effective, within limits, in reducing reoffending (Hollin, 1999; McGuire, 1995). The findings of these meta-analyses regarding the characteristics of effective practice (in terms of reduced reoffending) thus defined the boundaries of "what works". The impact of the meta-analyses has been widespread in that it has focused the thinking of academics and practitioners (e.g. Harland, 1996; McGuire, 1995; Van Voorhis, Braswell & Lester, 1997) and policy-makers (e.g. Bonta, 1997; Underdown, 1998; Vennard, Sugg & Hedderman, 1997) in seeking to develop services for offenders according to these "what works" principles.

The findings of the meta-analyses, with their focus on the statistical aggregate of a large number of studies, are not the only way to approach the task of defining effective practice. The Blueprints Program Review, with a remit to focus on reducing violence, approached the task of defining a model programme by setting the evaluation standards by which to judge the strength of the outcome evidence (http://www.colorado.edu/cspv/blueprints/Default.htm). In all, four strict criteria were established by which to judge the evidence in support of a particular programme (http://www.colorado.edu/cspv/blueprints/about/criteria.htm).   Thus, when programmes were presented to the Advisory Board for the Blueprints Program the evaluation standards for outcome evidence relevant to the programme were:

(1)   a strong research design, ideally an experimental design with random allocation, the presence of high rates of completion of the programme and robust measurement of the appropriate variables;
(2)   outcome evidence that speaks to the programme's effectiveness in significantly preventing or deterring violent behaviour;
(3)   that the effects of the programme have been replicated across multiple sites;
(4)   that the outcome evidence shows that gains during the delivery of the programme are maintained for at least 1 year post-intervention.

These criteria, stringently applied, have had the consequence that only 10 programmes have qualified as model programmes.

Regardless of the approach taken, be it meta-analysis or judgement of the strength of empirical research, the task for applied psychologists, among others, lies in turning empirical research into effective, deliverable services.

In attempting to turn research into practice there are two critical steps to take. The first is to translate the research findings into principles for effective practice; the second, which is a task now facing many service agencies, is to turn the principles into practice.

RESEARCH INTO PRINCIPLES

The task of translating research into workable principles for evidence-based practice is the first step towards the formulation of effective service delivery. The focus in the remainder of this chapter lies on the developments that have followed the "what works" agenda. Thus, the focus here is on structured multimodal treatment programmes that are cognitive-behavioural in orientation.

In their synthesis of the meta-analyses Andrews and Bonta (1994, 1998) established several principles to inform the development of practice aimed at reducing reoffending. The first principle is the *risk principle* which states that an important predictor of success is that offenders of medium to high risk of recidivism should be selected for treatment programmes. The *need principle* draws on the distinction between *criminogenic* and *non-criminogenic* needs. Criminogenic needs are the dynamic aspects of an offender's risk level which when changed in a positive direction bring about a commensurate change in the probability of reoffending.

The *responsivity principle* refers to the delivery of treatment programmes that will engage offenders. This principle means that programme delivery must always be cognisant of the offenders' social and cultural background, levels of verbal ability and motivation to engage in treatment. Finally, the *integrity principle* relates to the standards of the management systems necessary to support the effective delivery of offender treatment programmes. As will be seen, this principle makes a high level of demand on service providers, cutting across the whole spectrum of organizational structures and hierarchies (Hollin, 1995; Hollin, Epps & Kendrick, 1995; Lösel & Wittmann, 1989).

The formulation of these evidence-based principles has been driven primarily by researchers: however, as we move closer to practice there is a role for those who can bridge the gap between principles and practice. It is at this stage that the specialist consultant takes centre stage. The points made below are based primarily on my personal experience, taking into account the comments of colleagues who have undertaken similar work. My thoughts are offered here in the spirit of sharing my experiences rather than claiming any special insight or knowledge.

PRINCIPLES INTO PRACTICE

As the research informing the "what works" ideal began to gain an ever wider audience, in the mid-1990s the Prison Service in England and Wales gathered a group of academics and practitioners to formulate a methodology by which principles could be translated into practice (Lipton, Thornton, McGuire, Porporino & Hollin 2000). The task for those assembled was, in essence, to define the gold standard for programme design. This gold standard was finally encapsulated in a set of 10 criteria against which to measure the fit of a treatment programme with the "what works" principles. These 10 criteria became the accreditation criteria employed by the Prison Department's Accreditation Panel (Thornton, 1996). Briefly, HM Prison Service took the position that programmes for use with prisoners should comply with the gold standard defined in conjunction with its consultants. Thus, an accreditation panel was convened to judge the fit between pro-grammes submitted for scrutiny and the established standards (i.e. the accreditation criteria).

The Prison Service, as an organization, assigned itself the target, as a published key performance indicator, that a set number of prisoners would complete programmes accredited as effective in reducing reoffending. The Prison Service accreditation criteria were revised over time, as the research base grew and the panel became more sophisticated in its task, but essentially continue to address the same issues (Thornton, 1998). The initiative started by HM Prison Service has moved, as it were, into the com-munity and is now a major influence in the work of the Probation Service (Vanstone, 2000).

As a member of the initial group developing the criteria and as a member of the Accreditation Panel from its inception in 1996 until standing down in 1999, inevitably I have developed a working knowledge of programme design and development. Having worked, through my university, as a con-sultant to several probation services the practical issues in implementing the accreditation criteria have become increasingly clear. The general format for my consultancy work is to join a small team of probation staff who have been set the task of developing a programme. The discussion of the issues that typically arise in this style of work can be presented for discussion via the 10 accreditation criteria.

1. Explicit, empirically-based model of change

This criterion is defined as "An explicit model of how the programme is supposed to work. There should be evidence to justify the assumptions in the model" (Thornton, 1998). It is not a coincidence that theory is the first of the accreditation criteria. One of the guiding principles of underpinning the whole approach is that theory is the foundation upon which any treatment programme is built. It follows that theory informs the conceptualization of criminal behaviour, the understanding of risk factors, identification of the targets for change and so on. In working with agencies developing programmes according to "what works" principles, cognitive-behavioural theory is indicated by the meta-analyses as the theory of choice. However, in working with teams of practitioners developing programmes, there is always an initial drive to "get on with the job": there is a wish to start by developing practice, to begin by writing programme manuals and planning sessions. It is the role of the consultant to work with the programme developers initially to set practice towards one side and to focus on theory. The best vehicle for this shift to theory is the accreditation criterion itself: as agencies move towards programmes that are of an accredited standard, the criteria have taken on a reinforcing quality of their own.

The important task at this stage in the proceedings is to provide accessible reading material on both cognitive-behavioural theory and its application to understanding criminal behaviour. Again, this development of theoretical appreciation and application is not a process that can be rushed: some of the theoretical concepts need time to be worked through, so that exercises that help the team to make cognitive-behavioural formulations of increasingly complex behaviour can be very useful. The important process for the consultant with respect to theory development is not to act as an expert and lecture on theory, rather the task is better framed as helping the team to develop their own understanding of theory and how it can apply to their programme.

2. Targeting criminogenic need

"The programme should change factors which have been closely linked to the offending of those taking part" (Thornton, 1998). There are two key issues with respect to this criterion: first, defining criminogenic needs in the correct theoretical terms; second, identifying programme-relevant criminogenic needs. In cognitive-behavioural terms, criminogenic needs can be expressed in terms of cognitive functioning, skill level, educational ability and so on that are risk factors for continued offending. In describing criminogenic needs it is inadvisable to mix and match theory and targets: mainstream cognitive-behavioural theory does not, for example, incorporate concepts such as a dysfunctional ego, so it would not make sense to have this as a criminogenic need in a cognitive-behavioural programme. There can be difficulties here for the consultant as the work unfolds and begins to clash with the theoretical views held by other team members. It can be helpful to try to recast other theoretical concepts in cognitive-behavioural terms: thus, a dysfunctional ego might be translated as self-esteem, or content of self-talk, or even overly assertive behaviour.

Identification of relevant criminogenic needs can be achieved in two ways. First, the research literature can be used to help identify criminogenic needs: among the obvious examples are limited social problem solving skills, alcohol and drug misuse, and delinquent peers. Second, the programme developers might gather their own evidence regarding specific criminogenic needs: for example, a service may conduct research to identify criminogenic needs for a population about which there is limited knowledge, such as female violent offenders. The identification of criminogenic needs is critical as these become the focus for assessment of offenders regarding their suitability for the programme. In some instances, a robust assessment of need can be made using a standardized assessment instrument, such as the Level of Service Inventory-Revised (LSI-R; Andrews & Bonta, 1995). Of course, the identified criminogenic needs should be addressed during the programme!

3. Responsivity

"The methods used to target these criminogenic factors should be the ones to which those participating in the programme are responsive" (Thornton, 1998). It is a fundamental aspect of good practice that programmes are delivered in a manner that will motivate and engage participants. The role of the consultant is to keep the programme developers on track in this respect; although this is generally not a difficult task as most practitioners are highly sensitive to client issues.

In making a case for responsivity issues, the consultant can help services formulate policy. For example, it is not clear from the literature whether male and female offenders have similar criminogenic needs (Andrews & Dowden, 1999), but it is likely that males and females differ in terms of responsivity, particularly when working in groups (Bloom, 1999). This gender difference has obvious implications when it comes to policy on mixed or single-sex groups, style of presentation of programme materials, staff training and so on.

4. Effective methods

"Programmes should employ methods which have been consistently effective with offenders" (Thornton, 1998). A cognitive-behavioural programme will, by default, use cognitive-behavioural methods of behaviour change such as anger management, self-control training, social skills training and so on. There is a substantial literature that supports the efficacy of these methods with offenders (e.g. Hollin, 1990; Ross & Fabiano, 1985). Again, with experienced practitioners the consultant's task will be to refine the application of these methods.

A more difficult issue will come when working with programmes that come from a different theoretical tradition to the cognitive-behavioural one. In this case the consultant's task will be both to assist the programme developers in searching and making sense of the extant literature, and to help set up studies that show the methods are effective. The latter strategy can take more time, but a well-designed and implemented in-house study can provide convincing evidence that an approach has merit.

5. Skills orientated

"Programmes should teach skills which will make it easier to avoid criminal activities and to engage successfully in legitimate ones" (Thornton, 1998). There is a range of established techniques widely used in skills training, including modelling, instruction, role play, and feedback and coaching. The premise here is that behavioural change can be brought about by showing examples of the skill (modelling) so as to capitalize on our innate ability to learn from other people; directing the trainee's attention to the relevant aspects of the model's actions (instruction); allowing newly developing behaviours to be tried during role play; and feedback and coaching by the trainers to fine-tune and reward the trainee's developing skills. The task of the consultant is first to help in the identification of which skills are to be taught; then to move the programme developers to consider the more technical aspects of skills training, such as the sequencing of the skills to be trained, the level of skills to be attained and development of appropriate exercises for skills training. There is a substantial literature to inform this work, both with non-offender (Hollin & Trower, 1986a, 1986b) and offender populations (McGuire & Priestly, 1985).

6. Range of targets

"Given the complexity of criminal behaviour the panel will be looking for programmes which address a range of conceptually distinct factors in an integrated and mutually reinforcing way" (Thornton, 1998). As an exercise in stating the obvious, human behaviour is highly complex and it is unlikely that an intervention that seeks to address a single criminogenic need will be effective in reducing reoffending. While obvious it is not without precedent that interventions with offenders concentrate on a single factor. For example,

the modification of anger has become the principal target in many programmes for violent offenders. While it is the case that violent acts are
committed by people in angry states (Zamble & Quinsey, 1997), it would
be wrong to assume that anger is the main cause of violence or that all
violent offenders must be angry. Indeed, some studies suggest that propen-
sity to anger, in and of itself, fails to distinguish violent and non-violent
offenders (Loza & Loza-Fanous, 1999). It follows that to design treatment
programmes for violent offenders simply based around anger management
would be an error. A more realistic approach would be to design programmes to address a range of criminogenic needs in order to reduce
violent behaviour. For example, Aggression Replacement Training (ART)
is concerned with the violent person's social and communication skills,
moral maturity and anger management (Goldstein, Glick & Gibbs, 1998).

One of the issues the consultant may face lies in encouraging programme
designers to develop complex programmes. The objections that may be
raised are that the programme is becoming too involved, or too difficult,
or that delivery staff will not be able to take on programmes that are too
complex. These are, of course, entirely legitimate practical objections:
however, if programmes are going to be effective all the evidence tells us
that they *must* address a range of targets. As the process of programme
development is driven by evidence, then the evidence not the practicalities
must, within reason, be the prime concern. The opposite case is found when
a team begins to design fantastically complex programmes: on the principle
of having your cake and eating it, the consultant can appeal to the practical
issues with respect to what is attainable given the available time and
resources!

The prime concern is to develop programmes that address a range of
critical targets in the time available. It has been my experience on at least
one occasion to say to a service that, in my view, an effective programme
could not be developed within the constraints the organization was placing
around the programme developers.

7. Dose

"The amounts, intensity, sequencing and spacing of treatment should be
related to seriousness and persistence of offending, and to the range and
seriousness of the criminogenic factors typical of participants" (Thornton,
1998). This criterion directly follows the risk principle and, while manifestly
true empirically, it is difficult to translate into practice. Indeed, of all the
issues faced in programme development, it is the operationalization of this
criterion that invariably causes the most difficulty. There are two reasons for
this difficulty: first, the lack of substantial empirical evidence on the issue;

second, the very real time constraints that apply in the criminal justice system, be it a custodial sentence or a probation order.

One route to a solution is to draw a parallel with an established programme, such as ART (Goldstein et al., 1998), and base an argument for treatment dosage on that basis. Another, more utilitarian, possibility is to consider how much time is available and tailor the programme on that basis. The task of the programme development team if the latter strategy is adopted is to mount a convincing case that sufficient work can be carried out in the time allotted. The consultant's role here is often to be as realistic as possible in what can be achieved in a given time span.

8. Throughcare

Throughcare is a particular concern for programmes conducted in prisons. Effective throughcare means that the agency responsible for the prisoner on his or her release from custody is aware of and can continue the work started in the prison. The consultant can help the process by asking questions about the likely points of contact, preparation of documentation for the next agency and clarity of information about the programme to inform the work of the next agency.

For offenders in the community, the principle then changes to one of passing programme information across the organization. Of course, those working inside an organization know the pitfalls and the role of the consultant is to work with the team in developing strategies for effective communication. At a more complex level, there is the issue of the passage of information across different organizations in the community. Again, the consultant may help teams to brainstorm their way to effective strategies.

9. Monitoring

"Programmes should have a built in commitment to monitor their operations, and correcting and improving performance when it deviates from required standards" (Thornton, 1998). The force of this criterion, perhaps more than any other, demands that service managers must take a direct, hands on, role in the development and running of programmes. If the running of programmes is to be effective then there must be high levels of treatment integrity (Hollin, 1995). The need for integrity demands that managers must, for example, address the training and supervision of the staff conducting the treatment; the need for integrity demands that those individuals responsible for the management and supervision of treatment are involved in all the operational phases of the programme; the need for integrity demands the assurance of quality; and the need for integrity demands that evaluation is an essential component of treatment so that failing programmes can be rescued. In other words, managers need to be aware of all aspects of programme delivery. It follows that programme developers need to build management information systems into their programme. The role of the consultant is to assist in the development of such systems, both in terms of the nature of the information gathered and the systems for data collection. There are no hard and fast rules for the construction of information systems as they must be flexible to meet local needs and circumstances.

In formulating monitoring systems one aspect which will raise problems is the need to record treatment sessions. The issue of taping (audio or video) sessions for later evaluation is fraught with pitfalls. First, there are concerns simply about being taped; second, there are concerns, from both group leaders and participants, about who has access to the taped sessions. It seems to me that both these concerns are entirely reasonable. The role of the consultant in this regard is to guide the service in its policy formulation around these issues. The guiding principle is that the policy must be absolutely transparent, there should be absolutely no doubt about the boundaries placed around who has access to the tapes and for what purpose.

10. Evaluation

In working with services, it is generally the case that the practitioners and managers involved in the project are not researchers. This criterion is about evaluation of one's work, which is a task not beyond the scope of practitioners (McIvor, 1995), although complex outcome studies may require funding above and beyond what is possible at a local level.

The first task of the consultant is to help services distinguish the various levels of assessment that can be used to evaluate programmes. There are four levels of assessment data that I find helpful to define: these four levels are monitoring data, process data, integrity data and outcome data. Monitoring data are principally the details about the running of the programme: this might include background details of the participants, attendance rates, length of sessions and so on. Process data are related to the measures linked to targets for change in the programme: this might include, for example, changes in skill level, social problem solving ability or anger control. These data may well be collected through the use of psychometric measures, which require some specialist input from the consultant.

Integrity data are related, for example, to the video monitoring, group-worker assessment of sessions and so on. A great deal of careful planning is needed at this stage to produce integrity data that are both useful and manageable. It is the case that having videotaped sessions, services are unsure how best to utilize this source of information. The consultant can help guide services towards parsimony through the introduction of effective sampling schedules, concise checklists and so on. Finally, outcome data can be very difficult to collect when defined in terms of reconviction. However, as shown by Raynor and Vanstone (1996) in their evaluation of a community-based programme for offenders, rates of reconviction can be assessed in various ways. While comparison with a matched control group (even randomly allocated) is the ideal, an alternative is to gather reconviction rates for the treated group and then compare them with the predicted rates via some standardized protocol. As many services routinely collect data which would allow predicted reconviction rates to be calculated, a little help from the consultant should allow outcome studies to be produced.

CONCLUSION

The major strength of accreditation is that it points agencies in the direction of evidence-based practice. This drive towards evidence-based practice should lead not only to well-designed programmes, but critically to interventions that are implemented with rigour, in terms of staff training, selection of participants and monitoring and evaluation of effectiveness of process and outcome. Having said that, there are several emerging issues that merit an open discussion.

A major weakness in an accreditation system, which is perhaps beginning to creep into current thinking, is that accreditation becomes a bureaucratic, rather than an empowering process. In working as a consultant I have always taken the line that accreditation is good news for practitioners: accreditation should drive an organization to support practitioners in every way possible—through giving support and supervision, and by making available training and resources. The danger of an accreditation machine, driven by administrators for administrators, is that the process becomes a punishing dictator rather than an enabling facilitator of good practice. Thus, agencies see accreditation as an imposition, another paperwork exercise, that presents an impossible hurdle to hinder and interfere with their efforts to work with offenders and reduce reoffending.

Most important, it should be a central tenet of the whole process that nothing is fixed: as the evidence base unfolds, at both a local and international level (including the literature), so programmes and accreditation criteria and systems must change and develop accordingly. This means that somewhere in the process there needs to be someone responsible for seeing the "big picture": in dreadful management speak, there needs to be a "keeper of the vision". One of the tasks of a consultant, at times when everyone is lost in detail and chronically overworked, is to remind services where they started from and what they set out trying to achieve.

There are no simple answers, but some thoughts occur. First, might there be a requirement that those responsible for accreditation should have to serve their time with direct involvement in the running of programmes? Second, might the limits of accreditation be defined so as to reduce the demands placed on those running programmes? At the most basic level, ever increasing demands on service providers to serve the needs of accreditation runs the risk that the whole process simply becomes too expensive to be sustained.

References

Andrews, D. A., & Bonta, J. (1994). *The Psychology of Criminal Conduct*. Cincinnati, OH: Anderson Publishing Co.

Andrews, D. A., & Bonta, J. (1995). *LSI-R: The Level of Service Inventory-Revised*. Toronto: Multi-Health Systems.

Andrews, D. A., & Bonta, J. (1998). *The Psychology of Criminal Conduct*, 2nd ed. Cincinnati, OH: Anderson Publishing Co.

Andrews D. A., & Dowden, C. (1999). A meta-analytic investigation into effective correctional intervention for female offenders. *Forum on Corrections Research*, **11**, 18–21.

Blueprints Program Review. University of Colorado at Boulder. Website at: http://www.colorado.edu/cspv/blueprints/about/main.htm http://www.colorado.edu/cspv/blueprints/about/criteria.htm

Bonta, J. (1997). *Offender Rehabilitation: From Research to Practice*, User Report No. 1997-01. Ottawa: Ministry of the Solicitor General of Canada.

Bloom, B. (1999). Gender-responsive programming for women offenders: Guiding principles and practices. *Forum on Corrections Research*, **11**, 22–27.

Goldstein, A. P., Glick, B., & Gibbs, J. C. (1998). *Aggression Replacement Training*, Rev. ed. Champaign, IL: Research Press.

Harland, A. T. (Ed.) (1996). *Choosing Correctional Options that Work: Defining the Demand and Evaluating the Supply*. Thousand Oaks, CA: Sage.

Hollin, C. R. (1990). *Cognitive-Behavioral Interventions with Young Offenders*. Elmsford, NY: Pergamon.

Hollin, C. R. (1995). The meaning and implications of "programme integrity". In J. McGuire (Ed.), *What Works: Reducing Reoffending*, pp. 195–208. Chichester: John Wiley.

Hollin, C. R. (1999). Treatment programmes for offenders: Meta-analysis, "what works", and beyond. *International Journal of Law and Psychiatry*, **22**, 361–372.

Hollin, C. R. (2001). To treat or not to treat: An historical perspective. In C. R. Hollin (Ed.), *Handbook of Offender Assessment and Treatment*. Chichester: John Wiley.

Hollin, C. R., Epps, K., & Kendrick, D. (1995). *Managing Behavioural Treatment: Policy and Practice with Delinquent Adolescents*. London: Routledge.

Hollin, C. R., & Trower, P. (Eds) (1986a). *Handbook of Social Skills Training, Volume 1: Applications Across the Life Span*. Oxford: Pergamon.

Hollin, C. R., & Trower, P. (Eds) (1986b). *Handbook of Social Skills Training, Volume 2: Clinical Applications and New Directions*. Oxford: Pergamon.

Lipton, D. S., Thornton, D. M., McGuire, J., Porporino, F. J., & Hollin, C. R. (2000). Program accreditation and correctional treatment. *Substance Use and Misuse*, **35**, 1705–1734.

Lösel, F., & Wittmann, W. W. (1989). The relationship of treatment integrity and intensity to outcome criteria. In R. F. Conner & M. Hendricks (Eds), *International Innovations in Evaluation Methodology: New Directions for Program Evaluation*, No 42, pp. 97–108: San Francisco, CA: Jossey-Bass.

Loza, W., & Loza-Fanous, A. (1999). The fallacy of reducing rape and violent recidivism by treating anger. *International Journal of Offender Therapy and Comparative Criminology*, **43**, 492–502.

McGuire, J. (Ed.) (1995). *What Works: Reducing Reoffending*. Chichester: John Wiley.

McGuire, J., & Priestly, P. (1985). *Offending Behaviour: Skills and Stratagems for Going Straight*. London: Batsford.

McIvor, G. (1995). Practitioner evaluation in probation. In J. McGuire (Ed.), *What Works: Reducing Reoffending*, pp. 209–219. Chichester: John Wiley.

Raynor, P., & Vanstone, M. (1996). Reasoning and rehabilitation in Britain: The results of the Straight Thinking on Probation (STOP) programme. *International Journal of Offender Therapy and Comparative Criminology*, **40**, 272–284.

Ross, R. R., & Fabiano, E. A. (1985). *Time to Think: A Cognitive Model of Delinquency Prevention and Offender Rehabilitation*. Johnson City, TN: Institute of Social Sciences and Arts.

Thornton, D. (1996). *Criteria for Accrediting Programmes 1996/1997*. London: Programme Development Section, HM Prison Service.

Thornton, D. (1998). *Criteria for Accrediting Programmes 1998/1999*. London: Programme Development Section, HM Prison Service.

Underdown, A. (1998). *Strategies for Effective Offender Supervision*, Report of the HMIP What Works Project. London: HM Inspectorate of Probation.

Vanstone, M. (2000). Cognitive-behavioural work with offenders in the UK: A history of influential endeavour. *The Howard Journal*, **39**, 171–183.

Van Voorhis, P., Braswell, M., & Lester, D. (Eds) (1997). *Correctional Counseling and Rehabilitation*. Cincinnati, OH: Anderson Publishing Co.

Vennard, J., Sugg, D., & Hedderman, C. (1997). *Changing Offenders' Attitudes and Behaviours: What Works?*, Home Office Research Study 171. London: Home Office.

Zamble, E., & Quinsey, V. L. (1997). *The Criminal Recidivism Process*. Cambridge: Cambridge University Press.

INDEX